D1601121

Lost Promises

Debt, Austerity, and Development in Latin America

About the Book

The origins of the debt crisis, the principal institutional actors involved, and the structure of related policies are well documented. Less studied and less understood is the impact of austerity on the people of Latin America. In this collection of original essays, leading Latin American and U.S. researchers map the political economy of austerity in Latin America. Each essay focuses on a specific aspect of social relations—urban, rural, demographic, or economic. Exploring the theoretical and substantive implications of austerity in Latin America, the contributors show that the study of the region's debt crisis can contribute to an understanding of the impact of internationalization on national social structure and development.

The book begins with a historical analysis of global economic and institutional changes that presaged the rapid growth of debt in Latin America and determined the implementation of austerity policies. In Part 2, several essays focus on the structure of national economic stabilization policies and their impact on income distribution. Part 3 examines the effects of austerity on various dimensions of social structure including demography, urbanization, organized labor, and regional development. Popular responses to austerity policies are explored in Part 4.

Lost Promises
Debt, Austerity, and Development in Latin America

EDITED BY
William L. Canak
Tulane University

Westview Press
BOULDER & LONDON

Copyright © 1989 by Westview Press, Inc.

Published in 1989 in the United States of America by Westview Press, Inc., 5500 Central Avenue, Boulder, Colorado 80301, and in the United Kingdom by Westview Press, Inc., 13 Brunswick Centre, London WC1N 1AF, England

Library of Congress Cataloging-in-Publication Data
Lost promises : debt, austerity, and development in Latin America /
edited by William L. Canak.
    p. cm.
Includes bibliographies and index.
ISBN 0-8133-0552-7
ISBN 0-8133-0553-5 (pbk.)
    1. Debts, External—Latin America.   2. Latin America—Economic
policy.   I. Canak, William L. (William Leigh), 1947–
HJ8514.5.L68   1989
338.98—dc19   88-20812
                                                                        CIP

Printed and bound in the United States of America

The paper used in this publication meets the requirements of the American National Standard for Permanence of Paper for Printed Library Materials Z39.48-1984.

10   9   8   7   6   5   4   3   2   1

Contents

Tables and Figures

Acknowledgments

I was warned about the terrors and frustrations that inevitably plague the life of anyone with the temerity to organize a text of orginal essays. Forewarned, I plunged ahead. I must conclude that the alarmists were correct, but the contributing authors and my editors at Westview Press were not the source of my trials and tribulations. Rather, it was the task itself that I greatly underestimated. The editors at Westview Press, Miriam Gilbert, Constance Clark, and Martha Leggett, were good humored, experienced, supportive, and insightful. Marian Safran, a copyeditor at Westview, earned my admiration and respect for her work on this book. When needed, Westview's editors were always at hand with encouragement and sound advice. The contributors proved to be a wonderfully responsible and hardworking bunch. Of course, I originally solicited their contributions because they each have that reputation.

My graduate research assistants at Tulane University, Harry Crumpler and Danilo Levi, each provided yeoman service when it was required. Dan's translation of Alejandro Rofman's chapter is especially good. Harry was always there when the work needed to be done. His good humor and intelligence made the work enjoyable and gave me added confidence that we would complete the project in good shape. It was my wonderful good fortune to have Harry and Danilo working with me. One could not want better assistants. In addition, the Department of Sociology at Tulane has a very special collegial atmosphere where hard work and good fun seem to mix easily. Jane Kuroda helped prepare the tables for this book.

Special thanks go to Tulane's Roger Thayer Stone Center for Latin American Studies, a unique organization with a staff and resources that greatly facilitate scholarship. In large part this reflects the leadership provided by its director, Richard Greenleaf. Tom Niehaus of Tulane's Latin American Library provided excellent bibliographic support when it was needed. Tulane's Murphy Institute for Political Economy provided funding for the purchase of a computer and software that significantly reduced the time and energy required to perform many of the more mundane tasks associated with producing this text. That help is much appreciated.

I dedicate this book to my parents, Marion Bates Canak and Peter R. Canak.

William L. Canak

Introduction

William L. Canak

Debt and austerity, two compelling features of the new international division of labor, are transforming class relations and the political economies of Latin American nations. Public sector institutions and programs are being dismantled. In the private sector, agriculture, manufacturing, and finance increasingly reflect global economic and political forces. As national policies are adjusted to meet the institutionally defined priorities of the international economy, austerity is producing domestic depression, undermining social progress, and restricting the capacity of recently established democratic governments to consolidate their legitimacy. Thus debt, austerity, and development link the changing structure of the global economy to the daily economic, political, and social reality confronting Latin Americans.

The origins of the debt crisis, the principal institutional actors involved, and the structure of related policies are well documented. Less studied and less understood is the impact of austerity on the people of Latin America. This collection of original essays maps the political economy of austerity in Latin America. Each essay focuses on a specific context or set of social relations, for example, urban, rural, demographic, or economic. Through their study of austerity policies' impact on Latin American social, economic, and political life they contribute to a new understanding of how internationalization is transforming national social structure and development processes.

The book begins with a historical analysis of global economic and institutional changes that presaged the rapid growth of debt in Latin America and determined the implementation of stabilization policies. The terms of conditionality and structural adjustment under which Latin American domestic social and economic policy currently operate are extracting a fearsome toll on the daily lives of people, dismantling state institutions and programs, and restructuring local economies to function as short-term "cash cows" for commercial banks. Under the necessity of satisfying institutional performance criteria for continued access to credit, and under the close scrutiny of their accountants, Latin American governments are opening their national economies to the logic of international accumulation. They are doing so in order to acquire and maintain a creditworthy rating as they separately confront a coordinated set of institutional controls from commercial banks, multilateral finance agencies, and the Organization for Economic Cooperation and Development (OECD). In this new international division of labor (NIDL), Latin America is generating a massive outflow of capital, domestic economies are deteriorating, and state structure and programs are increasingly responding to an institutional logic divorced from the welfare and security of local populations. This process is mediated by the organization and struggle of local classes (see Chapters 6, 8, and 10), but the internationalization of production processes, capital markets, and labor markets has transformed the institutional environment within which individual states mobilize resources and implement policies. Austerity policies mark a fundamental shift in the relationship of Latin American states with domestic classes and the process of national accumulation. The impact of these policies on Latin American social, political, and economic structures is the subject of the following chapters.

In Part 2 Paul Singer and Adriana Marshall each focus on the structure of national economic stabilization policies and their impact on income distribution. In a number of Latin America's most heavily indebted nations the debt crisis has coincided with a return to political democracy. Singer presents a closely argued and theoretically sophisticated historical analysis of hyperinflation's impact on Brazilian society, specific policies (including "orthodox" and "heterodox shock") that have been initiated to control inflation, and the relationship of both economic policies and inflation to democracy. Marshall uses the Argentine case to consider one of the consequences of a principal International Monetary Fund (IMF) condition for loan rescheduling, namely, declines in real wages. She reviews the processes of income concentration and declining wages that predate the debt crisis and then determines the impact of those changes on the structure of consumer demand and manufacturing production in Argentina. In Argentina and elsewhere in Latin America, wage increases could have an immediate impact on idle manufacturing capacity. Indeed, for much of the continent, given the current world economy and export potential, increasing workers' wages may be the only alternative to a long-term period of economic stagnation.

Part 3 contains four chapters that detail the impact of austerity policies on Latin American social structure. Under the fiscal constraints of the IMF and the international commercial banks, Latin American governments' domestic social and economic policies are extracting sufficient surplus to meet debt payments. In addition, their economies could support increased imports and generate investment capital necessary to continue industrial growth or continuation of the state's economic and social functions. They cannot do both. With the examples of Brazil and Peru to inform their decisions, Latin governments are choosing to service the debt.

Each chapter in Part 3 focuses on a specific dimension of Latin American society: demographic structure and processes, regional development, urban social structure, and political structure. Hakkert and Goza's analysis of austerity policy's impact on Latin American demography presents a broad-ranging survey of demographic phenomena. Popular press accounts of Latin American life under austerity commonly turn to graphic anecdotal descriptions of mortality, migration, epidemics, and so forth. In contrast, Hakkert and Goza contribute a closely argued effort to separate out the impact of austerity from long-term demographic processes. Their study builds a comparative historical analysis of changing labor force opportunities—including the informal urban economy—and income effects. In turning to demographic crises and social control, Hakkert and Goza first distinguish twentieth-century demographic responses to crises from earlier periods, particularly in terms of short-term responses to deteriorating economic and institutional conditions. Latin American health and mortality trends in the 1980s present a diverse pattern of responses to austerity. Hakkert and Goza's portrait of mortality by cause shows the need to make cautious judgments regarding the impact of austerity programs. They extrapolate from existing data to assess diseases, homicides, suicides, and childhood mortality. Austerity's long-term impact on fertility, marriage patterns, and migration is also considered.

Alejandro Rofman's study of Argentine austerity policies and regional development builds on a review of Argentina's recent economic history and its impact on state structure and policy. Drawing parallels with other Latin American states, he then considers the postwar history of regional planning programs in Argentina and Latin America. He examines the relationship between traditional regional planning policy and the current economic crisis. Rofman concludes by considering the principles of an alternative regional planning strategy for Latin America within the context of internationalization processes that have made austerity policies necessary.

Portes and Johns review the impact of austerity on trends in Latin American urbanization. Their analysis focuses on such characteristic phenomena as urban primacy, the urban informal sector, housing, and the rise of popular organizations. They conclude that the debt crisis and austerity policies are exacerbating spatial polarization, accelerating growth of the urban informal economy, and broadening the range and focus of militant protests.

Part 3 concludes with William C. Smith's comparative study of austerity, "heterodox shock" stabilization policies, and their impact on political culture and political relations in Argentina and Brazil. Smith provides a comprehensive review of macroeconomic policy under the Austral and Cruzado Plans. He then links this analysis to the political initiatives of the regimes that devised these "stabilization" policies and relates subsequent social transformations to the overall process of democratization occurring in each country. He develops a thorough analysis of the "social pact" initiatives characterizing these fledgling democratic regimes. Finally, Smith concludes that external adjustment programs cannot be legitimated by elections alone but must be negotiated through an incorporation of labor and domestic capital into macroeconomic policy formation processes.

In Part 4, three chapters focus on responses to austerity policies in Latin America. Edward C. Epstein's analysis of organized labor's response to austerity policies in seven Latin American countries contrasts economic and political explanations for the observed pattern of strike behavior between 1976 and 1984. Union behavior is measured in terms of the number of strikes and popular strike support. Regimes are characterized in terms of their proclivity toward violence and modes of official control of unions. Edwards concludes that strike frequency and militancy is best understood in terms of the impact of variations in political control and unemployment.

Merilee S. Grindle's analysis of agrarian social relations under austerity draws on the Mexican case to examine peasant household strategies for survival in the face of economic adversity and adverse state policies. With an eye toward the general conditions of peasant life in Latin America, Grindle uses 1985 data from four *Municípios*. Diversification of crops, wage labor, commercial pursuits (including handicraft production), and, most important, labor migration define the complex strategies adopted in rural areas to cope with austerity. In many areas austerity has produced a process of class differentiation as a class of wealthier landowners has emerged, in part based on their relationship to local and international markets. Her analysis reveals the striking interaction of local economies with regional, national, and international political and economic developments.

John Walton and Charles Ragin's study of popular protest against austerity policies demonstrates the limitations inherent in analyses of the debt crisis that focus only on decisionmaking in powerful national and international institutions. Popular protests, they note, have played an integral role in shaping state policy. Their quantitative analysis of protests against IMF-mandated austerity and stabilization programs examines several hypotheses for variations in protest. First, they consider the hypothesis that protest has a linear relationship to the severity of austerity policy. Second, they examine whether it is the "urban" impact of austerity that determines variations in popular mobilizations. Third and fourth hypotheses analyze the state's ability to control unrest and the *power of capital and labor* respectively. Walton and Ragin conclude that whereas the hardship imposed by austerity policies affects protests, the pressure for stabilizing reforms, when linked to excessive urbanization and unionization, is a more important determinant of the occurrence and severity of protests. Moreover, Walton and Ragin conclude that economic dependency is negatively associated with dissent activity and that authoritarianism is unrelated to such activity. Finally, the intermittent course of austerity policies in Latin America and the shifting demands of multilateral agencies and commercial banks during ongoing negotiations show that the unrelieved pressure to implement austerity creates contradictions in the form of protest. These demands have moderated into a more flexible managed discounting, partly in response to such protests.

Part 1
The Global Economy and Austerity

1

Debt, Austerity, and Latin America in the New International Division of Labor

William L. Canak

In 1982, the Mexican government's near fiscal collapse highlighted the vulnerability and risk inherent in the massive debt burden Mexico had acquired in the previous decade. The sense of immediate crisis articulated by the press, political and economic leaders, and the academic community, however, reflected the historically new conditions of the world economy. The threatened insolvency of Mexico, and by extension that of other Third World governments with large debt burdens, now threatened the stability of capital markets and the leading international private financial institutions (Körner et al., 1986; Wiarda, 1987). It was, however, a crisis widely predicted throughout the 1970s (Payer, 1974; Rowen, 1977; Block, 1977; Abbott, 1979).

Subsequent to 1982, multilateral institutions—the International Monetary Fund, the World Bank—transnational banks, and governments in the advanced capitalist nations muddled and cobbled a flexible but coordinated policy directed at maintaining the institutional and interstate relations that defined the rules of the game from Bretton Woods until the 1980s (Dam, 1982; Dornbusch, 1984; Junz, 1981; Feinberg, 1987; Garten, 1982). Renegotiations and rescheduling for loans have allowed these creditors to search for a long-term solution while maintaining a steady outflow of capital from Third World nations, U.S. $29 billion in 1987 alone.

In the nations that acquired large foreign debts in the 1970s, the debt crisis itself and related domestic austerity policies have developed as cornerstone features of a new international division of labor (NIDL). Since the 1940s, the collapse of colonialism and consequent development of the interstate system have interacted with the internationalization of production processes and capital and labor markets and the emergence of multinational private enterprise to redefine the role of Third World nations in the world system. The contradictory processes of development characterizing that NIDL are most evident in the policy choices facing debtor nations. The agenda of stabilization and austerity policies mandated by the International Monetary Fund and other creditors as a condition for access to new financing for old loans and new capital now constrains the social and economic policy of many Latin American governments. The impact of these policies on the economic, political, and social structure of Latin America will be the focus of following chapters. The purpose of this chapter is to provide a brief introduction to the historical transformations in the international division of labor since the 1940s and their impact on the structure and policies of Latin American governments.

A New International Division of Labor

Latin American economic development, political structure, and policies are characterized by an uncertainty and volatility that reflects the region's position in the world system. In recent decades, principal regional trends have continued this pattern. Prior to the 1980s, rapid growth in conventional economic measures of development, for example, gross national product (GNP) per capita or energy use, has been accompanied by growing relative inequality and absolute poverty. In the past decade these latter trends have been exacerbated: Many Latin American nations experienced absolute declines in gross national product when world commodity prices declined, foreign investment and commercial-bank lending shifted to Asia, and domestic austerity and stabilization policies drove down wages and led to an expanded informal sector. Internationalization of local economies has intensified as finance, manufacturing, agriculture, and labor markets have become directly dominated by multinational institutions. Finally, whether authoritarian or democratic, national governments' organizational structure and policies increasingly have come to reflect the bureaucratic imperatives of international institutions and markets that are more intensively and extensively integrated and interdependent (Portes and Canak, 1981:229; Hirschman, 1987).

Latin American economic policies have been as volatile as the economies themselves. In the nineteenth century, export-oriented policies reflected extensive acceptance of the doctrine of economic liberalism (Portes and Walton, 1981; Skidmore and Smith, 1984:340). In the 1930s, reacting to world depression, economic nationalist sentiments gained wide acceptance and legitimated increased state intervention in the form of public sector corporations and policies subsidizing national industries. When the 1940s brought a boom in primary exports, economic liberals staged a brief comeback but were whipsawed when world prices once again plummeted.

In the postwar era, Latin American economic analysis generally and subsequent national policies were strongly influenced by ECLA, the Economic Commission for Latin America, an agency of the United Nations. ECLA's impact derived from its unique capacity to articulate a Latin American perspective on development, train researchers, and establish a hemispheric forum, which facilitated communication between policymakers and researchers throughout Latin America. Under the directorship of Raúl Prebish, ECLA established a historical-structural explanation of Latin "underdevelopment" and proposed that international trade agreements to reduce volatility in world commodity markets and import substitution industrialization would reduce Latin America's dependence and lead to self-sustained development.[1] Large-scale state economic intervention and development of state enterprises became components of this strategy for development.

This path of "national capitalism" placed constraints on the economic and political options open to domestic capitalists and thus increased the capacity of organized labor and working-class political parties to effectively mobilize and influence state policy. Populist demands for increased state spending and higher wages were matched by domestic business's fears of socialism, capital flight, and a search for international allies. This capital-labor relationship characteristic of import substitution industrialization has been identified as the structural basis for the emergence of repressive authoritarian regimes in many Latin American nations during the 1960s and 1970s (Canak, 1984; O'Donnell, 1973, 1978; Collier, 1979). The capacity of these regimes to repress working-class political mobilization and enforce an opening of local economies to international market forces became a cornerstone for IMF and commercial-bank loans in the 1970s. Nevertheless, during the recession-prone 1970s the semi-industrialized Latin American countries (Brazil, Mexico, and Argentina), which were the major recipients of private loans, continued import substitution policies, high rates of accumulation, and state sector growth financed by debt growth and resisted "stabilization" policies (Thorp and Whitehead, 1979; Fitzgerald, 1981).

Throughout the postwar era the complex institutions overseeing official capital transfers aimed at fostering development and introducing orderly market processes in the international economy have functioned—in Europe and Third World nations—to limit the capacity of nationalist and socialist groups to influence state policy (Block, 1977; Payer, 1982; Pastor, 1987; Wood, 1986). First the Marshall Plan and later the IMF-sanctioned lending served to transform national class relations and political power and reinforce processes of internationalization. Aid, grants, loans, and subsidized investment were in each case linked to the liberalization of national economic policies and evidence of a domestic capacity to "control" populist demands. National regimes were presented with a limited repertoire of acceptable development policies (Sanderson, 1985:20–21). Thus the debt crisis of the 1980s is not a crisis that threatens the monetary and fiscal stability of the core countries. Rather, it is a structural feature of a new stage in core-periphery dependency, in which the integration of Latin American nations in the world market is conditioned by the disciplinary authority of supranational agencies over national regimes.

Theorists attempting to conceptualize the structure and developmental processes of this new international division of labor have drawn distinct themes. The postimperialism theorists (Becker et al., 1987) have focused on development of multinational corporations and processes of class formation in the Third World. They viewed "indebted industrialization" in countries like Brazil and Mexico as the expression of an alliance between domestic elites and international financiers that is transforming the political and economic structures of *both* OECD and Third World nations. They asserted that internationalization of dominant class interests from OECD nations and the development of a dominant national bourgeoisie in Third World nations make the framework of *dependency* and of *imperialism* obsolete.

Fröbel, Heinrichs, and Kreye (1985) also identified the new patterns of trade and the relocation of production from OECD countries to the Third World as evidence for an NIDL. Based on cheap labor, fragmented production processes, and new technologies of transportation and communication, a world market is now possible. They argued that in the 1960s these conditions first became operative and set in place tendencies that on the one hand are transforming the historical division between industrialized and developing countries and on the other hand are encouraging the increased geographic and operational division of manufacturing processes (Fröbel et al., 1985:45).

One set of theorists has focused on the developmental *logic of capital accumulation* in the world system (Sanderson, 1985; Marcussen and Torp, 1982; Nyilas, 1982). These analyses depicted world economic processes as "a function of the expansion of capital and its valorization and reproduction at a global level" (Sanderson, 1985:9; see also Barkin and Rozo, 1983; Barkin and Suárez, 1982; Hymer, 1972; Palloix, 1977). Although this perspective recognizes the importance of multinational corporations and national states, it subordinates them to fundamental processes of capital accumulation that are both national and international. Thus capital accumulation, that is, the expanded reproduction of capitalist social relations through the transformation of surplus to new constant and variable capital, is the driving force that incorporates and integrates specific institutions and locations into a capitalist world economy. As capitalist social relations (proletarianization) become a global reality and the transnational coordination of capital (bank and production) occurs, the significance of trade has been reduced by the capacity to internationalize production (Sanderson, 1985:15).

Finally, international production and global coordination of capital increasingly require the "structural adjustment" of national economic policies. In contrast to the predictions of postindustrialization theorists, this perspective asserts that transnational production undermines the autonomous political capacity of national regimes. Protectionism is not an option for countries whose critical "resource dependency" is tied to foreign debt refinancing and structural adjustment programs presented as a condition for access to world credit markets.[2]

Global coordination of capital and the direct sanctioning of national regimes have been focused on a set of institutions that were founded in the 1940s. The following section briefly reviews these multilateral institutions and their developing role in the new international division of labor.

Rationalizing the World: The IMF, World Bank, and General Agreement on Tariffs and Trade

The system governing international monetary and trade relations from 1945 until the early 1970s was negotiated at Bretton Woods in 1944. Forty-four nations were present, but the proceedings were dominated by the two principal industrial powers, Britain and the United States. At Bretton Woods, U.S. officials wanted the postwar monetary system to avoid the uncertainties and instability created by floating exchange rates and uncontrolled devaluations of the 1920s and 1930s (Dam, 1982:88). It was hoped that this monetary system would sustain free trade and avoid the protectionist policies of the interwar period. This was to be achieved through the creation of multilateral institutions: the International Monetary Fund (IMF), the International Bank for Reconstruction and Development (the World Bank), and the International Trade Organization. The latter was short-lived, but the first two became fundamental components of the postwar internationalization process. In sum these institutions were a preliminary effort at global coordination of capital accumulation within a system of sovereign states. The more complete fulfillment of that intention necessitated the global integration of trade, finance, production, and labor markets.

The transformation of international financial markets in the 1970s and consequent debt crisis/credit crisis of the 1980s produced a transformation in the role of those institutions and their relationship with national states and private financial institutions. That process continues as recent calls for solutions to problems created by uncoordinated national economic policies have presented the need for a world currency and an international federal reserve system (*Economist*, 1988:9; Bell, 1988:24). The IMF's functions were quite specific. It was to establish fixed exchange rates and currency convertibility. In addition, it was to help governments through short-term liquidity crises, resulting from a negative balance of payments. The aim was to eliminate the impact on international trade of seasonal and short-term fluctuations. Loans were tied, at least in theory, to each government's contributions (Moffitt, 1983; Brett, 1985; Pastor, 1987). Although conceived as an international organization, governance was to be weighted to reflect each nation's quota, thus guaranteeing the United States and Great Britain a dominant role in defining policy. At base, the goal was to replace the function of the gold standard with a set of fixed exchange rates and reserve currencies that would be amenable to "regulation." Exchange rates were to be regulated by multilateral organizations, which would control a fund comprised of members' contributions. The system was based on the ability of nations to maintain stable exchange rates, the convertibility of currencies, and national policies supporting free trade and balance-of-payments equilibrium (Brett, 1985:111–112).

The World Bank, also created at the Bretton Woods conference, was to make long-term loans at commercial rates to finance infrastructure development projects in economically weaker nations. Had it been endowed with sufficient resources, the World Bank might have functioned to increase development investments and promote more balanced international trade (Brett, 1985). The Americans at Bretton Woods worked to constrain government contributions to the bank. Forced onto private credit markets, the World Bank reinforced commercial rates and credit policies while it absorbed the risk of loans to countries that were otherwise unable to obtain credit. In addition, project loans were guided by performance criteria. In 1956 and 1960 additional components were created to form the World Bank Group; the International Finance Corporation (IFC) to provide loans to private corporations (without government guarantee); and the International Development Association (IDA) to provide very long term loans (fifty years) to governments. Since IDA money was targeted for countries with weaker economies, little went to Latin America. Indeed, the original purpose of these organizations was to reestablish trade in the industrialized world. The foundation of this system was a stable U.S. currency, backed by gold reserves. When that system collapsed in the 1970s, the World Bank, like the IMF, was compelled to find its way in a newly uncertain international division of labor.

In the 1960s the World Bank's priority was agriculture; after 1973, bank project loans focused more on poverty.[3] Bank statements consistently asserted that economic criteria were the sole basis for its lending decisions, but the distribution of World Bank loans has favored regimes that encouraged foreign investment, free trade policies, and unrestricted capital flows, even when these policies have exacerbated inequality and poverty and reinforced the use of violence by national regimes in defense of international interests (Bornschier and Chase-Dunn, 1985:44–45). In essence, the World Bank's policies subsidized development of a national capitalist class allied with international business and antagonistic to autonomous national economic policies (Payer, 1982:117).

The third multilateral institutional pillar of the postwar international economy is GATT (the General Agreement on Tariffs and Trade). It is not an organization per se, but a treaty first signed in 1947 by industrial and developing countries—currently 105 countries participate—formally ratifying their commitment to end the protectionism that they viewed as one cause for the intractable nature of the 1930s Great Depression. It was originally conceived as part of the International Trade Organization (ITO), which was to complement the IMF and World Bank's governance of the postwar international system. Ironically, the ITO was established by the Havana Charter in 1948—53 nations signed the original agreement covering trade, foreign investment, and business practices—and provided with extensive regulatory powers, but it failed to secure U.S. government support when U.S. business and Congress protested external controls on trade policy.

Financed by members according to their share of world trade, GATT promotes trade equity by providing that any restrictions on trade be in the form of tariffs and not discriminate against any member. Whereas members automatically have most favored nation status with each other, countries applying for membership may be required to restructure their economic policies.[4] GATT influence has promoted policies that reduce constraints on trade and capital transfers. In its forty years, average tariffs of industrialized nations dropped from roughly 40 percent to 5 percent. Nevertheless, in the 1970s growing protectionism—particularly in the United States and Common Market countries—and glaring gaps in GATT controls (such as in agriculture, services, information) have undermined its credibility.

Parallel to trends in relations between the World Bank and IMF and the individual governments, GATT as an institution has emphasized development of standardized negotiation procedures for disputes and institutionalized performance criteria. The principal industrial and dominant trading powers (the European Economic Community, the United States, and Japan) have dominated past policies, but developing countries have often violated the principles of the GATT. Nevertheless, they have been unable to establish a coordinated set of proposals. Indeed, in common with the functioning of the World Bank and IMF, the GATT negotiations have reinforced the disunity of Third World interests.

In the immediate postwar years the functioning of these multilateral institutions was somewhat dampened by the Marshall Plan's massive transfer of resources to Europe. U.S. intentions at Bretton Woods and in the Marshall Plan were directed at establishing an international economic order in which "national capitalism," that is, state interventions limiting free trade and investment, would be controlled (Wood 1986; Dietz 1987). European recovery and the defense of capitalism against the alleged Soviet threat, however, also would be based upon the development of Third World markets for industrial products and raw materials exports to the United States (Wood 1986:40–41). Indeed, between 1950 and 1980 developing countries as a whole experienced considerable growth (Srinivasan 1982:92). It is significant that the Bretton Woods system did not distinguish between advanced industrial nations and the Third World. Thus no specific mechanisms were developed to direct external finance from countries with a surplus to developing countries. Nevertheless, in the postwar decades a succession of actors did play this role. In the 1950s foreign direct investment burgeoned; in the 1960s—after the Cuban revolution—official aid programs expanded; and in the 1970s—seeking to recycle petrodollars—international banks provided funds. The debt crisis of the 1980s stems in part from the lack of new external financing for Latin American development (Griffith-Jones, 1984:5).

By the 1960s, however, contradictions inherent in the Bretton Woods agreement began to compel changes. First, the U.S. economy's inability to eliminate deficits meant that foreign liabilities were outstripping its capacity to fulfill gold exchange commitments. Although the dollar functioned as the reserve currency for the international monetary system, U.S. balance-of-payments deficits tied to its military obligations and the Vietnam War meant that those nations with a surplus were paying for the U.S. policies if they did not convert their dollars into gold. However, if the United States had ended its balance-of-payments deficits, gold production at the fixed value of $35 per ounce would have been insufficient to meet the needs of an expanding world economy (Triffin, 1978). The leading industrial nations worked within the structure of the IMF to create new forms of credit that would counterbalance the U.S. deficits. In 1967 the leading industrial nations and IMF created an additional reserve asset called Special Drawing Rights (SDR), which was available to all IMF members. But this did not halt the flow of dollars from the United States, and fixed exchange rates and dollar convertibility for gold were increasingly anachronistic commitments, which eventually fell in 1971.

The Floating Palace

Nixon announced a devaluation of the U.S. currency and began an era of floating exchange rates (Dam, 1982). As U.S. economic hegemony declined, the multilateral institutional arrangements created in the 1940s were transformed. Thus it was the U.S. debt crisis of the early 1970s that marked the emergence of a new international monetary regime. The processes unleashed in the new environment of the 1970s would lead directly to the debt crisis associated with the Third World and especially Latin America in the 1980s. Latin America's economic relationship—particularly of the largest markets and most industrialized economies—with the world changed from one based on trade, aid, official loans, and direct investment to one dominated by government debt to private banks and multilateral financial agencies. Floating exchange rates greatly increased the uncertainty and volatility of international commerce. Multinational corporations were compelled to enter the currency markets in order to protect their positions and hedge against losses. Dollar devaluations transformed the business logic for private commerce. They also triggered the political logic leading to the Organization of Petroleum Exporting Countries (OPEC) cartel's actions six months later.

Certain historical events capture the essential focus of a decade because they redefine the meaning of existing social relations and, through their impact on major actors, reshape the social and institutional relations of succeeding years. In 1973 the OPEC cartel's imposition of a 400 percent rise in petroleum prices had an immediate impact on the international monetary system. Because oil was traded in dollars, the U.S. currency's 25 percent devaluation since 1971 and predicted continued decline motivated the OPEC nations to take action. This meant deficits for the oil-importing nations and an unprecedented infusion of capital for the international banking system. International private capital markets expanded rapidly. Increased commercial-bank lending to Latin American governments rapidly transformed the relationship between the IMF and Latin America. For the remainder of the decade, IMF financing for Third World countries dropped to roughly 3 percent of the total (Dam, 1982:296).

In the 1970s, high inflation and OPEC surpluses combined to yield very low real-interest rates for external debt (Sjaastad, 1983:309). Large commercial banks faced enormous liquid reserves with few outlets in the industrial nations, particularly in the United States, due to a prolonged and severe recession. They focused their loans on a small group of Third World countries that were viewed as good risks because of their large domestic markets, industrial base, and strong exports. Two countries, Mexico and Brazil, accounted for half the loans to non-OPEC countries, and most of the rest were directed to less than a dozen others (Stallings, 1987). Latin American operations rapidly became an important source of bank profits. In 1976 the U.S. Federal Reserve Board eased credit as a means to aid the economic growth that began in 1975. Over the next two years, however, an expanded money supply produced the double-digit inflation that eventually undermined the Carter administration. After 1979, however, under a new chairman the Federal Reserve Board began to stress a "tight money" policy aimed at reducing inflation, whatever the cost.[5] Resulting high interest rates broke both inflation and the economic recovery; as credit dried up, thousands of U.S. businesses went bankrupt; in Latin America and much of the world economy closely tied to the U.S. market, recession followed. Given the supposed security of loans to governments, international banks greatly increased the proportion of their assets committed to Latin American loans. Total private and multilateral loans to Latin America in 1976–1979 equaled a net transfer of $52 billion (ECLAC, 1986). In spite of this growth, the external debt did not reach historically unprecedented levels (Lewis, 1980). The cost of *debt service*, however, grew rapidly throughout the 1970s, especially after 1978, linked closely to Federal Reserve Board policies discussed above.

The relationship between international banks and the IMF also changed. In the 1960s U.S., European, and Japanese commercial banks had rapidly extended and intensified their international operations (Brett, 1985; Moffitt, 1983). Between 1971 and 1976 the overseas branches of the fifty largest international banks increased over 60 percent (Furtado, 1987: 30). Following U.S. corporations, and driven by U.S. controls on capital under Nixon, the largest U.S. banks soon discovered that their control of information and newly developed communication infrastructures provided them with significant advantages over local capitalists in currency speculation. Therefore, by the 1970s, if the IMF were to continue operating as a source of liquidity for nations with balance-of-payments deficits, it would be competing with private banks, which were now eager to recycle OPEC cash and were facing severely reduced investment opportunities in the industrial nations.

Particularly after an unsuccessful effort to influence Peru's loan repayments in 1976–1977, the commercial banks began to coordinate their loans with the IMF's evaluation of national economic policies, as a precondition for access to its funds. Thus IMF's functions began to change after 1973. In an era of floating exchange rates, IMF lending itself grew rapidly,[6] but shifted its rationale to one closely linked to bank interests: preventing debt crises and bank failures (Vaubel 1983:291–292). The IMF, originally the functional equivalent of a credit union (Kenen, 1986), was led by modifications in the face of a weak U.S. currency to act as a commercial bank enforcing fiscal responsibility on chronic debtors (Conway, 1987:196).

"Substantial Justification": *IMF Conditionality and Latin America*

The IMF's function as fiscal disciplinarian was initiated in the 1950s via a set of rules that addressed new problems relating to Third World members' currency requests. Within a defined proportion—"tranche"—of each country's contribution quota, applications were approved virtually automatically. Beyond this threshold, approval was to be conditioned on evidence that the funds would be used to support "an effective program for establishing or keeping the stability of the currency of the member country at a realistic exchange rate" (IMF, 1958:404). In later years IMF standby agreements increased in importance and a formal bureaucratic protocol for applications and supervision came to dominate IMF activities. Thus the IMF's relationship with less developed nations became that of an auditor and fiscal disciplinarian (Frenkel and O'Donnell, 1979:174–175). The rationale for its actions rested on self-defined technical and objective criteria regarding the general welfare of the national and international economy.

The specific set of measures imposed on borrower countries includes: (1) devaluation; (2) reduced public spending; (3) elimination of public subsidies; (4) wage restraint; (5) increased interest rates and taxes related to demand curbs; (6) elimination of state-owned or -supported enterprises and greater access for foreign investment; (7) reform of protection for local industries, export promotion, and application of new foreign exchange to the debt service. The general thrust is to promote market-oriented open economies geared to export production (Loxley, 1984:29).

Prior to the 1970s these "conditions" had only minor importance for Latin America. In the 1960s, 75 percent of net capital flow was composed of direct investment and official credits (Ffrench-Davis, 1985). By 1980, however, bank lending's proportion of net capital flow had reached 70 percent. In the rush to recycle petrodollars, international commercial banks engaged in aggressive loan policies that often were unaccompanied by analysis or judgment of client solvency. Throughout the 1970s easy access to private loans and high inflation combined to encourage many governments' acquisition of debt. Third World public debt increased from $75.1 billion in 1970 to $634.4 billion in 1983 (Wood, 1986:130). When U.S. Federal Reserve Board policies initiated an era of high interest rates and tight money to break inflation, bank lending terms reversed. Higher interest rates and short-term amortization and refinancing created a *credit crisis* that annually produced large increases in total indebtedness.

In this new environment, balance-of-payments deficits and bank debt compelled a rise in requests for standby loans from the IMF. As the central institution defining the terms for access to credit, the IMF's role was magnified. Coordination of creditor policies (IMF, World Bank, private banks, bilateral aid, and so forth) effectively prevented debtors from playing one credit source against another;[7] differences in specific debt conditions, trade structure, and national resources combined with variations in the actual implementation of conditionality (Körner et al., 1985:61; Walton, 1987) to undermine the possibility of *debtor cartels*.[8] Debtor governments seeking to travel their own course and place national development priorities ahead of debt payment and IMF-mandated structural adjustments had nowhere to turn. Without IMF approval, foreign investment and credit flows declined precipitously.[9]

Negotiations and Renegotiations:
The Role of Institutional Logic

The harsh IMF and World Bank conditionality and structural adjustment terms for debtor government access to new credits and renegotiation of old loans are commonly noted to have a creditor bias. The impact of these policies on the population and economic structure of debtor countries is viewed as a necessary price to pay for maintaining orderly markets and the financial stability of international institutions. Calls for a more equitable distribution of the costs of the debt crisis receive little sympathy from these agencies and/or international banks.[10] Thus the $52 billion (ECLA, 1986) in net capital transferred to Latin America between 1976 and 1979 was more than matched by a net outflow of $113 in 1983–1986 (Feinberg, 1987:205). In short, 5 percent of Latin American GNP has been exported in order to meet the conditions imposed by the commercial banks and the IMF.

The mandate of the IMF and World Bank is to stabilize and regulate the international financial order and sustain open international trade. The private banks' objectives are to lower their potential losses, increase payments, and provide the minimum necessary credit to guarantee that debtor countries continue to pay (Foxley, 1987:101). However, the capacity of debtor countries to implement the "structural adjustment" policies upon which new loans and credit are contingent is limited by the processes of internationalization that characterize the new international division of labor.

Internationalized production processes, labor markets, and financial markets, when coordinated through the organization of multilateral institutions and corporations, have effectively undermined national regimes' capacity to use traditional monetary, trade, and fiscal policies to control the economy (Furtado, 1987:40). Heterodox stabilization policies and austerity policies are fraught with contradictions that threaten the political legitimacy of national governments (see Chapters 2, 7, 8, and 10). Caught within these compelling cross currents, debtor governments have found themselves forced to accept a routinized process for rescheduling loan payments. They must present a plan for economic stabilization, a plan that conforms to the conditionality and structural adjustment criteria demanded by the IMF and World Bank as the basis for certification of creditworthiness. Negotiation with agencies of industrial nations' "aid regime" follows in order to obtain official loans on below-market terms and secure trade agreements within GATT. Finally, negotiations with the commercial banks determine access to new private credit (Garten, 1982:280).

In practice, these routine negotiations with one set of institutional actors present contradictory demands that, ironically, are contingent upon satisfactory negotiation with another set of creditors. These separate negotiations create an environment of institutionally determined performance criteria unrelated to the welfare and security of the debtor country population or traditional development goals, but that redistribute organizational power within debtor states. The IMF annual review procedures create an imperative for debtor governments to establish economic monitoring procedures and state institutions that allow continued supervision and standardized reporting procedures. In addition, the World Bank's shift from project-specific to broad structural adjustment policies and more short-to-medium-term lending reduces the role of special-purpose institutions and increases the importance of central banks and finance ministries within national regimes (Carvounis, 1984:62–84). The convergence of IMF and World Bank loan policies has increased the leverage of multilateral institutions by centralizing information and negotiation strategies for creditors. The effectiveness of IMF conditionality and the negotiated "rescheduling process" in controlling the overall *policy mix* in debtor countries is based on the ability to monitor borrowers' economic performance (Williamson, 1982:25). Indeed:

The negotiating procedure brings the IMF into the process of fashioning the economic policies for the debtor nation, including decisions that have powerful effects on domestic conditions. At the same time, the Fund insists that adjustment take place without recourse to heightened trade and exchange controls, and this also disposes the IMF to go beyond policy approval and into policy-making (Carvounis, 1984:68; see also Neu, 1979: 239).

In the 1980s, Latin America's principal debtor nations have produced a strong net outflow of capital based on reduced wages, reduced imports, and dismantling of state sector programs and institutions, especially public sector capital investments. Conditionality has required that surpluses generated by balance-of-trade surpluses be used to satisfy multilateral and international creditors. National regimes are constrained from shifting resource dependence to the local economy by raising domestic revenues. Thus the functions of all state institutions are increasingly buffered by those state agencies that negotiate access to new credit. And as a result, IMF conditionality is viewed as a set of institutional criteria that are incompatible with development goals and that delegitimate the sovereignty of national governments.

In addition, satisfaction of IMF "conditions" has become the routine first step required for debtor country loan negotiations with OECD nations through the Paris Club.[11] This structure has produced a maximum amount of uncertainty for debtor nations and maximum amount of flexibility and control for creditors. Debtors seeking bilateral loans and debt rescheduling face ad hoc procedures, short-term loans, which require constant negotiating, domestic policies aimed at rapid measurable results, and official indifference to the domestic consequences of required policies (Carvounis, 1984:73).

Finally, commercial creditors' loans are conditional upon Paris Club agreements, and the negotiation process for rescheduling loans follows no established routine. Again, this increases debtor uncertainty. The information search by debtor countries attempting to reschedule loans incorporates them into a perpetual round of prenegotiations, negotiations, and renegotiations, wherein they must respond to new demands for information on policies and policy performance. In order to "play the game" debtor country negotiators find themselves compelled to conduct three separate sets of parallel negotiations with creditors, who place mutually contingent but independent performance demands upon the debtor government's economic and social policies.

To conclude, Latin American debtor nations find themselves operating in a new international division of labor wherein internationalization has produced profound shifts in trade, production processes, finance, and investment. More important for the processes of policy formation and implementation, however, the coordination of multilateral, official, and commercial finance capital has created an environment of organizational priorities that are divorced from the functioning of the domestic economic and political marketplace in debtor nations. The consequences of compliance with the policies mandated by those international organizations are the subject of the following chapters.

Notes

1. Manuel Pastor, Jr. (1987: 21–22) briefly summarized the import substitution industrialization (ISI) model. "ISI was an attempt to develop local industry by having domestic enterprises take over the market for which there was a known demand: the market for imported consumer goods. High tariff walls would protect the domestic substitute, whereas overvaluation, dual exchange rates, subsidies, and other devices would cheapen the intermediate imports of raw materials and capital equipment necessary for final goods production (Hirschman, 1968; 1979). In addition to these trade policies, the state would take an activist role domestically by managing demand and sponsoring the construction of infrastructure—often paying for this by borrowing abroad" (Nolt, 1983:7–11).

2. "Whether in cases embracing the *low state* neoliberal authoritarianism of Chile or the *high state* mobilization of Brazil, the political capacity, or power, to guide industrial and agricultural internationalization shrinks before the transnational locus of production changes. The imperatives of export promotion, debt refinancing, import constraint, regressive wage policies, competitive devaluation (*realistic exchange rates*), and fiscal austerity dictate that the states of Latin America have less real capacity to negotiate their entry into the new international division of labor" (Sanderson, 1985:21).

3. Payer (1982:43) noted that this shift closely tracked changes in U.S. aid marked by the U.S. Foreign Assistance Act.

4. When Mexico joined the GATT in 1986, the cost involved an end to existing policies on import licenses, reduced tariffs, and lowered subsidies.

5. Hirschman (1987:32) in a typically sensible and colorful passage contrasted the "wallflower" and "garden path" metaphors that represent bankers' and Latin Americans' respective descriptions of the loan environment that continued until the "Volker shock" of high interest rates.

6. The OECD calculated that multilateral lending increased from $10 billion in 1971 to $76 billion in 1982. Private loans to Third World countries rose from $20 billion to $265 billion and the capital market's share of total loans reached 42 percent of the total by 1982 (OECD, 1983).

7. "Governments in industrial countries, led by the United States, are working to increase the collaboration among these three (IMF, World Bank, IDB) multilateral institutions in order to ensure that they offer consistent advice backed by the maximum degree of leverage" (Feinberg, 1987:206).

8. Indeed, coordinated actions by private bank advisory committees and the IMF have ensured that negotiations with major debtors are staggered, thus undermining one structural basis for debtor leverage in negotiations (Riding, 1988:1).

9. In early 1987 a decline in currency reserves led Brazil to suspend virtually all payments on its $113 billion foreign debt. The immediate goal was to step outside the rules of formal negotiation to compel improved terms from creditors. Other debtors were hopeful but passive. The international financial community and OECD governments acted. Foreign investment declined, credit flows were reduced, and trade sanctions were applied.

10. ECLA (1986:30) summarized the IMF and World Bank rationale as follows: "They assume that . . . the problem is one of short-term liquidity, that is a temporary conjunctural crisis caused by factors beyond the control of the agents involved . . . , it is claimed that this crisis will automatically be resolved when the world economy recovers, since financial equilibrium will then be restored within a few years and normal international credit operations resumed. In other words, it is assumed that, on recovering their capacity to service external debts, the developing countries will regain their image of creditworthiness and their former access to the international credit markets."

11. The Paris Club was created in 1956 as a multilateral organization to coordinate the policies of OECD creditor nations that have bilateral loans with Third World nations. Creditor nations have thus been able to centralize negotiations and routinize procedures. Debtor nations therefore must confront creditors in a negotiating framework where bilateral loans and rescheduling of loans are uniform across sources of credit.

References

Abbott, George C. *International Indebtedness and the Developing Countries.* London: Croom Helm, 1979.

Barkin, David, and Carlos Rozo. "L'Agriculture et l'internationalization du capital," *Revue tiers-monde,* 88: 723–745, 1983.

Barkin, David, and Blanca Suárez. *El Fin de Autosuficiencia alimentaria.* Mexico: Nueva Imagen, 1982.

Becker, David, Jeff Frieden, Sayre P. Schatz, and Richard L. Sklar. *Postimperialism: International Capitalism and Development in the Twentieth Century.* Boulder, Colorado: Lynne Rienner Publishers, 1987.

Bell, Daniel. "Some Simple Predictions About Planet Earth in 2013," *The Washington Post National Weekly Edition,* p. 24, February 22–28, 1988.

Block, Fred. *The Origins of International Economic Disorder: A Study of United States International Monetary Policy from World War II to the Present.* Berkeley: University of California Press, 1977.

Bornschier, Volker, and Christopher Chase-Dunn. *Transnational Corporations and Underdevelopment.* New York: Praeger Publishers, 1985.

Brett, E. A. *The World Economy since the War: The Politics of Uneven Development.* New York: Praeger, 1985.

Canak, William L. "The Peripheral State Debate: State Capitalism and Bureaucratic Authoritarianism in Latin America," *Latin American Research Review* 19: 3–36, 1984.

Carvounis, Chris C. *The Debt Dilemma of Developing Nations: Issues and Cases.* Westport, Connecticut: Quorum Books, 1984.

Collier, Cavis. *The New Authoritarianism in Latin America.* Princeton, N.J.: Princeton University Press, 1979.

Conway, Patrick. "Baker Plan and International Indebtedness," *The World Economy* 10: 193–204, 1987.

Dam, Kenneth W. *The Rules of the Game: Reform and Evolution in the International Monetary System.* Chicago: The University of Chicago Press, 1982.

Dietz, James L. "Debt, International Corporations, and Economic Change in Latin America and the Caribbean," *Latin American Perspectives* 55: 508–515, 1987.

Dornbusch, Rudiger. "On the Consequences of Muddling Through the Debt Crisis," *The World Economy* 7: 145–162, 1984.

ECLAC (Economic Commission for Latin America and the Caribbean). *Debt, Adjustment, and Renegotiation in Latin America: Orthodox and Alternative Approaches.* Boulder, Colorado: Lynne Rienner Publishers, 1986.

Economist. "Get Ready for the Phoenix," *The Economist*, p. 9, January 9, 1988.

Feinberg, Richard. "Multilateral Lending and Latin America," *The World Economy* 10: 205–218, 1987.

Fitzgerald, E.V.K. "The New International Division of Labour and the Relative Autonomy of the State: Notes for a Reappraisal of Classical Dependency," *Bulletin of Latin American Research* 1: 1–12, 1981.

Foxley, Alejandro. "The Foreign Debt Problem," *International Journal of Political Economy* 17: 88–116, 1987.

Ffrench-Davis, Ricardo. "The External Debt Crisis in Latin America: Trends and Outlook," in Kim, Kwan S., and David R. Ruccio (eds.). *Debt and Development in Latin America.* Notre Dame, Indiana: University of Notre Dame Press, 1985.

Frenkel, Roberto, and Guillermo O'Donnell. "The 'Stabilization Programs' of the International Monetary Fund and Their Internal Impacts," in Richard A. Fagen (ed.). *Capitalism and the State in Latin America.* Stanford: Stanford University Press, 1979.

Fröbel, Folker, Jurgen Heinrichs, and Otto Kreye. *The New International Division of Labour: Structural Unemployment in Industrialised Countries and Industrialisation in Developing Countries.* Cambridge: Cambridge University Press, 1985.

Furtado, Celso. "Transnationalization and Monetarism," *International Journal of Political Economy* 17: 15–44, 1987.

Garten, Jeffrey. "Rescheduling Sovereign Debt: Is There a Better Approach," *The World Economy* 5: 279–290, 1982.

Griffith-Jones, Stephanie. *International Finance and Latin America.* London: Croom Helm, 1984.

Hirschman, Albert. "The Political Economy of Import-Substituting Industrialization in Latin America," *Quarterly Journal of Economics* 82: 1–32, 1968.

———. "The Turn to Authoritarianism in Latin America and the Search for its Economic Determinants," in Collier, David (ed.). *The New Authoritarianism in Latin America.* Princeton, N.J.: Princeton University Press, 1979.

———. "The Political Economy of Latin American Development: Seven Exercises in Retrospection," *Latin American Research Review* 22: 7–36, 1987.

IMF (International Monetary Fund). *International Reserves and Liquidity: A Study by the Staff of the International Monetary Fund.* Washington, D.C.: International Monetary Fund, 1958.

Hymer, Stephen. "The Internationalization of Capital," *Journal of Economic Issues* 6: 91–111, 1972.

Junz, Helen B. "How to Assure the Stability of the Financial System," *The World Economy* 4: 263–270, 1981.

Kenen, Peter. *Financing, Adjustment and the International Monetary Fund.* Washington, D.C.: The Brookings Institution, 1986.

Körner, Peter, Gero Maas, Thomas Siebold, and Rainer Tetzlaff. *The IMF and the Debt Crisis: A Guide to the Third World's Dilemmas.* London: Zed Books, 1986.

Lewis, W. Arthur. "The Slowing Down of the Engine of Growth," *American Economic Review* 70: 556-564, 1980.

Loxley, John. *The IMF and the Poorest Countries.* Ottowa: The North-South Institute, 1984.

Marcussen, Henrik Secher, and Jens Erik Torp. *The Internationalization of Capital: The Prospects for the Third World.* London: Zed Press, 1982.

Moffitt, Michael. *The World's Money: International Banking from Bretton Woods to the Brink of Insolvency.* New York: Simon and Schuster, 1983.

Neu, Carl R. "The International Monetary Fund and LDC Debt," in Lawrence G. Franko and Marilyn J. Seiber (eds.). *Developing Country Debt.* New York: Praeger Publishers, 1979.

Nolt, James Herbert. "Conditions for the Predominance of Import Substitution Industrialization in the post-World War Two Era: An International Class Analysis," masters thesis in Economics, University of Massachusetts, Amherst, 1983.

Nyilas, Józef. *World Economy and its Main Development Tendencies.* The Hague: Martinus Nijhoff Publishers, 1982.

O'Donnell, Guillermo. *Modernization and Bureaucratic-Authoritarianism: Studies in South American Politics.* Berkeley: Institute of International Studies, University of California, Berkeley, 1973.

———. "Reflection on the Patterns of Change in the Bureaucratic-Authoritarian State," *Latin American Research Review* 13: 3–38, 1978.

OECD (Organization for Economic Cooperation and Development). *Economic Outlook.* Paris: OECD Publications, 1983.

Palloix, Christian. *Las firmas multinationales y el proceso de internacionalización.* Mexico: Siglo XXI, 1977.

Pastor, Manuel, Jr. *The International Monetary Fund and Latin America: Economic Stabilization and Class Conflict.* Boulder, Colorado: Westview Press, 1987.

Pastor, Robert (ed.). *Latin America's Debt Crisis: Adjusting to the Past or Planning for the Future.* Boulder, Colorado: Lynne Rienner Publishers, 1987.

Payer, Cheryl. *The Debt Trap: The International Monetary Fund and the Third World.* New York: Monthly Review Press, 1974.

———. *The World Bank: A Critical Analysis.* New York: Monthly Review Press, 1982.

Portes, Alejandro, and William L. Canak. "Latin America: Social Structures and Sociology," *Annual Review of Sociology* 7: 225–248, 1981.

Portes, Alejandro, and John Walton. *Labor, Class, and the International System.* Orlando, Fla.: Academic Press, 1981.

Riding, Alan. "Brazil's Reversal of Debt Strategy," *New York Times*, pp. 1 and 30, February 22, 1988.

Rowen, Hobart. "Poorer Nation Crisis Said to be Resolved," *Milwaukee Sentinel*, October 10, 1977.

Sanderson, Steven E. *The Americas in the New International Division of Labor.* New York: Holmes & Meier, 1985.

Sjaastad, Larry A. "International Debt Quagmire—to Whom do We Owe It?" *The World Economy* 6: 305–324, 1983.

Skidmore, Thomas, and Peter Smith. *Modern Latin America.* New York: Oxford University Press, 1984.

Srinivasan, T. N. "Why Developing Countries Should Participate in the GATT System," *The World Economy.* 5: 85–104, 1982.

Stallings, Barbara. *Banker to the Third World: U.S. Portfolio Investment in Latin America, 1900–1986.* Berkeley: University of California Press, 1987.

Sunkel, Osvaldo. *América Latina y la crisis económica internacional: ocho tesis y una propuesta.* Buenos Aires: Grupo Editorial Latinoamericano, 1985.

Thorp, Rosemary, and Lawrence Whitehead (eds.). *Inflation and Stabilization in Latin America.* London: Macmillan Press, 1979.

Triffin, R. "Reshaping the International Monetary Order," *International Social Science* 30: 301–314, 1978.

Vaubel, Roland. "The Moral Hazard of IMF Lending," *The World Economy* 6: 291–304, 1983.

Walton, John. "Urban Protest and the Global Political Economy: The IMF Riots," unpublished manuscript, Department of Sociology, University of California, Davis, 1987.

Wiarda, Howard J. *Latin America at the Crossroads: Debt, Development and the Future.* Boulder, Colorado: Westview Press, 1987.

Williamson, John. *The Lending Policies of the International Monetary Fund.* Washington, D.C.: Institute for International Economics, 1982.

Wood, Robert. *From Marshall Plan to Debt Crisis.* Berkeley: University of California Press, 1986.

Part 2
The National Economy
and Austerity

2

Democracy and Inflation, in the Light of the Brazilian Experience

Paul Singer

Democracy and Capitalism

In less developed countries (LDCs), macroeconomic policy is designed not only to sustain economic activity but also to foster industrialization. State ownership of transportation and energy infrastructures, as well as of heavy industry, is common. This compensates for the relatively small size of social expenditures and allows the public sector to implement effective fiscal policy. Nevertheless, the macroregulation of the economy is far from being a purely technical task. It is in fact a battlefield of opposed interests. For example, international business and local business may have opposing interests; likewise for wage workers and small producers (who benefit from high levels of employment) versus people who own and control large businesses and who are in high-income strata (who are worried by the pressure for wage increases, budget deficits, and inflation).

The fight over policies of macroregulation is highly ideological. On the right are those who think that state intervention should be minimal, just sufficient to keep price stability and balance-of-payments equilibrium. On the left are those who want the state to keep the economy near full employment and redistribute income by means of social expenditures, industrial policy, and regional development schemes. The resulting political disputes and theoretical controversies make up a complex scenario.

In Latin American democracies much of the haggling over prices (including wages, rents, and interest) is transferred from the market to the political arena. The demand for state assistance comes, not only from low-wage labor, unemployed, old, sick, and disabled persons, but also from peasants, regional interest groups, small businesses, and even big corporations. Such demands influence electoral struggles, and elected officials, in order to retain support of their constituents, tend to expand public expenditure. This requires, of course, higher taxes, which meet a growing resistance by taxpayers.

In LDCs the pressure on the treasury is compounded by the demand for public investment in transport, energy, heavy industry, technology, and other sectors that also provide "external economies" to private capital. In a country like Brazil where a sizable part of the labor force is unable to get "formal" employment, the state's role as an employer is important. Low-pay public sector employment is a sort of substitute for the nonexistent "dole," benefiting only supporters of winning candidates.

Inflation

Since World War II, inflation in capitalist democracies often has been exacerbated by the refusal of monetary authorities to restrict the money supply. This probably reflects their recognition that working-class voters show more tolerance for low inflation than for frequent recessions. Monetary and fiscal policies have been used mainly to keep inflation at a low (or tolerable) level, but not to eliminate it altogether.

There are, however, important differences between inflation of differing amounts, above or below certain thresholds. The so-called crawling inflations are so small that their corrosive effect on real income is hardly perceived. However, once inflation increases, the losing parties—wage earners, creditors, landlords—do become aware and start to fight for legal and contractual defenses against the prospective devaluation of their incomes and assets. Such defenses are, of course, the periodic readjustment of nominal values—wages, debts, rents—according to some legal index of average price-level increases. This is known as indexation.

The indexation of an economy takes time. Brazil, for instance, had yearly two-digit inflation during most of the 1940s and 1950s. Wage indexation was instituted only in the middle of the 1950s and financial assets were officially indexed only after 1964. Indexation takes time because employers, debtors, tenants, and other interest groups resist having their costs periodically raised by some index while at the same time having no guarantee that their own incomes will rise at least as much. In addition, inflation is always seen as an evil that should be eliminated at once. Indexation seems to prolong it. It takes years and several attempts and failures before the majority becomes convinced that the costs of eliminating inflation (usually through recession) are more unbearable than inflation itself.

The Indexed Economy

Once inflation becomes relatively large and permanent and most strategic prices—wages, rents, debts, exchange rates, and taxes—are indexed, economic relations change considerably. First, the indexation system is far from homogeneous. The time interval for adjusting nominal prices is not the same for all commodities and services. For instance, during the early 1980s in Brazil, rents were readjusted each semester, wages each month, the exchange rate each day. Indexation cannot compensate for all the loss caused by inflation, but the smaller the time interval between readjustments, the larger the compensation. In general, exporters have a much better defense against inflation than wage earners, and the latter have smaller inflationary losses than landlords.

Second, the indexation system is managed by the government. The rules of indexation in Brazil are defined and at times revised by the government. The rules refer to the time interval between readjustments as well as to the index applied to each price. When inflation is high, different indexes offer considerably different results. For instance, 1987 Brazilian wages were readjusted by a cost-of-living index based on consumption habits of low-income families. Previously, wages were readjusted by an index based on a much wider income-range. When relative prices change, as they do frequently under high inflation, each of these indexes may show quite different variations. Foodstuffs have a much bigger weight in the low-income index; thus, when food prices rise above other prices, this index indicates more inflation than the wider income range index.

Besides wages, financial assets face different indexation rules. Savings accounts, real estate installments, time deposits, fiscal debts—each has its own rules, which have been frequently altered as part of the monetary policy. The same may be said about the indexation of taxes. Income tax, for example, is heavily dependent on the readjustment of income brackets and—for firms—on the readjusted value of assets.

When inflation becomes truly high—in Brazil it has been in the three-digit range since 1980—*indexation rules* play a decisive role in income distribution. By changing such rules, the government can favor profits to the detriment of wages, debtors to the detriment of creditors, tenants to the detriment of landlords, or vice versa. Through indexation, the state can redirect the income flow to different economic sectors or classes, depending on the purposes of the economic policy. The state may step up the readjustment of the exchange rate and slow down the readjustment of nominal wages in order to increase exports and reduce imports and thereby create a larger trade surplus.

In an indexed economy, governmental intervention is much broader, and given the intricate mathematics involved in indexation, its meaning for real incomes is not easily perceived by the public. On the one hand, the government becomes more powerful and gains more freedom to practice macroregulation. On the other hand, the government is held responsible for the ongoing inflation and its damaging effects on real incomes. Even if wage earners or small business owners do not know exactly why they are getting poorer, they certainly blame the government.

In a high-inflation, indexed economy, like that of Brazil and many other Latin American nations, distributional struggles cease to be fought among classes or class fractions and become increasingly directed toward the state. Each class fraction (landlords, exporters, financiers, manufacturers, organized workers) struggles for more favorable indexation rules. This leads to faster and larger readjustments of prices, wages, and rents. If the government yields to such demands, the result is still higher inflation. At the same time, however, all classes together want the government to somehow stop or, at least, slow down inflation. Thus the government's ability to pursue a consistent economic policy is more apparent than real.

A perfect indexation system would give each income earner instantaneous and complete compensation for the current rise of his or her costs. The result would surely be hyperinflation. When prices, wages, and rents go up daily or even several times a day, as is common during hyperinflation, no further income redistribution is possible. The market economy founders, barter replaces monetary exchange, activity contracts dramatically, and almost everybody suffers. Once an economy reaches this point, all resistance against relative income losses vanishes and a monetary reform can easily extinguish the inflationary wildfire. Obviously, no government would choose this solution to the dilemma of high inflation. Therefore, government refuses demands to improve indexation and tinkers with the rules so as to convince people that they will be better off and that inflation will soon stabilize and later decline.

The Fight Against Inflation:
The Orthodox Treatment

Although high inflation is generally regarded as a scourge, orthodox anti-inflation policies that reduce demand inflict heavy losses on both business and wageworkers. It is not surprising that opposition to recessionary policies becomes very strong. Such opposition is frequently able to moderate orthodox policies or to force government to adopt compensatory measures, which alleviate some hardships. However, such measures reduce the effectiveness of the anti-inflationary drive. More often than not, the final result is that inflation is merely stabilized, but at the cost of economic stagnation.

This was Brazil's experience between 1981 and 1983. In 1980 inflation reached the three-digit level and external creditors forced the Brazilian government to adopt a rigidly orthodox adjustment policy designed to reduce inflation and produce a surplus on the trade balance. Growth of the money supply was checked, occasioning a harsh credit squeeze. The nominal value of loans to the private sector expanded 73 percent against an inflation of 110.2 percent, which implies a 17.7 percent reduction of the loans' real value. At the same time, public expenditure was cut and interest rate controls were dropped. Internal demand declined, particularly for consumer durables. Industrial sales declined precipitously, production dropped and employment decreased. In 1981, the Brazilian economy plunged into recession: In real terms, the gross domestic product (GDP) fell 3.3 percent and GDP per capita fell 5.7 percent. Manufacturing output was reduced by 10.4 percent. However, the impact on inflation was minor; inflation was reduced from 110.2 percent in 1980 to 95.2 percent in 1981.

In 1982, facing a decisive year-end election for state governors and the congress, the government eased somewhat the orthodox attack on inflation. Agriculture and exporters continued to get subsidized loans. The nominal value of loans to the private sector expanded 91.6 percent against a 95.2 percent inflation, implying a real decline of 1.8 percent. Recession had visibly eroded the social basis of support to the government, without a compensating reduction of inflation. The military regime then in power was eager to gain a majority in congress and in as many states as possible in order to win a majority in the Electoral College—composed by the federal congress and by delegates from state assemblies—that was going to choose the next president in 1985. The real value of loans to the private sector declined another 2 percent, but the global deficit of the public sector rose from 5.9 percent of GDP in 1981 to 6.6 percent in 1982. Real output of manufacturing fell, in 1982, 0.44 percent and real GDP increased 0.92 percent. Per capita GDP still declined by 1.5 percent. In 1982, recession was replaced by stagnation and inflation reached 99.7 percent.

The small improvement in the economic situation helped the government to reach its electoral objective. Although the opposition won a large majority in the popular vote, the underrepresentation of the large states in the Electoral College gave a majority of seats to the official party. Thus the continuation of the military regime—probably in a civil guise—seemed assured. Nevertheless, support for the government continued to deteriorate. The orthodox economic policy was obviously failing; the much needed growth was absent, whereas unemployment and inflation remained high.

In September 1982, the Mexican moratorium provoked panic in the Euromarket, and all forthcoming loans to Latin American countries were cut at once. In common with other debtor nations, Brazil was servicing its already enormous external debt by means of new loans. In 1982, international interest rates were still high. The London Interbank Offering Rate (LIBOR), a measure of international loan rates, was 13.40 percent and the prime rate stood at 14.59 percent. Brazil's trade balance was U.S. $817 million. The interest on the debt, to be paid to external creditors, was $12.55 billion. Technically, the Brazilian state was insolvent, but the government tried to hide this fact from the public in order to avoid an election defeat in November. The government decided to pay the debt interest with the country's foreign exchange reserves. The reserves quickly fell from $7.50 billion in 1981 to US $3.99 billion in 1982.[1] After the election, the government asked the IMF for a standby loan.

Under IMF surveillance the orthodox policy was intensified. In February 1983, the currency was devalued 30 percent *above* current inflation. This accelerated inflation to a still higher level. The government had already exported food reserves. Thus, when bad weather further reduced the supply of foodstuffs, their prices increased enormously. At the end of 1983 inflation reached 211 percent. The government's credit squeeze was intensified, but even so the nominal value of loans to the private sector grew 143.4 percent, declining 21.7 percent in real terms. Fiscal policy was made stricter: The public sector deficit fell to 2.5 percent of GDP (below the target of 2.7 percent programmed with the IMF). Government investment, which had already declined 3.42 percent in 1982, fell another 6.42 percent in 1983.

Inevitably, another harsh recession occurred. Manufacturing output decreased 6.13 percent, real GDP fell 2.5 percent, and per capita GDP declined 4.9 percent. Thousands of workers were fired, increasing social tensions in a country with no unemployment compensation. The large industrial towns in metropolitan São Paulo, Rio de Janeiro, and Belo Horizonte were severely hit by the decline in industrial activity. A large number of families became homeless, and street violence increased remarkably, culminating in the organized looting of supermarkets in working-class districts.

Until the external debt debacle, the government managed the indexation system in such a way that low incomes were somewhat preserved. In 1983, under the pressure of IMF and external creditors, the government decided to change the rules of wage indexation in order to bring about a cut of real wages. Such a move required congressional approval (the official party had a majority in Congress). Opposition was widespread and included business groups that demanded a cut in interest rates, not in wages, and argued that they were suffering losses under the weight of excessive financial expenses and that a further cut in real wages would depress even more an already contracted domestic market. As time went on, a common front of business and workers emerged and directed its protests against the wage squeeze and more generally against the whole orthodox stabilization policy. Public opinion against wage cuts became so strong that the ruling party split and Congress rejected the proposed change of wage indexation rules.

In early 1984, opposition to economic orthodoxy changed into opposition to the military regime. A campaign for "direct elections" for President brought millions to the streets. The split in the official party widened, giving opposition parties a majority in the Electoral College. In January 1985, Tancredo Neves and José Sarney were elected president and vice president, respectively, marking the start of a new era in Brazilian history, officially called the New Republic.

The failure of orthodoxy proved decisive for the defeat of the military regime. The stabilization policy failed on its own terms. It imposed heavy costs on employment, wages, profits, and consumption but failed to reduce inflation. The mechanics of the failure are clear: Orthodox stabilization cut internal demand by means of price "adjustments" (currency devaluation, increase of tariffs and indirect taxes, elimination of subsidies), which initially *accelerated* inflation; finally in order to bring inflation down, monetary and fiscal policies became very severe, inflicting large losses on indebted groups, such as farmers and small business owners, as well as on beneficiaries of the social programs, for example, poor regions, public school students, recipients of public health assistance and "social" housing programs, and so on.

The orthodox treatment of high inflation in an indexed economy brings about a time sequence in which either: (1) indexation rules are changed to the detriment of the working classes in order to intensify the contraction of effective demand, or (2) recession works through the economy and reverses the trend of price increases. From the experience of Brazil as well as of other indexed economies, one may conclude that the latter time sequence is politically fatal, at least if there is some measure of democracy. No government that must face elections every four, five, or six years can hope to win the battle against inflation in time by means of the orthodox treatment. Orthodoxy has been successful in industrialized countries in which inflation climbed above the two-digit frontier without going beyond the indexation threshold. In such cases, relatively short-lived recessions were able to bring inflation down to a bearable level. Without indexation, even a moderate two-digit inflation inflicts heavy losses on wage earners, comparable to the hardships caused by unemployment. In this way, a trade-off between inflation and unemployment may come about. Wage earners, the majority of the electorate, may define at the polls the terms of the trade-off. However, in the fight against much higher inflation in indexed economies, orthodoxy does not have much chance. The cost of unemployment quickly eliminates the popular support needed by orthodoxy if it is to become effective against inflation.

The Fight Against Inflation: The Heterodox Treatment

Orthodoxy fails in the fight against high inflation in indexed economies because the costs to eliminate an inflation, which is to a large extent a legacy of the past, are too high. The heterodox treatment is essentially a strategy to eliminate "inertial" inflation. Heterodox treatment assumes that the "active" inflation, resulting from current disequilibrium between global demand and supply, must be dealt with according to the orthodox treatment.

The heterodox treatment of inflation has two parts: (1) the elimination of active inflation by means of conventional monetary and fiscal policies; (2) the elimination of inertial inflation, by means of a currency reform, which allows government to define specific rules of conversion of wages, debts, and rents into the new currency. Conversion rules should be devised with the aim that each income in the new currency be equal to its average during a past period. This period is determined by the timing of readjustments, defined by the previous indexation system.

Conversion by average real values replaces indexation. Inflation is, in this way, eliminated at once, assuming that any remaining excess demand or undersupply has already been corrected by conventional monetary and fiscal policies. Ideally, the heterodox treatment is to be applied when inflation is already completely inertial. This is defined not only by its constancy but also by equilibrium of external accounts and of the public sector.

This approach and its resulting strategy to eliminate high inflation in indexed economies was originally conceived in 1984 by two young Brazilian economists—Persio Arida and André Lara Rezende. Although the approach was intended as an alternative to the orthodox treatment of inflation in Brazil, its first practical applications were made elsewhere. In the middle of 1985, "heterodox shocks" against extremely high inflations were applied in Argentina, Israel, and Peru. Finally, after the heterodox experiences in other countries had been widely discussed, on

February 28, 1986, the Brazilian government announced its Cruzado Plan.

The assumption that the Brazilian inflation at that time was exclusively inertial was based on its constancy (it was 211 percent in 1983, 223.8 percent in 1984, and 235.1 percent in 1985), on the equilibrium in the balance of payments, and on the presumed elimination of the public sector deficit by a fiscal reform, enacted at the end of the preceding year. The Cruzado Plan introduced a new currency—the cruzado—worth 1,000 cruzeiros (the old unit of currency).

All wages and rents were converted into cruzados by proportions that aimed to maintain their real average value. Wages, however, got an additional bonus of 8 percent and the legal minimum wage got a bonus of 15 percent. Moreover, the decree also conceded to wage earners the following: an escalator clause according to which wages were to be readjusted every time inflation reached 20 percent and an unemployment insurance scheme. All this was done to mollify the expected opposition of trade unions, given the sharp reactions against heterodox shocks of trade unions in Argentina and in Israel.

In order to avoid anticipatory price increases and wage demands, the Cruzado Plan was prepared in strict secrecy. Its authors (a team of about ten economists, among them Arida and Lara Rezende) intended to convert by the "average" income *and* prices. However, the government lacked the necessary data for calculating the conversion factors of prices into cruzados. Therefore, prices were converted by the spot rate of 1,000 to 1 and immediately frozen. For Arida and Lara Rezende, the price freeze was just a tactic to win time (it was supposed to last three months) in order to bring prices to their "equilibrium" level. For the president and the political leadership, the price freeze became the most important element of the Cruzado Plan. They knew that the wage laborers wanted to stop prices from rising. The politicians correctly deduced that the price freeze would assure wide popular support for the plan.

In fact, the announcement of the Cruzado Plan was greeted with almost universal enthusiasm. President Sarney—Neves had died before his inauguration—spoke over a nationwide TV network and enjoined every citizen to be a *Fiscal do Presidente* (president's watchman) in order to enforce the price freeze. In response, millions of Brazilian citizens swarmed into supermarkets, stores, cafeterias, and so forth, to check prices. Many vendors tried to increase their prices at the last minute and were caught red-handed. Managers of supermarkets were arrested by the police, mainly to rescue them from the crowds. In some instances of excess enthusiasm, stores were plundered. TV coverage transmitted the most sensational scenes, whipping up popular fervor through frequent denunciations of the "saboteurs" of the Cruzado Plan. Columnists proclaimed that the monetary reform would redeem the country by banishing financial speculation and usury and rewarding honest work and productive investment.

The popular outcry expressed the intensity of popular outrage over inflation. Only the left-wing opposition to the government protested. The main criticism of the Left was of the unequal treatment given to wages and prices. Wages were reduced to the average, whereas prices were frozen at their peak value. Defenders of the Cruzado Plan replied that many prices under state control had not been readjusted recently and therefore prices in general were frozen at an average level. Since no accurate information on the recent behavior of individual prices was available, the issue remained unresolved.

Labor union members were particularly outraged because all wage contracts were changed at once, by decree, without any prior consultations. Union members were convinced that the conversion of wages by the "average" meant a large loss for workers, and they tried to mobilize rank and file to demonstrate and strike against the plan. The majority of union rank and file, however, did not feel injured by the Cruzado Plan: They were faced with a slightly reduced real wage if prices remained constant. And initially—for the first time in decades—the cost-of-living index stabilized.

From the beginning of the Cruzado Plan, a remarkable increase in consumption took place, the outward signs of which were traffic jams, overfull restaurants, cinemas, hotels, and even hospitals. Sales of clothes and consumer durables increased rapidly. An increase in real income may have accounted for part of this consumer spending. To a large extent, however, it was paid for with past savings. Savings accounts lost almost 10 percent of their balances in three months; over U.S. $2 billion was withdrawn, probably because the end of inflation eliminated the monthly readjustment of savings balances, a readjustment of about 15 percent per month right before the monetary reform. A widely held monetary illusion led many savers to regard such readjustment as a sort of "interest." Under the Cruzado Plan this adjustment fell to 0.5 percent per month. This perceived disincentive to save, together with the very peculiar atmosphere linked to the first relief from inflation in their lifetimes, probably explains the frenzy of consumption that overtook Brazilians.

In fact, some prices continued to rise. The freeze never reached prices of nonstandardized articles such as garments, shoes, furniture, repair services, and so on. Cost-of-living indexes did stabilize because foodstuff prices were actually declining. The Cruzado Plan was deliberately timed to coincide with the end of the main harvests (autumn in the Southern Hemisphere begins in March) so as to take advantage of the seasonal expansion of agricultural supply. This effect was limited to the first few months of the plan.

Large manufacturing firms responded to the increase of demand by expanding output without raising prices. Economies of scale gave them a margin of windfall profits, which gradually were eliminated by the steady increase of costs. Even labor costs grew as employment rose rapidly and firms began to compete for skilled labor by offering better pay. A wave of strikes in small and medium-sized enterprises, which had expanded production, succeeded in winning ad hoc wage increases. The real upswing in prices, however, came from industries producing raw materials. These industries were working already at full capacity and soon their output became very scarce. For example, not enough glass containers were available for the beverage and pharmaceutical industries. Stocks of building materials were rapidly exhausted when suddenly millions of homeowners decided to paint and renovate their dwellings. Even if large companies were unable to escape the price freeze, dealers could and did. Scarce raw materials were channeled to the black market. Dealers began charging an *agio* (overprice), a practice that became widespread throughout the economy.

At the height of the euphoria, Finance Minister Dilson Funaro announced that the price freeze would be ended after three months. There were immediate strong protests. President Sarney called Funaro and instructed him to inform the public that the price freeze would last until demand and supply were balanced. This became the official line. Consumers were happy; businesses began to devise tactics to evade the price freeze whenever market conditions allowed it.

The government issued official price lists with several hundred consumer items—categorized by types and trademarks—which became the main weapon of the president's watchmen. Gradually more and more of these items disappeared from the conspicuous shelves of the supermarkets where their prices could be easily checked. They were only to be found in smaller stores, often under the counter, with *agios* added to their price. The government promised that the official apparatus of price control would be greatly reinforced and would thus support the efforts of Sarney's watchmen. In reality nothing was done. The economists in charge of the heterodox policy did not want the freeze and were anxious (although not in public) to eliminate controls. Their view of the Cruzado Plan was completely different, and to some degree opposite, from that of most Brazilians and the political authorities. For the average Brazilian, the plan meant the end of inflation through the price freeze, enforced by political power against "speculators and saboteurs." For the economists, it meant a sophisticated change of the unit of account through which average incomes are stabilized and inflation is painlessly eliminated from the economy.

In a few months, the concealment of commodities completely defeated the president's watchmen. Initial enthusiasm was replaced by anxiety over where scarce articles could be found. The practice of preventive stockpiling by consumers became widespread. This reinforced the excess demand. Inflation returned, but at this stage mainly as "repressed" inflation in which the main cost for purchasers was not so much the price charged but the time and effort spent to make the transaction.

At the same time, an unanticipated redistribution of income took place through the half-enforced price freeze. Small businesses and self-employed workers quickly escaped the price freeze, due to the non-standardized nature of their products, and thereby increased their gain. Given low barriers to entry for such businesses, many people were attracted to them and the number of small businesses multiplied. Their demand for manpower expanded accordingly, and they competed for semiskilled and even unskilled labor by increasing wages. This led to sizable wage increases for nonunion and low-wage workers. Large firms had much less opportunity to raise prices illegally. They had to support growing costs with constant prices. Their profit margins declined until (in some cases) they became negative. Such firms refused to accede to demands for increased wages. As a result workers who had been at the forefront of wage battles and who used to get the highest pay bore losses similar to their employers. In the São Paulo metropolitan area during 1986, the income of registered employees rose 20.3 percent, that of unregistered employees rose 39.3 percent, and that of the self-employed rose 66.4 percent (Amaro et al., 1987, Table 20).

This income redistribution soon became unsustainable. The large businesses in less competitive markets stopped investing and soon reached full production capacity. This limited the expansion of the rest of the economy. Excess demand for consumer goods and capital goods produced inflation, which at the start was repressed by the price freeze, but which gradually went into the open.

The heterodox team employed an "orthodox" policy to fight against this new inflation. The aim of this policy was to eliminate excess demand through fiscal and monetary policies. However, political authorities did not feel any enthusiasm for cutting public expenditures or for squeezing credit and driving up interest rates. Moreover, given the fact that general elections were taking place at year's end, it was obviously the worst time to start an unpopular stabilization program. In July, a first attempt was made to extract a sizable share of middle-class income through forced loans on the purchase of cars and fuel and on foreign travel. Instead of lowering demand, the forced loans were regarded as price increases, signifying a violation of the price freeze by the government itself. For the first time since the enactment of the Cruzado Plan, public opinion turned against the government's economic policies.

Income-distribution-related conflicts, fought through successive price increases, soon returned. The government could have stopped the process by enforcing the freeze, with the support of the president's watchmen, and by creating a framework for negotiations through which relative prices could be decided. The logic of the heterodox approach implied that there are relative prices that are mutually consistent and may therefore be kept stable, moving only in response to changes in demand or supply. In the aftermath of a high inflation, which was just repressed for some months by a price freeze, such "equilibrium-relative prices" could not be determined through the market because all sorts of price spirals immediately brought inflation back. Negotiations, under public control and arbitration, could have linked whole sets of interdependent prices.[2] This would have required the creation of permanent negotiation boards, in which government, employers, employees, and the self-employed were represented.

The Brazilian government enjoined employer groups and labor union confederations to negotiate a so-called Social Pact but failed to put forward any concrete proposal for new regulation of prices and wages. The negotiations ended in complete failure. The talks were headed by the minister of labor; the economic ministries were conspicuously absent. The minister of finance and the Central Bank did not wish to give up any fraction of their power over economic policy. This obstinacy effectively undermined any attempt to negotiate strategic prices. The Brazilian economy plunged back into inflation. One week after the November 15 election, a last drive against excess demand was made. The government increased indirect taxes on nonessential consumption items (such as cigarettes, beverages, cars) and increased tariffs on public services. Indirect tax increases imply a corresponding rise of prices, which, through indexation, is transmitted to wages, which again induce new and more general increases of prices. Since the increase of taxes and tariffs tended to reduce real incomes, its affect on wages was impeded by a complete reformulation of the official inflation index, from which all nonessential items were eliminated. Once again, the whole package was prepared secretly and enacted by decree.

This clumsy attempt at effective demand management proved to be political folly. The package unleashed an uproar of indignant protests from left, center, and right. The timing of the unpopular measures was regarded as an aggravation. The government had waited until after election day to implement the policy. Thus it did not adversely affect the chances of its candidates. In fact, the Brazilian Democratic Movement party (PMDB), which was in the government, won a landslide, electing twenty-two out of twenty-three state governors and more than half of the Constituent Assembly. The new economic policy was regarded as treason by the electorate and particularly by wage earners who were harmed by the change of indexation rules. A general strike was scheduled by both labor confederations (General Labor Confederation, or CGT, and United Federation of Labor, or CUT), for December 1986, and the government hastily revoked the change in the cost-of-living index. The Cruzado Plan, which originally was greeted by fervent applause, ended in utter disaster. Officially measured inflation reached 7.3 percent in December 1986 and 16.8 percent in January 1987.

The failure of Brazil's heterodox shock policy can be ascribed to a misunderstanding: The economists intended to ease the application of orthodox measures by eliminating at once the deadweight of past inflation that was preserved through the indexation system; the political authorities viewed the heterodox shock as a sort of magic, the logic of which was beyond their comprehension. They marveled at the ease and rapidity with which inflation was apparently subdued and concluded—like most laymen—that the shock freed them from the constraints imposed by high inflation.

However, the misunderstanding does not explain everything. Resistance to the "management" of effective demand came not only from the political leadership. There was a general revulsion, stemming from the experience of three years of orthodox treatment, toward recessionary policies. The proof that excess demand was not the only—not even the main—cause of the return of inflation was provided by the follow-up to the Cruzado Plan, the so-called Bresser Plan (named after L. C. Bresser Pereira, the new minister of finance), enacted in June 1987. By this time, the economy was already in recession and real wages suffered a deep cut through a change in indexation rules. There was always an orthodox component to the shock: In addition to the real wage squeeze, tariffs and prices of basic inputs were sharply increased just at the moment when prices and wages were frozen. As a result, in August and September inflation fell to about 5 to 6 percent per month and then began to accelerate again, reaching almost 15 percent in November 1987. There was no revival of demand during this period. The return of inflation this time had the same basic cause as the previous one: the readjustment of relative prices, always in response to higher costs and in anticipation of future increases of the same costs.

Democracy and Inflation

Orthodox and heterodox economic policies share the assumption that the state will macroregulate the economy from a position *above* sectoral or class interests. For the common good, these interests must be defeated by means of authoritarian policies, prepared in strict secrecy and enacted by surprise. Both approaches regard excess demand as the root of inflation and conclude that it must be cut by means of a credit squeeze, a reduction of public expenditure, and an increase in taxes and tariffs. Heterodoxy is an extension of orthodox policies, designed to facilitate the management of effective demand in high-inflation indexed economies. The political feasibility of such policies is not explicitly considered.

Democratic capitalism is prone to inflation mainly because most distributional conflicts are disputed in the public sphere. The state budget acts as the biggest redistributor of income and in less developed countries (LDCs) as the main locus of capital accumulation (and also as the main employer). Voters and elected officials exchange political and economic favors, the exchange being facilitated and vitiated by inflation.[3] Once an economy is indexed, the production of excessive demand by public and private overspending becomes structural. Conventional theory sees the culprit only in public spending because the state is supposed to be the only one to have the power to create purchasing power from nothing, by the issue of fiduciary money. But that is far from being true. The main issuers of money are banks, which finance all sorts of expenditures, public as well as private. So, in an indexed economy, the fight against inflation requires, not an authoritarian macroregulation, highly centralized and consequently ignorant of how its policies affect individual industries and consumers, but a democratically disputed and negotiated micro-regulation of strategic prices.

If inflation is the ultimate product of democracy, then the remedy must be sought in democracy itself by extending it from the political to the economic realm. Some microdecisions, like price and wage setting, cannot be left to private bargaining in an indexed economy. Such microdecisions, particularly where capital is highly concentrated, must be made consistent with price stability. Consistency must be achieved not through shocks but systematically, through an elaborate set of negotiation boards, in which the clashes of sectoral and class interests can be constrained by monetary discipline.

To sum up, if effective demand should not grow beyond global supply, the allotment of demand among competing sectors and classes becomes the main problem. This is in essence a political question. When agents have not only economic but also political resources, then the market is not a self-disciplining mechanism. Therefore, a new form of regulation must be invented in which interests are represented by their purchasing power *and* their voting power. The state's responsibility is to identify the real limits of what can be allocated. Once microregulation is instituted, the democratization of macroregulation becomes feasible because the functioning of the former educates people and enables them to participate intelligently in the latter.

Notes

1. In 1982, Brazil still obtained U.S. $12.51 billion in new loans, from which $6.95 billion was used to amortize past debt.

2. These negotiations replace, in a certain way, bargaining in the marketplace. But market bargaining results in private contracts that can be freely changed, whereas the outcome of negotiations is enforced by the state, under the control of consumers and periodically revised. Distributional conflicts are fought openly, all parties gaining some control over their *real* incomes.

3. Vitiated, of course, because inflation takes away much of what is given in the form of nominal values.

References

Amaro, M. N., C. A. Ramos, M.G.P. Pinto, and M.M.J. Costa. "Desempenho do Mercado de Trabalho Brasileiro em 1986." Brasilia: Ministério do Trabalho (mimeo), 1987.

Arida, P. *Inflação zero: Brasil, Argentina e Israel.* Rio de Janeiro: Paz e Terra, 1986.

Singer, P. *O dia da lagarta: democratização e conflito distributivo no Brasil do cruzado.* São Paulo: Brasiliense, 1987.

3

The Fall of Labor's Share in Income and Consumption: A New "Growth Model" for Argentina?

Adriana Marshall

Introduction

Low wages and the resulting low consumption capacity of most of the population in Latin America and in other underdeveloped economies often have been regarded as a basic constraint on economic growth.[1] This view challenged the conventional economic wisdom that greater income concentration at the top is favorable to growth because it would presumably foster investment while also being the best option for increasing consumption. In contrast, it was argued that a more equal distribution of income would be the optimum alternative for expanding the domestic market, including the market for modern manufacturing production.[2] In this latter view, inequality is at the root of stagnation.

In the 1980s, this debate has once again become important as prolonged economic stagnation and declining wages throughout Latin America have brought to the fore the crucial role of consumption in the process of economic growth. In Latin America there is a new wave of interest in designing policies capable of raising the purchasing power of wages and boosting effective demand without accelerating inflation and weakening the trade balance.

During previous decades, low-income urban wage earners in Latin America were an important market for manufactured goods. Although it is possible, as many Latin American examples demonstrate, to develop an industrial base with a market concentrated in the medium- and high-income strata, consumption of manufactured goods by lower strata is actually quite substantial.[3] In 1970, for example, the poorest 50 percent of the population in Buenos Aires, Santiago, Lima, and Caracas accounted for about one-third of all expenditures on food and beverages and for one-fifth or more of the market for clothes and footwear. More surprising,

47

they constituted over one-quarter of the market for "modern" household appliances. In other cities, such as Quito, the figures were only slightly lower.[4]

The wages and other income sources of working class households in Latin America have been reduced in the 1980s by the cumulative impact of deindustrialization, the consolidation of "speculative" economies (speculation having replaced productive investment), economic recession in core countries, unprecedented levels of external indebtedness, and finally, by "austerity" programs implemented to deal with domestic inflation and to obtain the resources for servicing the external debt. Shrinking consumption levels, interrupted by minor short-lived recoveries and a slow pace of export growth, make prospective sales uncertain for business. This uncertainty has wide repercussions, ranging from no new investment (with its correlate, the persistence of obsolete infrastructure) to the diffusion of lax contractual practices. The irregularity of income and spending power associated with precarious employment reinforces the very instability of effective demand, the uncertainty of which had fostered irregular employment in the first place. The generalization of irregular forms of employment and mounting open unemployment both contribute to the contraction of private consumption, adding to the impact of low wage levels. This of course has been detrimental to the wage earners' standard of living, but in many Latin American countries it also has become a strong constraint on sustained economic growth.

In this chapter I address the issue of labor's falling real income and its impact on the domestic market. The analysis focuses on Argentina, a nation where the decline in real wages has been one of the most severe in Latin America. The decline occurred well before 1980 and was due to the monetarist policies implemented by the military regime that ruled from 1976 to 1983. Of seven Latin American countries with such declines, only in two, Guatemala and Peru, was the fall of labor's share in the GNP greater than in Argentina.[5] In Argentina, as in several other Latin American countries, labor's income fell more than the GNP per capita did, and the consumption of wage earners dropped more than did overall personal consumption. This notwithstanding, the decline in labor's consumption was reflected in the reduced size of the domestic market.

The remainder of this chapter is organized in three sections. First, I discuss some aspects of Argentine economic strategy since 1985. Next, I review the adverse evolution of labor's income and the increasing income concentration after 1975. Finally, I analyze how those changes affected the level and structure of consumer demand and manufacturing production. The Argentine experience has several unique characteristics.

Nevertheless, the impact of falling wages on consumption and its implications for economic growth may be generalized to other Latin American economies.

The Economic Program (1985–1987) and the Domestic Market

In the second half of the 1980s, the Argentine government adopted a growth strategy based on promoting the expansion of nontraditional, industrial exports. In the context of broader industrial export promotion schemes, some steps were already taken via tax rebates and credit lines. The incentives will probably increase manufacturing exports, in particular. Some of the regional agreements, such as the recent one between Argentina and Brazil, are already yielding positive results.[6] However, the global effects of these agreements are not likely to be spectacular in the short and medium term. First, there is intensified competition among countries with internal-market crises. Many of them are implementing similar manufacturing-export-led growth strategies. Second, in core economies protectionism, which limits access to these markets, is rising. Thus the possibility for manufacturing exports to play a central role in the growth process withers away. In addition, in Argentina, apart from the constraints shared with other Latin American countries, the starting point for increasing manufacturing exports is particularly unfavorable. The participation of manufactures in total Argentine exports decreased between 1973 and 1984. Their value in constant dollars fell at a cumulative annual rate of 0.8 percent (CEPAL, 1986:67). Moreover, although the effects of an expansion of manufacturing exports on domestic economic activity would undoubtedly be positive, practically no objective assessment has been made of the potential capacity of Argentina's industrial structure to engage in a more dynamic export behavior (CEPAL, 1986:69).

Argentina's manufacturing sector exports only 8 percent of its output.[7] The main destination of Argentine manufacturing production continues to be, as it always has been, the internal market. Only in fifteen industrial categories is more than 10 percent of production sold in the external market. About 70 percent of all industrial activities are oriented almost exclusively to the domestic market, which absorbs more than 95 percent of their output. The industries exporting more than 10 percent of production account for a mere 14 percent of total manufacturing production.

The economic strategy of the current Argentine government not only assigns to the external market a decisive role in future growth but also includes as an essential prerequisite a stabilization program designed to control spiraling inflation in the short term. The program was launched in mid-1985 with the policy package popularly known as the Austral Plan. This was to be followed by successive versions in 1986 (the Australito) and 1987 (the Austral II).[8] A crucial component of these plans was to freeze (in its tighter form) or to control wages and prices, including public utility tariffs. The Austral Plan was successful in slowing down inflation, particularly in the initial stages when public support was widespread, but wages lagged vis-à-vis the still rapidly rising prices.

Apart from the goal of reducing the fiscal deficit, these austerity policies, as with stabilization programs elsewhere, impose a severe constraint on the domestic market via strict wage control. These policies take for granted that wage increases have a doubly negative impact. On the one hand, such policies assume an effect on prices (because firms pass along wage costs in higher prices). On the other hand, they assume an adverse impact from labor's increased consumption: In Argentina the latter has been blamed as much for small export surpluses and for inducing "excessive" imports leading to trade balance deficits[9] as for a "premature overheating of the economy" accelerating the inflationary process. In contrast, the positive side of labor's increased consumption capacity, the widening of the domestic market, has been neglected. But even the basic negative assumptions of austerity programs regarding labor consumption need closer scrutiny. In Argentina neither the fact that consumption out of wage incomes seldom exceeded 60 percent of total private consumption nor its implications have been generally acknowledged.[10] And the presumed adverse effects of rising wages on the trade balance have yet to be demonstrated. The fear that wage increases would induce excessive imports seems unfounded. For instance, corroborating Cline's finding in the early 1970s that downward income redistribution had virtually no impact on imports in either Mexico or Brazil (Cline, 1972), a recent simulation of the effects of a wage increase on imports in Ecuador showed that the impact was not significant (García, 1987).

Thus Argentina is characterized by both external and internal limitations (including here the uncertain response of Argentine manufacturing firms to government export incentives) on the growth of manufacturing exports. In light of these limitations and of the domestic market's overwhelming role in the absorption of manufacturing production, it is important to assess the trends in labor's income and consumption and their impact on the size and structure of overall consumer demand. This is done in the following sections.

The "Legacy" of the Military Regime, 1976–1983: Low Wages and Income Concentration

After 1976, the distribution of income in Argentina soon changed from having been one of the least unequal in Latin America to one comparable to Colombia's or Chile's in the late 1960s (Altimir, 1986). The wage policies (wage freezes accompanied by liberalized prices) applied by the military government's economic team produced a rapid and drastic fall in real wages. No subsequent recovery was able to restore real wages to previous levels. In consequence, labor's participation in the GNP declined dramatically from 50.6 percent in 1970 to 39.3 percent in 1983 (see Table 3.1).

The loss of real income by wage earners was accompanied by an increase in the concentration of personal income between 1975 and 1981. The 10 percent in the highest income class had a considerable gain. At the expense of all but the very poorest citizenry, the share of income of the highest group rose from 27.7 percent to 34.9 percent.[11] The concentration of income and wealth may have been even larger than is registered by household surveys and national accounts: In addition to the underdeclaration usual in the high-income classes, the very substantial "capital" flight of the late 1970s and early 1980s conceals part of the total income of households at the top of the income scale (Altimir, 1986:547).

The large decline in labor's income share and, furthermore, the size of registered and unregistered property and entrepreneurial income suggest that increased inequality was the result of the widening cleavage between labor's wages and income from profits (Marshall, forthcoming). The impact on income inequality of changes in wage differences among workers was minor. In the longer term these hardly varied. Although between 1976 and 1982 the economic team attempted with some limited success to foster wage heterogeneity within both private and public sectors, later measures, that is, homogeneous percentage increases for all wages and raises in the minimum wage, counteracted the effects of the previous policies (Marshall, 1987). However, the growing distance between the wage levels of the bulk of the work force, including manufacturing and construction workers, sales and other white collar employees, and the salaries of a small elite in well-paid positions, such as executives in manufacturing, banking, and finance, also contributed to the worsening of income distribution.

In addition to wage policy, the military government introduced certain tax reforms and changed the amount of labor's direct contributions to

52

Table 3.1 Wages, Income Distribution, and Consumption, 1970-1986

Year	Real Wage Industrial Worker 1983=100 (1)	(2)	Wage Bill/ GNP[a] (%)	Consumption Per Capita 1970=100	Wage Bill[ab] 1970=100	Wage Bill[ab]/ Consumption (%)
1970	113.2	127.6	50.6	100.0	100.0	57.1
1971	119.2	132.6	51.8	102.4	106.4	58.3
1972	111.9	123.5	46.9	102.4	97.5	52.6
1973	118.8	133.5	51.9	103.9	113.4	59.2
1974	132.4	146.8	56.0	110.7	134.1	64.7
1975	134.3	136.2	49.9	110.1	146.8	70.0
1976	94.9	95.3	36.1	97.9	92.9	49.0
1977	81.2	85.8	34.3	97.9	85.7	44.5
1978	77.0	81.4	38.3	93.7	93.1	49.7
1979	88.9	95.3	39.0	104.7	98.0	46.1
1980	99.0	108.1	45.6	109.9	118.0	52.0
1981	93.0	99.1	39.0	104.4	96.2	43.9
1982	80.6	84.1	31.9	91.5	70.1	35.9
1983	100.0	100.0	39.3	93.4	98.3	48.6
1984	127.1	121.8	--	--	--	--
1985	111.6	114.0	--	--	--	--
1986	105.2	114.6	--	--	--	--

(1) Deflated by consumer price index of same month.
(2) Deflated by consumer price index of next month.

a Refers to the nonagricultural wage bill and nonagricultural GNP.
b Deflated by the implicit prices of private consumption.
Sources: No estimates on income shares were published by the Central Bank of Argentina (BCRA) after 1973. Figures are my own estimate on the basis of data on sectoral wage bill and sectoral product for all sectors except agriculture (BCRA, unpublished figures): Unpublished data of the Economic Commission for Latin America (CEPAL) for real wages (between 1970 and 1976, refer to basic wage only; from 1976 on, to total remuneration).

the social security system. These policies reinforced the process of income concentration. By 1981 the groups that had seized power in 1976 had implemented their "social project." In the areas of taxation, social security, and state social expenditures, the most important reforms had been introduced. Social policy, instead of trying to compensate for the decline in wage incomes with collective services, increased labor's contribution to financing social expenditures. According to this social policy model, the costs of labor force reproduction and maintenance of retired workers would have to be borne solely by wage labor (Marshall, 1987).

In the area of taxation, several measures intensified the regressiveness of an already extremely regressive tax structure: tax exemptions for personal incomes that come from distributed profits (benefiting groups already exempted from paying taxes on incomes obtained from financial operations), preference for taxes on firms (easily shifted to the consumer) instead of taxes on persons, and extension of the value-added tax to wage goods such as food and medicines (Riavitz, 1985; Marshall, 1987). These changes increased the weight of indirect taxation, which falls disproportionately on the poorest sectors, while diminishing the already negligible proportion of taxes on personal income. In 1979, for instance, these taxes amounted to only 7 percent of the tax revenues.

In the area of social security, starting in 1975 the direct contributions out of wages were raised continually. In 1976, personal contributions to the state pension system were increased by implementing a decree originally formulated during the government of Isabel Perón. Contributions to the system of health care, the Obras Sociales, were raised in 1980. At the same time, employers' payroll taxes for the state pension scheme and for the public housing fund, Fondo Nacional para la Vivienda, were eliminated and replaced with an extension of the value-added tax. Moreover, after 1976 the workers affiliated with the health care system had to make partial payments for medical services previously supplied at no cost (Cortés, 1985). Similarly, after 1979, services provided free by the network of public hospitals were restricted to the very poor. Users had to pay a fee, unless they could demonstrate extreme poverty, for example, with a certificate from a social worker. In practice this meant that wage earners covered by the Obras Sociales would not have access to free hospital services any longer (Marshall, 1987).

In short, during the military regime numerous reforms were introduced that adversely affected labor's "nonmarket" consumption and disposable income. These reforms added to the negative effect of wage policies, reducing even more the purchasing power of the workers and restricting their free access to some social services. At the same time as labor's disposable income was being curtailed by increased direct and indirect taxation, several tax exemptions benefited those whose income derived from profits, enhancing their consumption capacity and further stimulating financial speculation. In this way, for labor, during the period between 1976 and 1983 the evolution of *after-tax* factor shares in the national income was as bleak as or worse than the trend in *pre-tax* factor shares (Marshall, 1988).

Although the impact of the military's wage and social policies undoubtedly was evident during the 1976–1983 period, many of their more permanent effects were felt later, perhaps even more severely, under civilian rule. And with some important exceptions, this particular legacy of the military regime was not transformed by the latter part of the 1980s.

Wages and Income Distribution Under the "Heterodox" Austerity Program, 1985–1987

In 1986, after one-and-a-half years of constitutional government and the implementation of the new stabilization program known as the Austral Plan, the work force, although better remunerated than between 1976 and 1983, still was earning less than in the early 1970s (see Table 3.1). Moreover, in 1985 labor's share of the national income was only 70 percent of what it had been in 1970.[12] Similarly, the distribution of personal income continued to be as unequal as at the end of the military regime. By 1985, after the change of government and economic policy, the degree of inequality still was much higher than in 1975.[13]

Since 1984, wage differentials in the private sector have tended either to be narrow or to remain stable because the minimum wage has been repeatedly raised and percentage increases have been applied, in principle, without distinction to all wages. Nevertheless, the proportion of workers with remunerations close to or below the minimum wage was larger in 1985 (24 percent) than in 1975 (17 percent).[14] In addition, public sector and private sector wages became increasingly unequal. In the context of the Austral Plan of 1985 and its follow-up, the management of government deficit spending to an important extent rested on cutting wages in public administration and in state-owned enterprises. Cuts in the absolute size of state employment have been much more difficult to implement. At the same time, wages in the private sector have been freed somewhat to move upward, presumably on the basis of productivity increases, although not beyond government-fixed limits (Marshall, 1988).

Indeed, the "heterodox" stabilization package, combining fiscal control with an "income" policy (Dornbusch and Simonsen, 1987) and implemented since 1985, left little scope for a basic transformation of labor's situation either through wages and employment or through the collective provision of services. First, wages have remained controlled. Fearing that wage growth once again would unleash a process leading to hyperinflation, the current economic team strongly opposed free collective bargaining for wages (still banned in 1987). According to Dornbusch and Simonsen (1987:226) the difference between heterodox and traditional stabilization programs lies in the fact that "income" policies of heterodox programs regulate both wages and prices while orthodox policies control wages alone. This distinction might be correct in theory. In practice, however, price control is more lax and more difficult to enforce than wage control, at least in the Argentine case. And business opposition to price control has certainly been strong. Reactions have ranged from provoking artificial shortages of diverse commodities to joint action demanding the lifting of controls.[15] The government succeeded in decelerating inflation, but still consumer prices have been rising quite rapidly, thus eroding the purchasing power of wages. In addition, prices, but not wages, rose just before the first freeze was enacted in 1985 and prior to each subsequent announcement of emergency policies. It is significant that the level of real wages of the late 1970s, itself much lower than that of preceding years, has become the established standard of reference for judging wage changes.

Moreover, efforts to stimulate employment growth have failed. The unemployment rate has been high, by Argentine standards. Although in Buenos Aires the rate stabilized in 1986 at a level of about 5 percent of the labor force, in many provincial cities it was much higher, occasionally reaching two-digit figures (Encuesta Permanente de Hogares). Brief economic recoveries were accompanied by more intensive use of overtime work, a well-established practice in Argentina, instead of by increased employment. In the manufacturing sector, for instance, by the end of the first quarter of 1987, the number of workers employed was considerably below that of 1970, and in many industrial branches employment continued to fall between 1985 and 1987.[16]

Employment stagnation cannot be attributed solely to economic policies, including the long-term maintenance of high interest rates: The private sector has often failed to respond to the diverse incentives introduced by the government in order to promote the export of manufactured goods. It is worth recalling that despite the upward redistribution of income between 1976 and 1983 due to wage cuts and to changes in taxation favoring profits, private investment did not increase, except momentarily in 1977. Between 1978 and 1985 gross fixed investment declined at an annual average rate of 8.0 percent, and its share of the GNP decreased after 1980. Moreover, private investment in productive equipment fell more than did total investment.[17] Distributed profits went abroad or were used for speculation at home. Conspicuous consumption increased, but as is discussed below in this chapter, it was not enough to offset the impact on the size of the domestic market of labor's shrinking consumption.

Finally, although after 1984 there were some changes in social expenditures, taxation, and the financing structure of social security, these changes were too few to redress the long-lasting consequences of the military government's policies for the "social wage." One such change was to increase the budget allocation for some social expenditures.[18] However, given the strict constraints that limit total public spending, the increase did little to improve social services. In addition, the national food plan, Plan Alimentario Nacional, which distributed basic food to deprived households, was implemented with varying success in different regions. The enduring decline of real wages and the growing proportion of households with low income expanded the demand for social services. If state expenditures were to increase sufficiently so as to meet that demand, then they would conflict with other policies aimed at reducing the fiscal deficit and at restricting the extension of state activity. These latter were both key objectives of the stabilization program of the late 1980s.

Another reform was the elimination in 1984 of the value-added tax on wage goods and the reinstatement of employers' payroll taxes for the state pension scheme, but only to half the previous level. The other half was to continue to come from general tax revenues. Later in 1986 a small increase in employers' contributions, from 7.5 to 9.5 percent of the wage bill, was proposed for implementation in 1987 (*Latin American Weekly Report*, 11 December 1986:8). In any case, the system collapsed for lack of funds, a predictable result of the contraction in the wage bill. Thus the pensions of retired workers, originally intended to equal 82 percent of the wage received prior to retirement, in 1986 amounted to little more than 20 percent. Beginning in 1987, a pension scheme administered by private insurance companies and expected to attract medium- and high-income groups coexists with the public system (*Latin American Weekly Report*, 20 November 1986:8). As for the health care system, after a long battle that prevented its radical transformation in accord with two projects of 1985,[19] a new bill was drafted in mid-1987. If approved, it will, inter alia, raise employers' contributions to the Obras Sociales.[20]

In 1985 a new tax, the "forced savings" (*ahorro forzoso*), was temporarily imposed on those with incomes above a certain level. After five years those taxpayers are to receive a partial return of their "savings." Apparently, this tax met considerable resistance. The forced savings plan was reintroduced in October 1987 together with the new stabilization package. But although this kind of income tax is progressive and although

the more intense campaign against tax evasion has succeeded in substantially raising total revenues, evasion has remained widespread.[21] Only
13 percent of the registered taxpayers paid taxes in 1984 (*LARR, Southern
Cone Report*, 11 September 1986:2). Just half of the revenues coming
from the value-added tax were estimated to reach the Treasury. About
one-third of the claims for tax rebates presented in industrial promotion
schemes were fraudulent. A mere fraction of import duties were actually
paid. And noncompliance with social security contributions is sizable
(*Latin American Weekly Report*, 20 November 1986:8). In addition, by
early 1986 less than half of the potential "forced savers" had actually
contributed (*Latin American Monitor, Southern Cone*, January-February
1986:259).

In sum, since 1984 the constitutional government has proposed or
enacted several important measures capable of improving the social wage
and nonmarket consumption of the low-income households. It is most
unlikely, however, that they have had or will have, in the short term,
a significant redistributive impact.

Labor's Consumption, the Domestic Market, and Manufacturing Production

The participation of labor in total private consumption mirrored the
trend in labor's share of the GNP.[22] It stood at 57 percent in 1970 and
reached a maximum of 70 percent in 1975. Since 1976 it has generally
been less than 50 percent (see Figure 3.1 and Table 3.1). As in other
Latin American economies, the fall in labor's consumption affected
overall household consumption (see Figure 3.2).[23] However, probably
because consumption from profits and other sources of high income did
not fall, per capita consumption declined at an average annual pace of
just 1.6 percent. Meanwhile, wages decreased at an annual rate of almost
4.0 percent. Nonetheless, the impact of labor's declining spending power
in relation to the level of aggregate consumer demand was important
enough so that in 1983 consumption per capita was some 7 percent
below its level of 1970 (see Table 3.1).

Data on consumption patterns of low-income households in 1970[24]
suggest that with the reduction of their disposable income, wage earners
attempt to preserve the level of food consumption by increasing the
share of household expenditures allocated to food. This is done at the
expense of the share of expenditures on traditional manufactures, such
as clothing and footwear, but not the share of expenditures on modern
household appliances. In any case, over time, worker households' consumption of both traditional and modern manufactures will eventually

58

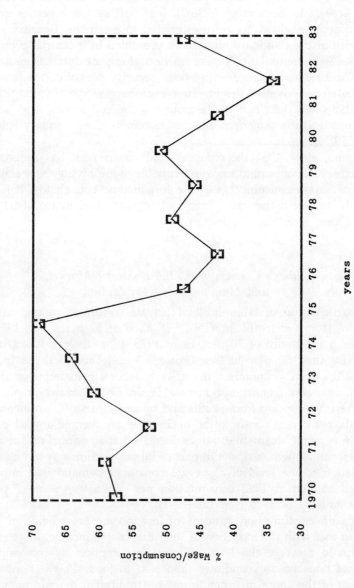

Figure 3.1 The Share of Labor in Personal Consumption, 1970-1983 (percentage)

Source: Based on data in Table 3.1.

59

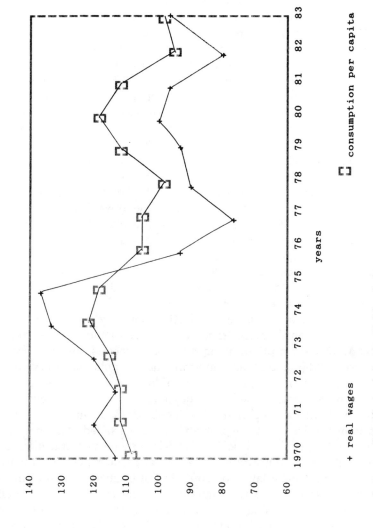

Figure 3.2 Real Wages and Consumption per Capita, 1970-1983 (1983=100)

+ real wages   [] consumption per capita

Source: Based on data in Table 3.1.

decrease with the fall in their total disposable income. In short, their standard of living will deteriorate.[25] This may be expected to affect the size of the domestic market for manufacturing production.

Data on sales and on consumption of diverse manufactured goods are very limited. Generally one must look at trends in production for indirect evidence of consumption trends. During the period from 1975 to 1985 the production of clothing, textiles, and leather goods, among the most sensitive to the decline in the consumption of low-income households, decreased at an annual rate of almost 5 percent. This was well above the average decline of manufacturing production as a whole (1.6 percent).[26] More specifically, between 1975 and 1982 the production of clothes and of footwear fell at an annual rate of 11.0 and 9.0 percent, respectively; of household electric appliances, 8.5 percent annually, and of radio, television, and communication equipment, 12.5 percent.[27] Car sales, which had risen in 1979 and 1980 due to the cheaper imported cars available at the height of the import liberalization period, during 1982–1985 were below the levels of 1974–1981. Significantly, in 1979 and 1980 sales of large cars increased, whereas sales of small cars dropped (CTI, several years), confirming the upward shift in consumption capacity toward the beneficiaries of the monetarist economic policies. In addition, although food production remained quite stable from 1970 to 1985 (actually growing at an annual rate of 0.5 percent), it fell slightly when wages declined most drastically, in 1976–1978, in 1981–1982, and again in 1985. Most remarkably, in 1985 food consumption per capita was below the levels of 1970 to 1980.[28]

Trends in manufacturing production not only provide some indirect evidence of consumption trends but in fact should also reveal how the decline of consumption, along with other factors, affected production. Between 1980 and 1983, anti-inflationary policies, overvaluation of Argentine currency, rapid reduction of industrial protection, and the rise of real interest rates added to the ongoing contraction of internal demand. The result was a deep crisis. The indebtedness of industrial firms went up dramatically, and their profitability was curtailed. Although the crisis hit manufacturing as a whole, it was felt more heavily in textiles, clothing and footwear, wood, furniture, and metal products, electrical machinery, and transport materials (Kosacoff, 1984:30). Liberalization of imports of consumer goods, in particular, was a critical factor affecting traditional industries like clothing, as well as the "modern" electronics industry. The adverse impact of foreign competition on the domestic productive structure lasted well beyond the relatively short period during which Argentina's economy opened up to imported consumer goods. But in any case, accompanying the fall of wages, the domestic output of clothes and footwear and of many household appliances and electronic goods decreased well before import liberalization.

The dismantling of the industrial sector and the fall in demand were such that in only a very few cases were 1984 production levels comparable to those of the early 1970s. These few included expensive goods sold in the high-income market, such as color television sets and air conditioners.[29] The changes in the structure of total personal consumption meant that not all industrial branches were affected to a similar extent by the fall in demand. This is reflected in the restructuring of manufacturing output. Between 1970 and 1985 the participation of food, beverages, and tobacco increased from 22 to 26 percent. The shares held by clothing, textiles, and leather goods and by metals, machinery, and equipment (including household durables) shrank.[30]

By the third quarter of 1986, industrial production showed some signs of recovery, although it was still below the 1974–1975 output level. However, not all industries shared equally in this progress.[31] Not surprisingly in light of the wage trends, a few months later a reduced demand for manufactures was reported once again. Of twenty-eight manufacturing industries surveyed, only four had experienced some increase in demand for their products.[32] In the late 1980s the trend in manufacturing production has been too unstable to reveal a definite pattern of industrial restructuring in Argentina.

Conclusion: Redistribution and Growth

There is substantial idle capacity in Argentine manufacturing. In this situation, wage increases could lead to output growth and increased profits, a prerequisite for sustained expansion. Some certainty about prospective sales constitutes an incentive for making better use of unused capacity and for undertaking new investment. Theoretically, the concentration of income and spending power also might lead to higher levels of total consumption expenditures. This, however, requires such an upward shift of income that the increased inequality and social polarization it would entail make this option not only socially unjust but simply not politically feasible under a democratic regime. Given the past decade's declining trend in the size of the internal market, in conjunction with constraints on the development of manufacturing exports, the policy option seems to be between either raising the income of the workers or prolonged economic stagnation.

Notes

1. For a review of the two versions of Latin American "underconsumptionism" see Lustig (1980). Dutt (1984) recently posited that under conditions of underutilized capacity and monopoly power, insufficient consumer demand would just

lead to economic stagnation, and that demand insufficiency is the outcome of large income inequalities; this model was applied to the case of India.

2. Two empirical studies in this area are worth citing: Lustig (1979) on Mexico and Wells (1974) on Brazil.

3. In contrast to the findings of some earlier studies (e.g. Wells, 1974), Bonelli and Vieira da Cunha (1981) argued that accelerated growth in Brazil (1970–1975) did not encounter any limitation originating in the consumption capacity of high income classes.

4. Data for all cities except Buenos Aires are from Musgrove (1978); for Buenos Aires, data cited by Pinto (1976). See also Wells (1977).

5. Data cited by PREALC (1986:63).

6. Despite the initial fears of Argentine managers that the outmoded domestic industrial firms would be unable to compete with Brazilian manufacturing, trade between Argentina and Brazil increased by 40 percent after the agreement (*Latin American Monitor, Southern Cone*, August 1986:317).

7. These data and those below are from CEPAL (1986).

8. The Austral Plan, or "heterodox shock," froze wages, prices, and public utility tariffs after granting a general money wage increase of 90 percent of the previous month's inflation. It also changed the Argentine currency from the peso to the austral, establishing a table for conversion that varied over time. For other features of this stabilization plan see, inter alia, Epstein (1987). Full price control was later replaced by "administered prices." By September 1986, fifteen months after the Austral Plan, a new set of economic policies was announced that again implemented wage-and-price controls (*Latin American Monitor, Southern Cone*, September 1986:330). A package of emergency economic measures was again applied in February 1987: a four-month wage-and-price freeze with a money wage increase to be implemented in two stages and a raise of public utility prices (*Latin American Monitor, Southern Cone*, March 1987:391). Since prices were increasing again at about 10 percent monthly, quite similar though more drastic measures were adopted in October of the same year (*El País*, 15 October 1987). The successive versions included other aspects, among which were currency devaluations.

9. For a critique of this conception see Cortés and Marshall (1986).

10. Cortés and Marshall (1986) and Table 3.1, this chapter. The share of labor in private consumption was over 60 percent only four times in thirty years. Here as below in this chapter, labor's consumption is equivalent to the wage bill.

11. Data on distribution of individual income in Altimir (1986:542).

12. Data in PREALC-ILO (1986:63).

13. Estimates based on data for Buenos Aires from the *Encuesta Permanente de Hogares* (EPH). The Gini coefficient for individual income distribution was .36 in 1975, .42 in 1981 (Altimir, 1986), and .42 in 1985 (October) (Marshall, 1988).

14. My own estimates on the basis of data from EPH. The figures are for Greater Buenos Aries, and they are not exact due to the form in which the data were made available. It is worth commenting that the proportion of self-employed

workers who earn up to two minimum wages also increased from 34 percent in 1980 to 45 percent in 1985, despite the fact that they generally worked full-time or even longer (Szretter, 1986).

15. For instance, the claims made by an alliance of several business groups in the middle of 1987 included the lifting of all price controls (*Latin American Regional Reports [LARR], Southern Cone Report*, 6 August 1987).

16. Data in INDEC (Instituto Nacional de Estadística y Censos), *Estadística Mensual*, no. 172, 1987:23.

17. My own estimates on the basis of data in BCRA, *Estimaciones trimestrales sobre oferta y demanda global*, 1986, and BCRA, unpublished figures.

18. However, the share allocated to education in the central government budget of 1985 (data in *Latin American Monitor, Southern Cone,* November 1985:232), as the proposals for 1986 (ibid., March 1986) and 1987 (*El País*, 15 October 1987), were below historical levels, similar to its share in 1976–1978 (Marshall, 1987).

19. In 1985 the health minister proposed a national health care system that extracted the health care insurance program, the Obras Sociales, from trade union ownership and gave a greater role to the state. Stress was placed on redistribution of revenue from rich to poor. The project also reduced workers' contributions while increasing payroll taxes; it was opposed by the unions and was not approved in Parliament.

20. No change is to affect the size of workers' contributions, and trade union ownership of funds is recognized (see *Latin American Monitor, Southern Cone,* June 1987:427).

21. According to information cited in the *LARR, Southern Cone Report*, 11 September 1986:2, tax revenues had increased by about 50 percent between the beginning of Alfonsín's administration and late 1986.

22. Most of this section is based on Marshall (forthcoming). Due to the nature and sparsity of the available data, the analysis is far from complete and the conclusions are open to further discussion.

23. Real wages and per capita consumption (1970–1983) are strongly associated (R square .63 [t = 4.5] and significant).

24. Data for Buenos Aires metropolitan area, from INDEC, Encuesta de presupuestos familiares, 1969/70, *Serie Investigaciones Demográficas*, n.d. More details can be found in Marshall (1988). There are no data on consumption patterns by income strata after that date. A survey of household incomes and expenditures was made in 1986, but at the time of my writing this chapter the results were not yet available.

25. Relative prices of consumer goods and services did not change in the longer run. Thus, the main impact on consumption patterns came from changes in total disposable income (Marshall, 1988).

26. My own calculations with data in BCRA, *Estimaciones oferta y demanda global* (1986) (annual average rates of change; constant australes of 1970).

27. My own estimates on the basis of BCRA data cited in Kosacoff (1984, Appendix).

28. My own estimate on the basis of data on food production in BCRA, *Estimaciones oferta y demanda global*, 1986, and on population growth.

64   Adriana Marshall

29. Data in CTI (diverse years).
30. From 13 to 9 percent, and from 26 to 24 percent, respectively (my own estimates with data from BCRA, *Estimaciones oferta y demanda global,* 1986).
31. Data in BCRA, *Boletín Estadístico* 34, no. 10–12, 1986:63.
32. According to the Latin American Investigations Foundation (FIEL), cited by *Latin American Monitor, Southern Cone,* December 1986:367. These periodic assessments are too affected by short-term, conjunctural variations to be significant for discussion of more structural trends: Demand fluctuated up and down from April to June and from June to December. In any case, with reference to consumer goods, it was noted that the growth of demand was localized in nondurables, particularly food (FIEL, *Indicadores de coyuntura,* nos. 241 and 243, 1986).

References

Altimir, Oscar. "Estimaciones de la distribución del ingreso en la Argentina, 1953–1980," *Desarrollo Económico,* 25(100):521–566, 1986.
Bonelli, Regis, and Paulo Vieira da Cunha. "Crescimento económico, padrão de consumo e distribução da renda no Brasil: uma abordagem multissetorial para o perído 1970/75," *Pesquisa e Planejamento Económico,* 11(3):703–756, 1981.
CEPAL (Economic Commission for Latin America). "Exportación de manufacturas y desarrollo industrial," *Documentos de Trabajo,* 22, 1986.
Cline, William R. *Potential Effects of Income Redistribution on Economic Growth,* New York: Praeger Publishers, 1972.
Cortés, Rosalía. "La seguridad social en la Argentina: las Obras Sociales." FLACSO–Programa Buenos Aires, *Serie Documentos e Informes de Investigación,* 28, 1985.
Cortés, Rosalía, and Adriana Marshall. "Salario real, composición del consumo y balanaza comercial," *Desarrollo Económico,* 26(101):72–88, 1986.
CTI (Consejo Técnico de Inversiones). *Anuario de la Economía Argentina.* Buenos Aires, diverse years.
Dornbusch, Rudiger, and Mario H. Simonsen. "Estabilización de la inflación con el apoyo de una política de ingresos," *El Trimestre Económico,* 54(214):225–281, 1987.
Dutt, Amitava K. "Stagnation, Income Distribution and Monopoly Power," *Cambridge Journal of Economics,* 8(1):25–40, 1984.
Epstein, Edward C. "Recent Stabilization Programs in Argentina, 1973–86," *World Development,* 15(8):991–1005, 1987.
García, Norberto E. "Remuneraciones, precios e importaciones de bienes, Ecuador, 1970–82," in *Política Salarial, Inflación y Restricción Externa,* Santiago: PREALC–OIT, 3–47, 1987.
Kosacoff, Bernardo P. "El proceso de industrialización en la Argentina en el período 1976/1983." CEPAL (mimeo; preliminary version), 1984.
Lustig, Nora. "Distribución del ingreso, estructura del consumo y características del crecimiento industrial,"*Comercio Exterior,* 29(5):535–543, 1979.

_____. "Underconsumption in Latin America," *The Review of Radical Political Economics*, 12(1):35–43, 1980.

Marshall, Adriana. *Políticas Sociales: el Modelo Neoliberal*, Buenos Aires: Editorial Legasa, 1987.

_____. "Income Distribution, the Domestic Market and Economic Growth in Argentina," *Labour and Society*, 13(1), 1988 (forthcoming).

Musgrove, Philip. *Consumer Behavior in Latin America*. Washington, D.C.: The Brookings Institution, 1978.

Pinto, Aníbal. "Styles of Development in Latin America," *CEPAL Review*, First Semester:99–130, 1976.

PREALC. See PREALC-ILO.

PREALC–ILO (Programa Regional del Empleo para América Latina-International Labour Office). *Ajuste y Deuda Social*, Santiago: PREALC-OIT, 1986.

Riavitz, Norma. "Incidencia de la estructura tributaria sobre los incresos de los asalariados." FLACSO–Programa Buenos Aires. *Serie Documentos e Informes de Investigación*, 22, 1985.

Szretter, Héctor. "La subutilización de la mano de obra en el Gran Buenos Aires: evolución y tendencias." *Estudios y Documentos sobre Empleo, Remuneraciones y Recursos Humanos*. Proyecto Gobierno Argentino-PNUD-OIT, ARG/84/029, 1986.

Wells, John. "Distribution of Earnings, Growth and the Structure of Demand in Brazil During the 1960's," *World Development*, 2(1):9–24, 1974.

_____. "The Diffusion of Durables in Brazil and Its Implications for Recent Controversies Concerning Brazilian Development," *Cambridge Journal of Economics*, 1(3):259–280, 1977.

Part 3
The Consequences of Austerity

4

The Demographic Consequences of Austerity in Latin America

Ralph Hakkert and Franklin W. Goza

Introduction

On May 28, 1984, a major São Paulo newspaper described the repercussions of the International Monetary Fund's recessionary economic policy prescriptions on the Brazilian population as follows:

> Seventeen months after the agreement with the International Monetary Fund, Brazil enters into its fourth year of recession, marked by hunger, unemployment, increasing crime, and rising numbers of *favelas* (zones of urban poverty). The figures are irrefutable and frightening: one in every six wage earners is unemployed; ten million Brazilians receive up to half the legal minimum wage; hunger already figures as one of the ten most frequent causes of infant mortality in the State of São Paulo; the looting of food and gas containers in Greater São Paulo health centers is increasing; and, the infant mortality rate in the *favelas* of Belo Horizonte is as high as 10 percent (almost the same number as the backlands of the Northeast) (*Folha de São Paulo*, May 28, 1984).

The notion that austerity policies implemented in several Latin American countries during the 1980s influenced prevailing demographic trends has a strong intuitive appeal. The reasons for this are fairly obvious. First, orthodox policy prescriptions had a strongly recessionary effect on all economies involved. Consequently, unemployment increased and wages fell, thereby throwing significant population segments under the subsistence minimum. In addition, these policies provoked a general decrease of social spending, especially in health and education. From 1979 to 1983, per capita real expenditures on health in Latin America declined by nearly 60 percent and educational spending by 59 percent (UNICEF, 1987). As a consequence, one might expect the following to occur:

- Increasing unemployment;
- Further income concentration;
- Deteriorating real average incomes;
- Increasing malnutrition, especially among children;
- Larger proportions of deaths due to malnutrition and infectious diseases;
- Increasing labor force participation of women and children;
- Reduced marriage rates;
- Lower birth rates;
- Increasing marital instability and divorce rates;
- Increasing crime rates, including child abuse;
- Changes in the prevailing patterns of internal migration; and
- Increasing emigration, where possible.

The following sections present a systematic analysis of most (though not all) of these phenomena and indicate to what extent they can be discerned as consequences of current Latin American austerity policies.

Despite the apparent irrefutability of the figures cited by the *Folha de São Paulo*, their interpretation as indicators of the demographic impact of austerity policies is somewhat elusive. Although undoubtedly employment and income levels have been negatively affected, the evaluation of health conditions, levels of nutrition, and especially of more strictly demographic factors like infant and child mortality, fertility, marriage trends, and migration is fraught with methodological pitfalls that are not always fully appreciated by the area specialists writing on the social implications of the Latin American debt crisis.

A UNICEF study looked at the Brazilian recession of the early 1980s and correlated rates of infant mortality. In the Northeast, infant mortality increased from 93.1 per thousand children under one year of age in 1982 to 116.1 in 1984, or an average increase of 25 %. The increase in infant mortality for that time period was 12 % for all of Brazil. . . . The Pan American Health Organization (PAHO) has figures that show reported cases of malaria in Brazil increasing from 197,000 in 1981 to 378,000 in 1984. There have been confirmed reports of the reappearance in Brazil of the bubonic plague and of leprosy—and not only in the rural areas. Brazil now has one of the largest numbers of AIDS cases in the world—and it is spreading rapidly. Many Brazilian observers see a clear link between social deterioration and the debt. Debt service has drained resources away from public sector expenditures for social service. The steady drop in health and educational standards has condemned a large part of the population to worsening levels of malnutrition and higher exposure to communicable diseases (Roett, 1987:21–23).

Several reservations have to be made regarding such accounts. First, few countries in Latin America possess a sufficiently efficient and complete civil registration system to produce accurate and up-to-date fertility and mortality statistics. Even seemingly straightforward questions, such as whether Brazil's infant mortality rate increased, as UNICEF (1987) suggested, therefore often become quite controversial. Reliable estimates of migration and household sizes can be obtained only from census and survey figures, which, in most countries, do not go beyond 1982. Moreover, as Martine et al. (1984) suggested, one of the consequences of decreased governmental spending in countries like Brazil has been precisely the cutback in the collection of migration data, which, unlike wage and employment statistics, have been available for the 1970s, but are virtually nonexistent for the 1980s. Conclusions concerning these issues therefore have to be based on partial or completely impressionistic evidence.

Even with current data available, a common problem is the impossibility or failure to refer to appropriate baseline figures for comparison. Data referring to only one point in time, distressing as they may be, convey a partial impression at best. The infant mortality rate of 10 percent mentioned in the *Folha de São Paulo* is undoubtedly high but hardly indicative of a recent increase, considering that infant mortality in Belo Horizonte (not only the *favelas*) during the early 1970s, the height of Brazil's "economic miracle," attained 125 per 1,000 births (Wood, 1977). Similarly, malnutrition is a serious problem in many parts of Latin America, but consistent time series data demonstrating an actual deterioration during the debt crisis are remarkably scarce.

Separating the demographic effects of austerity from structural long-term processes presents another challenge. Declines in fertility, increasing crime rates, and female labor force participation, or diminishing migration toward major cities may be so intertwined with secular trends that they become extremely difficult to isolate. The gradual return of leprosy in Brazil began at least as far back as the early 1970s and may or may not have been aggravated by cutbacks in health expenditures since 1980. Similarly, the spread of malaria (the number of reported cases has risen to 444,000 in 1986) and AIDS is a fact, but the underlying causes are quite specific and only indirectly related to the deteriorating economic situation.

Time lags are another complicating factor. According to a classic study by Brenner (1973) on the United States, fetal mortality normally increases within months after the first signs of recession and perinatal mortality after about a year, but postneonatal death rates may take several years to react. Ironically, at the time the article appeared in the *Folha de São Paulo*, infant mortality in the state of São Paulo was at a historical low: 41.9 per 1,000 during the period from May 1983 to April 1984. It was only in the second semester of 1984, with employment already recovering, that infant mortality increased somewhat.

Finally, there are counteracting mechanisms to be reckoned with that may push demographic trends in unexpected directions. For instance, in the face of deteriorating prospects, the most vulnerable segments of the urban labor force may seek refuge in subsistence agriculture and thus suppress the apparent impact of recession on the urban economy. Eyer and Sterling (1977) argued that adult death rates in the United States during the past century actually *decreased* most rapidly during periods of recession. Although suicide and some other violent causes of death tend to rise during such periods, the degenerative diseases that account for most adult mortality are more responsive to the stress, long working hours, and social disintegration characteristic of boom periods. Similarly, it has been suggested that the deterioration of health conditions in Greater São Paulo during the 1968–1974 boom was due, in part, to the very prosperity of the area, as intense in-migration, usually from high-mortality areas, made the periphery grow rapidly, without a concomitant expansion of urban infrastructure (Leser, 1975).

Changing Labor Force Opportunities

Shifts in the employment situation have a direct link to the increasing poverty and income concentration observed throughout Latin America during the 1980s, as well as to the changing migration patterns occurring in response to perceived opportunities. The austerity policies undertaken by several Latin American countries at the start of the decade had severe consequences for employment. The number of jobs created from 1978 to 1982 was so low that even though labor force participation declined, the decline failed to compensate increases in the economically active population (EAP), causing increased unemployment (Klein & Wurgaft, 1985). From 1980 to 1984, the weighted average of urban unemployment for twelve Latin American countries (Argentina, Bolivia, Brazil, Chile, Colombia, Costa Rica, Mexico, Panama, Paraguay, Peru, Uruguay, and Venezuela) increased from 5.8 percent to 7.9 percent (Klein & Wurgaft, 1985). During this period, Chile experienced the highest unemployment levels, increasing from 11.7 percent to 18.5 percent. In three other countries, Bolivia, Uruguay, and Venezuela, the urban rates doubled, from approximately 7 percent to between 13 and 15 percent (García & Tokman, 1985). Unemployment diminished somewhat after 1985 in countries like Brazil, Chile, and Venezuela, without, however, returning to its pre-1980 levels.

One form of labor force adjustment has been the increased participation of women in the work force since 1980. Although it is unlikely to be due to the debt crisis alone, this participation has been notable during the austerity era and apparently constitutes an important family survival strategy. The trend is incompletely reflected in the official statistics, because a major portion is probably accounted for by the domestic production of consumer goods that were previously acquired in the marketplace, a process in which women play an crucial role. Nevertheless, the official female labor force participation in Brazil increased from 33.6 percent in 1979 to 36.9 percent in 1985 (FIBGE, various years).

Costa Rican female labor force participation among non–household heads rose from 23.6 percent in 1979 to 26.7 percent in 1982 (PREALC, 1985a). The latter was part of a general increase in participation rates among both male and female non-household heads in an attempt to counteract the effects of high unemployment, falling real wages, and high inflation (PREALC, 1985a). The corresponding increase for male non-household heads was from 57.3 percent in 1979 to 63.5 percent in 1982. The most significant changes occurred among men over 50, as activity rates of the 50–59 and 60+ age groups rose from 89.8 percent to 98.6 percent and from 17.8 percent to 27.4 percent, respectively. Note, however, that in spite of the Costa Rican crisis, children apparently remained in school (PREALC, 1985a). In Bolivia, in contrast, where austerity policies were especially severe, the number of primary school dropouts increased dramatically, from 2.2 percent in 1980 to 8.5 percent in 1983, as a simultaneous increase in youth labor force participation was registered (UNICEF, 1987).

In Brazil, the youngest members of the work force seem to have been most adversely affected by recent labor force adjustments. In 1979, those aged 10–14 made up 6.7 percent of the employed population, a figure that declined to 5.0 percent in 1985. During the same period the 15–19 age group witnessed its percentage of total jobs drop from 15.4 to 14.0 percent. Even the 20–24 age group experienced a similar decrease, although of a smaller magnitude (FIBGE/PNAD, various years). Note, however, that the decline of the birthrate, which began during the late 1960s, may partially explain these findings. In Argentina, youths suffered no greater unemployment as a result of the crisis than did any other group. There, it appears quite the opposite occurred (United Nations, 1986).

One significant consequence of the 1980s debt crisis was the rapid growth of the informal sector (for a discussion of sector types see Chapter 6) in many Latin American economies (García & Tokman, 1985). This occurred primarily as employment opportunities in the formal sector failed to keep pace with the number of new labor force entrants (Sabóia, 1986; United Nations, 1986). In some countries this recent increase is also related to the nonexistence of an effective welfare system. Thus, recently dismissed workers, especially those supporting others, are obliged to find some form of employment as quickly as possible, whatever it may be.

In Brazil and Costa Rica, the informal sector contains many recently displaced formal sector workers and youths entering the labor force (Sabóia, 1986; PREALC, 1985a). Between 1981 and 1983, the informal sector expanded rapidly in ten of the twelve Latin American countries for which data are available (García & Tokman, 1985). Only in Chile and Uruguay did the growth of this sector decline slightly. Furthermore, in Brazil and Costa Rica, relative and absolute growth of the informal sector greatly exceeded that of the formal sector (World Bank, 1986; PREALC, 1985b). In general, as the informal sector expanded, the incomes of those there employed tended to worsen proportionately (García & Tokman, 1985). In Costa Rica, Brazil, Argentina, and Peru rapid informal sector growth during this period was associated with income declines of between 23.5 percent and 39.3 percent. Only in Colombia, where this sector grew little, did income improve. Infante's (1985) study of Brazilian incomes by sector of urban employment revealed that, in 1983, 65.8 percent of the informal (which he called nonorganized) sector workers found themselves in conditions of extreme poverty, that is, earning less than one minimum wage, slightly up from 63.9 percent in 1981. In the formal sector, only 23 percent earned less than one minimum wage. It therefore appears plausible that as the informal sector grows, so too will poverty.

Brazilian data indicate that during 1984 and 1985 the formal sector temporarily rebounded from the decline of the early 1980s. From 1983 to 1985 the formal sector, operationalized as those with a signed work card (which provides access to limited benefits), grew from 34.3 percent to 36.5 percent of those employed. It is, however, unlikely that this tendency has persisted after the second wave of recession hit Brazil in 1987. Meanwhile, it has become increasingly difficult for Brazilian youths to acquire formal employment, as their number in that sector dropped off significantly in both absolute and relative terms. This result echoes the aforementioned difficulty youths have finding employment in general.

Effects on Income

In real terms, the earnings of Latin American workers have been greatly reduced since the implementation of recent austerity policies. Between 1980 and 1985, average per capita income in the twenty-three Latin American countries fell 9 percent (UNICEF, 1987). The exception, at least through 1983, was Colombia (García & Tokman, 1985). In Costa

Rica, real wages fell nearly 40 percent between 1979 and 1982; a reversal of 19 percent occurred in 1983, followed by another increase of 6.2 percent in 1984 (MTSS, 1985). From 1981 to 1985, real wages declined 16 percent in Chile, while from 1981 to 1984 they dropped nearly 30 percent in Mexico and 18 percent in São Paulo (UNICEF, 1987). Although the Brazilian recession of 1987 has so far not been so devastating in terms of its employment effects as that of 1982–1983, its income effects actually have been more severe. From August 1986 to July 1987, real wages in metropolitan Brazil fell by over 38 percent (SEADE, 1987). Statistics from the Interunion Department of Statistical and Socio-Economic Studies (DIEESE) indicate an even steeper descent: From March to September 1987 real wages of São Paulo workers, according to these statistics, dropped 48.3 percent (*Estado de Minas*, 1987).

The result of such an erosion of earnings is an increased number of people living in poverty conditions. The legal minimum wage in several countries will not support one person, let alone a family. According to Walter Barelli, director of DIEESE, the Brazilian minimum (roughly the equivalent of U.S. $50) is insufficient for a worker to purchase his family's basic necessities. In order to provide for the minimum require-ments of an average-sized family, the 1987 minimum wage should have been raised over 600 percent (*Estado de Minas*, 1987). Since in 1983 only four minimum salaries were required, this represents a progressive and rapid deterioration in the living standard of Brazilian workers. In 1985, 42 percent of the Brazilian work force earned one minimum wage or less (FIBGE, 1987). Those earning less than two minimum wages, a conservative estimate of the poverty line, constituted 65 percent of the employed. In the poor northeastern region, nearly 80 percent of the employed fell into this bracket during the early 1980s. Although these figures improved slightly in 1984 and 1985, it was expected that they would indicate an increase in poverty level wages in 1987.

In Mexico, where a single minimum salary has also been insufficient to support the needs of a family, early 1980s statistics indicate that 31 percent of the EAP earned roughly this amount and 54 percent earned less (Carr, 1986). Similarly, in Costa Rica, the percentage of household heads earning a single minimum wage or less increased from 24.4 percent in 1979 to 30.8 percent in 1982 (PREALC, 1985a).

One Brazilian occupational group hit especially hard by the fall in real wages has been the agricultural laborers, who represent about 11 percent of the employed work force (FIBGE/PNAD, various years). This group experienced a precipitous decline of nearly 40 percent in real wages from 1981 to 1985. During 1986, their wages rebounded temporarily as a result of the Cruzado Plan. However, it is believed that they quickly fell once this plan terminated, worsening considerably during 1987. The number at poverty level among this group is thus extremely high and growing.

To compensate for these low wage levels, workers have been obliged to try to work longer hours, find second occupations, and find employment for their wives and children (Zurron Ócio, 1987). Furthermore, families have been forced to change their consumption patterns. In Chile during the early 1980s more than 60 percent of all urban families earned less than the income required to purchase a basic food basket (UNICEF, 1987). In Costa Rica, increases in the poverty rate between 1979 and 1982 lead to a documented decrease in milk and meat consumption (Céspedes, 1985). Per capita beef consumption in Brazil fell from 22 kg per year in 1977 to 15 in 1985 and 13 in 1987. Finally, although no quantitative data are available, there have been systematic reports in the Brazilian press about working-class families that had to give up regular housing and move to the *favelas* (e.g. Nitrini, 1981).

Although most researchers believe that a reconcentration of income occurred in Latin America as a result of the crisis of the 1980s (Sachs, 1987), it is difficult to obtain unquestionable results indicating this. This is because survey results are frequently limited to urban areas or contain so few households that the observed shift in income distribution could be due to random fluctuation. Thus the following results should be regarded with caution. In Chile, the Gini index apparently declined slightly from 1981 to 1982, in favor of the upper-middle deciles, as incomes among the bottom 40 percent declined about 10 percent in real terms (Altimir, 1984). In Costa Rica, income concentration increased slightly between 1979 and 1982 (Pollack & Uthoff, 1985). The Gini index for Brazil, after improving from 1979 to 1981, started to rise again in 1982 (FIBGE, various years).

Demographic Crisis and Social Control

Most existing studies on the more specifically demographic aspects of crises are found in historical demography or economic history rather than in the contemporary demographic literature. This is due partly to the benefit hindsight provides in sorting out the interplay of secular and short-term trends but especially to the dramatic proportions of past crises. The great famines of the early fourteenth century and the subsequent ravages of the Black Death, which decimated several European populations, are the best-known examples. There are, however, significant differences between these historical population disasters and contemporary crises. In the predominantly rural economy existent in Europe until the eighteenth century, ecological and demographic factors, particularly crop failures and Malthusian population pressures, were the major causes of epidemics and subsistence crises. A sharp increase in mortality was the clearest consequence of such situations, so that historical demographers actually define a demographic crisis as "an excess of deaths over births in a given area during a specific period of time" (Sogner, 1979). The extent of social control over the relevant demographic components—migration, marriage, fertility, and mortality—was limited to out-migration from the areas affected and delayed marriage. Whether there was any conscious fertility control is a matter of some dispute.

In contrast, demographic responses to the crises of the twentieth century are characterized by a wider range of social control mechanisms. Fertility has become subject to widespread individual control and is now one of the principal regulatory mechanisms by which populations adapt themselves to changing economic prospects. Mortality has become subject to the collective controls of basic sanitation, public health measures, and nutritional intervention, as well as individual education and hygienic awareness, to a degree that now makes it relatively insensitive to any but the most severe economic disasters. Infant mortality is often offered as a prime indicator of the general quality of life in a population. However, there is now considerable agreement that it does not respond directly to short-term deteriorations in living conditions and may, to a large extent, be controlled. Many of the controls are not immediately affected by cutbacks on social spending or by deteriorating living conditions. Existing basic sanitation may keep infant mortality from rising long after investments in this area have been suspended. Well-targeted nutritional assistance programs directed at the most vulnerable population groups may minimize malnutrition, and child deaths from diarrhea may be kept down now that oral rehydration therapy has proven to be a cheap and effective cure (e.g. UNICEF, 1987).

This does not imply that contemporary societies are immune to the health consequences of recessions. MacMahon & Yen (1971) have shown that certain congenital malformations in the United States increased during the 1930s, and the aforementioned study by Brenner (1973) revealed a decline of different components of infant mortality during periods of high unemployment. In parts of the Third World, where health conditions are especially precarious, mortality crises occur even today. Sogner (1979), citing Fernando, mentioned the malaria epidemic of 1934–1935 in Ceylon (Sri Lanka), which hit an undernourished and debilitated population after the economic depression of 1930–1934 and lifted infant mortality rates to well over 400 per 1,000 in some districts. Other examples of famines and their ensuing mortality in Bengal (1943) and Bangladesh (1974) were documented by Sen (1981), and more recently demographers have started systematic studies of the demographic consequences of famines (e.g. Bongaarts & Cain, 1982; Hugo, 1984; Kane, 1987).

Famine, however, is but one among a range of possible sequels of the breakdown of social support mechanisms. As a rule, the economic crises of the twentieth century in the industrialized or semi-industrialized countries have not had such extreme consequences, and on the whole their effect on death rates has been surprisingly modest. The Great Depression in the United States caused a 46 percent drop of the GNP between 1929 and 1933, while unemployment soared from 0.4 to 11.5 percent of the population over age 10. Immigration came to an abrupt halt, from 279,678 in 1929 to 23,068 in 1933. Marriage rates also responded promptly, falling from 10.1 per 1,000 in 1929 to 7.9 in 1933, whereas the crude birthrate dropped to 16.6 per 1,000 in 1933, a historical low not again attained until the 1970s. Nevertheless, infant mortality fell from 67.6 per 1,000 in 1929 to 57.6 in 1932, rose slightly to 60.1 in 1934, but then resumed its downward trend.

In Latin America, trends for this period were quite similar. Due to the economic crisis of the 1930s, most Latin American countries, with the exception of Mexico, suffered a marked, though temporary, decline in birthrates (Collver, 1965). In some, like Argentina and Chile, birthrates stayed relatively low for several years but eventually increased again. Marriage rates between 1929 and 1933 fell by 19 percent in Argentina, 25 percent in Uruguay, and 33 percent in Chile but recovered soon afterward. A sharp decline of marriage rates also occurred in Colombia. There is, however, little evidence of a systematic rise of infant mortality throughout the continent, although apparently minor increases did occur in Colombia and Argentina.

Life and Death Under Austerity

With reference to the debt crisis of the 1980s, a comparison of health and mortality trends in three countries, Chile, Costa Rica, and Brazil, shows a mixed and somewhat contradictory picture. The Chilean case in particular has been object of close scrutiny. On the one hand, this is because Chilean demographic statistics are of much better quality than those of most Latin American countries. On the other hand, interest has been awakened by the curious circumstance that almost a decade of free market economics, with the concomitant exacerbation of social inequality, declining consumption levels of the poorest population segments (Cortázar, 1983; Riveros & Labbé, 1984), and even a 14.4 percent drop of the GDP in 1975, failed to interrupt the country's downward infant mortality trend. This remained true even in the early 1980s, when

Table 4.1   Chile: Infant Mortality Rates,
1970-1985

Year	Mortality (per 1,000 births)
1970	82.2
1971	73.9
1972	72.7
1973	65.8
1974	65.2
1975	57.6
1976	56.6
1977	50.1
1978	40.1
1979	37.9
1980	33.0
1981	27.0
1982	23.6
1983	21.9
1984	19.6
1985	19.5

Source: Chile, Instituto Nacional de
Estadistica (INE), Anuario Demografico 1985.

the GDP once again fell by a spectacular 17.2 percent between the last semester of 1981 and the second semester of 1983, while unemployment reached the highest rates anywhere in the continent (Foxley & Raczynski, 1984).

Nevertheless, infant mortality fell continuously, from 82.2 per 1,000 births in 1970 to 19.5 in 1985 (see Table 4.1). Some slowdown has been apparent since 1982, but with the rate already approaching the theoretical limit of possible reductions, such slowing should be expected even under normal circumstances. According to Haignere (1983), the causes of the sharp decline in infant mortality are increased expenditures on maternal and child health and nutrition programs, which prevented an otherwise inevitable deterioration of infant and child health conditions. Essentially the same conclusion was reached by researchers from Chile's Corporación de Investigaciones Económicas para América Latina (CIEPLAN) (Foxley & Raczynski, 1984; Raczynski, 1985; Raczynski & Oyarzo, 1981), who emphasized the priority given to these programs at a time when overall health expenditures per capita were lower than in 1970. They also recognized some influence of improved education and a more favorable fertility distribution.

The Chilean situation is even more puzzling when contrasted with that of Costa Rica, a country known for its long-standing tradition of public health care. Rosero's study (1983) of Costa Rican infant mortality since 1910 detected systematic increases within a year after the onset of recessions. The study continued only until 1981, but more recent figures show that a small increase, from 18.1 to 18.8 per 1,000 births, did occur between 1981 and 1982. In 1983 and 1984, the downward trend resumed, although at a slower rate than before. Despite cutbacks of child nutrition programs, statistics from the Costa Rican Ministry of Health show that malnutrition among preschool children diminished from 8.6 percent in 1978 to 4.1 percent in 1982. For 1982, there are data showing significant reductions in food consumption and health care for the population in general. That infant mortality did not react more sharply may be due to the increase of breastfeeding (Mata et al., 1984) and to the relatively fast recovery of health investments in 1983 and 1984.

Despite the absence of a similar increase in Chilean infant mortality, there are indications that not all is well. The smallest declines occurred between 1973 and 1974 and between 1975 and 1976 and are probably related to the social turmoil of the 1973 coup and to the 1975–1976 recession. A breakdown by educational levels of the mothers showed an increase from 144.6 per 1,000 in 1973 to 157.3 in 1974 and again from 133.5 per 1,000 in 1975 to 136.5 in 1976 for mothers with no formal education (Foxley & Raczynski, 1984). Although the downward trend resumed afterward, these figures nevertheless indicated that social and economic disturbances did leave their imprint on infant and child mortality. Several authors (Haignere, 1983; Foxley & Raczynski, 1984; Raczynski, 1985; Solimano & Haignere, 1984) mentioned the secular increase, since the early 1970s, of reported cases of typhoid and para-typhoid fever as well as infectious hepatitis as possible signs of deteriorating health conditions. Despite the nutritional assistance programs, which have a long tradition in Chile and were intensified in the 1970s, statistics collected by the Ministry of Health showed that, after six years of steady decline, malnutrition among preschool children increased from 8.8 percent in 1982 to 9.8 percent in 1983. According to Raczynski (1985), the increase reflected budget cuts in the nutritional assistance programs. In 1984, when open unemployment diminished somewhat and nutritional assistance was intensified, the percentage fell again, to 8.4 percent.

In Brazil, nutritional assistance programs do not have the Chilean tradition or intensity. Brazilian infant mortality trends since the 1960s reveal a curious, roughly countercyclical pattern with respect to economic growth. Although the evidence is not entirely conclusive (Hakkert, 1984a), there are strong indications that infant mortality in the major cities increased during the 1968–1974 boom period, because of the deterioration of the legal minimum wage and the inability of basic sanitation programs to keep up with the intense growth of the urban periphery (Wood, 1977). Consequently, the authorities perceived a need for more investments in social and basic sanitation programs. The latter expanded considerably during the 1970s (Vetter, 1983) and became one of the main factors behind the 1975–1982 infant mortality decline, while the economy entered a phase of slower growth. Immunization campaigns were also expanded. The state secretariats of education provide nutritional supplements to school-age children and the Brazilian Legion for Assistance (LBA) distributes basic food rations to preschool children and pregnant women. However, unlike Chile and Costa Rica, Brazil has not systematically attempted to balance the effects of its austerity program by nutritional intervention.

An assessment of the recent evolution of Brazilian mortality is complicated by the scarcity of reliable statistics. Indirect estimates based on the 1970 and 1980 censuses and on the 1984 National Household Survey (PNAD) show considerable health improvements in practically all parts of the country. According to these estimates, infant mortality dropped from 113.8 per 1,000 in the late 1960s to 87.9 in the late 1970s and 68.1 in the early 1980s (FIBGE, 1986). Meanwhile, the percentage of malnourished children up to age 5-1/2 in the Northeast, as measured by the 1986 Demographic and Health Survey (BEMFAM/Westinghouse, 1986), diminished. Although the overall proportion of 38.8 percent of children with some degree of malnutrition is certainly high, it compares favorably with a 1974–1975 study by the Brazilian Census Bureau, which found a truly alarming proportion of 86.4 percent (FIBGE, 1982). Advanced malnutrition, in particular, decreased from 35.5 percent to 7.0 percent.

Encouraging as these results may be, they refer to fairly long periods and may not convey possible setbacks in the aftermath of the debt crisis. Moreover, some researchers (e.g., Silva, 1986) dismiss the apparent improvement of nutritional status as due to comparability problems. Whether infant mortality in Brazil has increased in recent years is a matter of some dispute. In a rather controversial study of vital registration data, circulated by UNICEF, Becker & Lechtig (1986) argued that, after several years of consistent decline, infant mortality once again started to increase in 1983. There is some empirical support for this assertion, but the numbers should be interpreted with caution. The ratio of registered infant deaths to births increased from 56.0 per 1,000 in 1982 to 57.0 in 1983 and 60.9 in 1984. However, infant deaths and especially births are subject to considerable underregistration, which may vary from year to year. Furthermore, for purely methodological reasons, the ratio experiences an artificial upward drift in times of sharp fertility decline, generally to be expected during recessions. After this effect is discounted, the slight increase in 1983 disappears. The larger increase in 1984 seems to be real, but in 1985 the ratio dropped again, to 49.2 per 1,000. A similar trend is apparent in data from the state of São Paulo, where registration is fairly reliable. After reaching a historical low of 41.9 per 1,000 in the period from May 1983 to April 1984, infant mortality in this state increased temporarily to 45.4 in November, before resuming a declining trend, reaching 34.4 in November 1987.

Further evidence may be obtained from mortality statistics by cause, which are published annually by the Brazilian Ministry of Health (Brasil, various years). See Table 4.2 for proportional mortality trends for some causes likely to be associated with deteriorating living conditions. Clearly, intestinal infections have been consistently on the retreat. The same occurred in Chile (Raczynski & Oyarzo, 1981). Brazilian researchers (Monteiro, 1982) have generally attributed this decline to investments in urban infrastructure, especially access to drinking water, undertaken during the 1970s. In Chile, this explanation has been given less frequently, but there too the availability of drinking water expanded considerably, according to the 1982 census. Oral rehydration, which became widely available during this period, may have reinforced this decline in deaths due to intestinal infections.

The steady increase of homicides in Latin America is worrisome. In Brazil, the number nearly doubled between 1977 and 1984 (see Table 4.2). Its relation to austerity policies is somewhat tenuous, except in countries like Peru, where political violence rose sharply as a consequence of the debt crisis. There, politically motivated homicides, virtually non-existent until 1980, rose to 3,587 in 1984, nearly 2 percent of all registered deaths (Figallo & Valderrama, 1987). In Costa Rica, however, there were actually fewer homicides in 1982–1983 than in 1980–1981, even though the number of theft convictions rose by almost 70 percent (figures from the Ministry of Justice). Suicides are more eloquent in revealing the national state of mind. In Costa Rica, they increased from 0.98 percent of all deaths in 1982 to 1.40 percent in 1983. A smaller increase in Brazil is apparent from Table 4.2. The relationship of suicide to economic trends stands out more clearly in a breakdown by suspected motives. From 187 in 1982, the number of suicides attributed to financial problems increased to 339 in 1983, the nadir of the financial crisis, when Brazil was forced to seek IMF assistance. In 1984, that number declined to 285, and in 1985, the first year of the short-lived 1985–1986 recovery, to 224.

For children under age 5, there was a clear increase in the proportion of deaths attributable to nutritional deficiencies, from 4.23 percent in 1983 to 4.99 percent in 1984. As there is no well-developed monitoring

Table 4.2   Brazil: Proportional Mortality by Some Causes, 1977-1984

Cause of Death (percent)

	Nutritional Deficiencies	Intestinal Infections	Tuberculosis	Pneumonia and Influenza	Homicide	Suicide
1977	1.52[a]	7.52	1.29	6.11	1.38	0.56
1978	1.59[a]	7.39	1.18	5.93	1.38	0.49
1979	1.66	6.07	1.00	5.06	1.57	0.49
1980	1.55	5.34	0.93	4.78	1.85	0.52
1981	1.43	4.81	0.85	4.64	2.03	0.54
1982	1.34	4.41	0.76	4.60	2.10	0.53
1983	1.28	4.08	0.70	4.30	2.26	0.59
1984	1.50	3.95	0.69	4.34	2.44	0.61
1985	na	na	na	na	na	0.58

Cause of Infant Death (percent)

	Nutritional Deficiencies	Intestinal Infections	Tuberculosis	Pneumonia and Influenza	Low Birth Weight	Suicide
1977	3.30[a]	23.77	0.14	12.78	6.68	0.70
1978	3.59[a]	23.53	0.16	12.46	6.23	0.69
1979	4.56	19.95	0.12	10.23	6.60	0.79
1980	4.34	18.16	0.12	9.71	6.48	0.76
1981	4.17	16.80	0.12	10.00	6.15	0.57
1982	4.12	16.22	0.11	10.45	6.06	0.50
1983	4.08	16.08	0.10	9.20	5.42	0.47
1984	4.78	15.59	0.09	9.22	5.17	0.69

[a] Not comparable to later figures, due to different classifications.
na Not available.
Sources: Brazil, Ministerio da Saude, Estatisticas de Mortalidade
Fundacao IBGE, Anuario Estatistico 1986.

system, actual malnutrition trends during the early 1980s are unclear. The percentage of deaths due to low birth weight, also an indicator of nutritional status, did not increase in the country as a whole. Data from the city of Santo André, near São Paulo, where the children's hospitals register the nutritional status of all patients, show a decline of malnutrition for those aged 1–3 months, from about 25 percent in 1980 to 18–20 percent in 1981. This level was maintained until the second half of 1985, when it dropped further, to 15 percent and then, in 1986, to 10 percent (FAISA, several years). This indicates that although malnutrition remained a problem, its incidence at least did not increase. Although quite exposed to the effects of unemployment, Santo André is also a relatively prosperous city, with possibly greater reserves that may have kept the situation from deteriorating. In contrast in Recife, in the poor northeastern region of Brazil, Dias et al. (1985) found that the percentage of children born with birth weights under 2.5 kilos increased sharply from 1982, in about the same proportion as the number of hours of work needed to acquire a basic food ration.

Infectious and parasitic diseases increased everywhere, due in part to a measles epidemic in 1984. For Brazil as a whole, the proportional mortality for infectious and parasitic diseases for children under age 5 increased from 19.45 percent in 1983 to 19.63 percent in 1984, but in Greater São Paulo, the percentage of infant deaths due to these causes reached 21.21 percent, compared to 17.36 percent in the previous year. To explain the measles epidemic, Macedo (1984) and others have suggested that three consecutive years of low wages and unemployment were beginning to take their toll on the infant population. Another interpretation attributed the problem to errors in the administration of the vaccination programs. Considering that an even larger outbreak took place in 1986, during the short-lived boom of the Cruzado Plan, the latter explanation cannot be ruled out.

Long-term Consequences

According to United Nations (1986), demographic phenomena are only weakly affected by economic cycles. Whether this is true depends somewhat on the time frame of the analysis and on how narrowly one defines "demographic phenomena." If the definition of demographic phenomena is limited to population size, growth, and age structure, then the impact of economic cycles is quite modest. Mortality data are clearly more responsive social indicators than such demographic phenomena. However, in the case of Latin America, the recession unleashed by austerity measures in the early 1980s did not last long enough to turn around prevailing mortality trends. In Chile, improvements continued, although possibly at a slower pace than before. In Costa Rica, a temporary infant mortality increase was quickly reversed once spending on health and nutrition programs resumed. Had Brazil's economic problems continued as acute as they were in 1981–1983, health and mortality indicators might have deteriorated further. By 1984, however, a temporary recovery was under way, and consequently the situation improved in 1985 and 1986. In the second semester of 1986, the Cruzado Plan began to falter, plunging the country into another recession, which reduced the legal minimum wage to its lowest real value (roughly U.S. $35) in history. One may wonder what will be the long-term consequences of a prolonged sequence of such crises and partial recoveries. Whereas the short-term effects of the 1982–1983 recession may have been attenuated by the accumulated effect of past investments in basic sanitation and health, the need to cut costs in these areas as part of a long-term austerity policy may render further prospects less favorable.

The lasting demographic consequences of economic crises are more likely mediated by fertility and migration behavior. This is not an exclusive characteristic of the Latin American debt crisis. As has been shown by Chen and Chowdhury (1977), among others, the impact of even such an extreme event as the 1974 famine in Bangladesh on local population growth trends was mediated by lower fertility and higher out-migration to a much larger extent than by actual death from starvation. Research in this area is, however, difficult, not only because birth and especially migration statistics are more deficient than death registration data, but also because the evaluation of the specific impact of economic trends on reproduction requires a long-term view. Fertility in most Latin American countries was falling long before the debt crisis. Moreover, recent trends in the different countries have been quite distinct. Major declines during the past ten years occurred in Brazil (BEMFAM/Westinghouse, 1986) and Colombia (CCRP/Westinghouse, 1986), but not in Argentina, Chile, or Costa Rica.

Although there is abundant historical evidence of the short-term decline in rates of marriages and births that normally accompanied the prewar recessions in the developed countries (e.g. Basavarajapa, 1971; Glass, 1938; Kirk, 1960; Pressat, 1969), the lasting effects of prolonged economic adversity are more difficult to assess. The major reason is that, unlike mortality, reproduction is subject to individual planning. Bongaarts and Cain (1982), for instance, have argued that although the immediate consequence of an acute crisis tends to be the reduction of birthrates, they may later return to unprecedented levels, to compensate unrealized fertility and ensure sufficient offspring to overcome possible mortality crises in the future. The argument is, however, limited to a context of famine, high expected mortality, and lack of institutional alternatives for providing support to the aged.

One of the first social indicators to be affected by any kind of social or economic crisis is nuptiality, as couples postpone marriage in the face of unfavorable prospects. Nuptuality does, however, tend to recover rapidly. Fertility is also sensitive but, for obvious reasons, takes longer to react. In Greater São Paulo, for instance, one notes a clear decline in the marriage rate, from 8.12 per 1,000 during the period from August 1981 to July 1982, to 6.75 two years later. When the economic situation improved somewhat in the second semester of 1984, marriage rates immediately increased, although not to pre-1982 levels. Similarly, birthrates recovered somewhat in 1985, closely following the increased marriage rates of nine months earlier. In 1986, however, the downward trend of both marriages and births resumed, despite the economic recovery. In June 1987, the birthrate over the past twelve months was at a historical low of 22.75 per 1,000 and the marriage rate at 6.34 per 1,000, the lowest recorded since the early years of the century.

From a short-term perspective, an interesting implication of the responsiveness of birthrates to economic cycles is that, in a rather perverse way, recession and therefore austerity policies may contribute to lower infant mortality. This point was made, for instance, by Hojman (1985), in his econometric analysis of Chilean infant mortality during the 1970s. The effect may occur for several reasons:

1. The smaller number of births may reduce the pressure on scarce infant and child care resources (Raczynski & Oyarzo, 1981).
2. If the birthrate falls disproportionately among the most disadvantaged population segments, the children actually born have a lower average risk of dying than earlier birth cohorts (Hakkert, 1984b; Solimano & Haignere, 1984).
3. Lower fertility usually implies a more favorable distribution of births by spacing and birth order. Trussell and Pebley (1984) estimated the potential impact of a better fertility distribution on infant and child mortality, controlling for several socioeconomic variables, at 10 percent and 21 percent respectively.

From a long-term perspective, the implication of these fertility fluctuations is that cohorts attaining reproductive ages during recessions may marry later and have their children at older ages, but this does not necessarily imply lower completed fertility. Analyzing the behavior of U.S. fertility during the period from 1927 to 1960, one notices, for instance, that the completed family sizes of actual cohorts of women varied much less than period fertility rates. The completed family size implied by the latter declined from 2.78 children per woman in 1927 to 2.10 in 1936, then gradually increased again to reach 3.58 in 1957, when another decline set in. Meanwhile, the completed family size of actual cohorts of women, classified by the year in which they reached the mean age of childbearing, varied from 2.53 in 1927 to 2.23 in 1936–1937, after which it increased to a peak of 3.12 in 1958. The reason for this greater stability of the completed family sizes of actual cohorts is that many of those who postponed childbearing in the 1930s ended up having their children later.

In demographic analysis, the problem of identifying this kind of behavior is known as the problem of *intensity* versus *timing*. In this context, the present fertility fluctuations in countries like Brazil and their evident correlation with economic trends allow two interpretations. According to one, the austerity policies of the 1980s have mainly affected the intensity component, by speeding up a process of structural fertility decline that otherwise would have occurred anyway, though at a slower pace. In this case, the demographic effect of austerity on population trends will, paradoxically, stimulate long-term economic growth, since it implies a more favorable relation between the labor force and the number of dependents in the three or four decades to come. The other viewpoint acknowledges the existence of an "austerity effect," but interprets this effect, to a large extent, as one of timing. If this view is correct, it means that extrapolations of the current fertility decline may grossly underestimate future birthrates.

With respect to Third World countries, demographic theory building has tended to favor the study of long-term trends over the analysis of circumstantial factors. "When we simultaneously analyze secular transformations and short term phenomena, our baggage of analytical techniques overwhelmingly favors the former" (Hogan, 1985). The demographic literature therefore tends to interpret the decline of current fertility in the Third World in terms of intensity, rather than timing. Recent studies of major fertility declines in Colombia (CCRP/Westinghouse, 1986), Costa Rica (United Nations, 1985), and Brazil (BEMFAM/Westinghouse, 1986) have listed a wide range of causes, from access to contraception to urbanization, female education, and "motivational factors," but have rarely addressed the question of to what extent these motivational factors may be reversed once economic conditions change. U.S. demographers learned a painful lesson in the 1940s, when they discovered that apparently secular trends towards lower fertility had actually been biased by the adverse economic circumstances of the Great Depression. Consequently, population projections made in the 1930s turned out to be embarrassingly low. Of course, the U.S. "baby boom" cannot be explained solely as a shift in the timing of fertility. Easterlin

(1962) and others (e.g. Boyer, 1984) have attempted to identify other, more structural, economic factors behind this phenomenon that may not apply to Latin America today. Nevertheless, if postponement of births, due to the sobering economic prospects of the IMF era, is occurring to any significant extent in countries like Brazil, it may profoundly alter the prospects for future fertility trends.

Migration

One option frequently considered by those in search of enhanced economic and social opportunities is migration. As a result of current austerity policies, some former migration routes have ceased to exist, and new ones have opened. Emigration from South and Central American nations to other parts of the world is expected to increase steadily while, as a reaction to the debt crisis, Latin American countries are expected to impose stronger restrictions on immigration to and within their boundaries. Internal migration, however, is expected to continue, given the difficulty of restricting this type of movement.

In the latter context, Martine et al. (1984) pointed out that migration totals could theoretically be affected in two radically opposed directions. On the one hand, the recessionary effects of austerity measures might bring about an overall increase in the number of moves, especially of the poor, in response to the need to find new means of subsistence. On the other hand, the decrease of opportunities in the urban economy and government-sponsored construction projects or settlement schemes might discourage such moves. The eventual outcome will obviously depend on the specifics of each particular area. Evidence for either hypothesis is difficult to obtain because of the lack of recent data from most Latin American countries. An interesting case is that of Bogotá. Although Colombia was not so severely affected by the debt crisis as some other Latin American countries, it has had the most recent census, taken in October 1985. The population of Bogotá enumerated at this date was 3.98 million, compared to a corrected total of 2.86 million in 1973. If the 1985 number is correct, it implies a rather sluggish average annual growth rate of 2.8 percent, which, if extrapolated, would bring the population in 2000 to slightly under 6 million, less than the most conservative estimate of 6.5 million so far prepared by the United Nations. Although no solid data are available, there have also been reports of a reversal of prevailing migration trends toward Mexico City. Similarly, the Brazilian press has regularly written about the return of migrants from the major metropolitan areas to the Northeast, as a result of urban unemployment (Martine et al., 1984).

Costa Rican results support a contrary hypothesis, namely that the economic crisis promoted rural-to-urban migration and increased urbanization. In this country, steady rural-to-urban migration continued at least until 1985 (MTSS, 1986). This finding is partly explained by the 1982 fall in average agricultural earnings to beneath the official minimum wage, where it remained until 1985, and by the fact that urban wages in all major sectors were substantially higher (MTSS, 1986).

An option frequently considered by Mexicans in search of economic and social opportunities is to go to the United States. During the past decade, Mexico has almost always been the country that provided the greatest number of legal immigrants to the United States, but no clear increase is apparent so far. Immigration and Naturalization Service (INS) data indicate that in 1986 there were 66,533 legal Mexican immigrants, slightly up from 57,800 in 1984, but not much more than the annual average of 64,030 during the 1970s. Concerning undocumented immigrants, however, most of whom are Mexican nationals, INS data indicate a steady increase, from nearly 1 million in 1980 to an estimated 1.8 million in 1986. Probably at least part of the observed increase is directly related to reduced economic opportunities at home. The same data also indicate that in the 1980s legal immigration to the United States from Bolivia, Brazil, Colombia, and Venezuela has continued to increase. Although some of this increase is certainly due to family reunification, adverse conditions at the point of origin must also be considered.

Recent changes in the immigration laws of Argentina and Venezuela, both former recipients of large numbers of workers from neighboring countries, stemmed at least partially from the Argentine and Venezuelan austerity programs, as both countries passed effective legislation limiting the future entrance of undocumented workers. Although the number of Latin American immigrants to Argentina in the 1970s declined compared to earlier decades (Carrón, 1979), the 1980 census counted nearly 700,000 nationals from neighboring countries (INDEC, 1981). Because of the undocumented nature of many, a stricter immigration policy designed to regulate their flow into and through the country was passed in 1981. No data permitting an evaluation of this law are available, but researchers believe that the tougher legislation, in conjunction with the falling real incomes of workers in Argentina, has greatly reduced the numbers of undocumented workers present (Villar, 1984).

Throughout the boom years of the 1970s, especially after 1974, Venezuela received many undocumented workers from Colombia and, to a lesser extent, Ecuador, Peru, and Chile. In 1980, Presidential Decree 616 was passed to register the more than 1 million undocumented foreigners believed to be in Venezuela. The Venezuelan immigration laws also appear to have produced the desired effect of stemming the flow of undocumented workers. The positive net migration of the 1970s became negative in the 1980s, so much that, from March to September 1983, 22,197 more foreigners left the country than entered (Van Roy, 1984). For the entire 1980–1985 period, net out-migration has been estimated at 126,625. For the Colombians alone, the number was 56,858 (Torrealba, 1987). Likely, it was the country's tougher immigration laws along with its diminished economic activity that best explain the rapid reversal in past migration patterns from neighboring countries.

Within Brazil, there is little concrete evidence to evaluate whether rural-to-urban migration patterns during the crisis have changed. It has been estimated that the state of São Paulo receives over 500,000 migrants per year, with 70 percent headed for the metropolitan area (Higobassi, 1987). Brasília is also expected to receive nearly 100,000 migrants in 1987. Employment opportunities in more remote areas have now all but vanished. One case in point is the Amazonian frontier state of Rondônia, first systematically opened to colonization in 1969. Although it is not possible to prove that migration to that state increased as a result of economic difficulties in other parts of the country, this possibility should at least be considered. This is because Rondônian-bound migration steadily increased during the early 1980s, from 37,000 in 1979 to 60,000 in 1981 to 167,000 in 1986 (SEPLAN, 1986). However, a major drop occurred in 1987.

The migrants arriving from this point on will have come too late to take advantage of the governmental land redistribution or any other projects to welcome migrants. Rather, because of constraints on the state and local governments, as well as high regional unemployment, delinquency, violence, and prostitution, the government of Rondônia decided in 1987 to allocate two million cruzados to pay for the passages of those willing to leave the state and return to their point of origin. In Campo Grande, capital of the state of Mato Grosso do Sul, a similar phenomenon occurred. Experiencing an unemployment rate of nearly 20 percent and serving as a stopping-off point for many migrants on their way from the southern region to the Amazonian frontier or vice versa, this local government too decided to pay for bus transport of those interested in moving to other regions. Several thousand such tickets were distributed form January to May 1987.

In response to the debt crisis of the 1980s, the number of Brazilians interested in or actually undertaking emigration has increased substantially. A recent survey of 1,390 São Paulo adults indicated that 34 percent had thought about emigrating (*Folha de São Paulo*, July 31, 1987). Of these, 57 percent declared the desire to leave behind the difficult economic situation as their principal motive. Those actually leaving the country may be divided into longtime foreign residents deciding to "sell out" and return home, and native-born Brazilians in search of a better life elsewhere. The countries issuing the greatest number of resident visas to Brazilian citizens over the past years have been Italy, Portugal, Spain, and Australia, in that order (Lessa, 1987).

During the early part of 1987, migration to Canada was frequently considered by Brazilians. This occurred when Canada was promoted in unofficial circles as a land of opportunity for those seeking employment. Thus, during the first half of 1987, over 1,500 Brazilian "tourists" arrived at the Toronto airport. Until that time no visa was required of Brazilian tourists arriving by air. This situation has since changed with the implementation of very strict controls. However, many of the early arrivals were reclassified as "economic refugees" and allowed to stay (Paoletti, 1987). Many of these, as well as later arrivals currently awaiting deportation hearings, now make their home among the 200,000 immigrants in the Portuguese enclave of Toronto, known as Portugal Village.

Conclusions

This examination has discerned several demographic consequences of recent austerity programs in Latin America. Most countries experienced sharp increases in unemployment and rapid growth of the informal sector. Given the lack of an effective social security system in many countries, the informal sector has necessarily grown as those in need had to do whatever was necessary to survive. We expect that as this sector grows in relation to the formal sector, so too will Latin American poverty.

One apparent household survival strategy adopted in several areas has been the increased labor force participation of women and aged men. In some more desperate areas, even the participation rates of children increased in an effort to help their families reach a minimum level of subsistence. The long-term consequences for those countries where many children drop out of primary school to begin work will likely be extremely negative. Although the population segments most affected by declining labor force opportunities vary between countries, it is usually the most disadvantaged group that suffers most, and within this group especially the rural poor. In addition, most informal sector workers, as well as those earning low wages in the urban formal economy, are extremely vulnerable to macroeconomic adjustments.

One of the first demographic consequences that would be expected is a deterioration of infant mortality and other health indicators. Surprisingly, the impact in this area has been relatively modest, at least in the countries considered. In Peru, Bolivia, or other countries where the social consequences of austerity have been more violent, health indicators may have deteriorated more acutely, especially among the poorest population segments, but unfortunately no data are available to confirm this suspicion. In Chile, Costa Rica, and Brazil, for the time being, past investments and social control mechanisms are still fairly effective in preventing a permanent increase of mortality. This may, however, not continue to be the case, as past investments are gradually depleted by a long-term need to cut back on social expenditures.

Any existing mortality increases are unlikely to have a major effect on population growth in the near future. The austerity crisis may, however, alter future growth trends through its influence on fertility, especially in countries like Brazil, where a major fertility decline was already under way. One of the unsolved questions in this context is to what extent the current economic situation has actually affected this trend and, if so, whether it has reinforced the structural trend toward lower fertility or rather led to a postponement of births. Latin America may not face anything similar to a baby boom in years to come, but if postponement is at all significant, it may profoundly alter future fertility prospects. For the time being, demographers have little certainty as to what is really happening and whether the fertility decline of the austerity era can be extrapolated into the future.

Available data, however limited, indicate that during the debt crisis of the early 1980s rural-urban migration continued at a brisk pace in some areas of Latin America. This can be partly explained by the extremely low wages earned by the rural agricultural workers and the general decreases of services provided in such areas. Concerning international migration, probably no Latin America country is willingly receiving low skilled immigrants. Undocumented workers in small numbers certainly continue to migrate to and from many areas. However, as a result of the crisis situation, fairly effective measures have been taken to halt this flow. Nevertheless, increasing numbers of Latin Americans consider the option of emigration outside of the area.

References

Altimir, Oscar. "Poverty, Income Distribution and Child Welfare in Latin America: A Comparison of Pre- and Postrecession Data." *World Development* 12, pp. 261–282, 1984.

Basavarajapa, K. G. "The Influence of Fluctuations in Economic Conditions on Fertility and Marriage Rates, Australia, 1920 to 1938 and 1946 to 1967." *Population Studies* 25 (1), 1971.

Becker, Roberto A., and Aaron Lechtig. *Brasil: Evolução da Mortalidade Infantil no Período 1977–1984.* Ministério da Saúde, Brasília, 1986.

BEMFAM/Westinghouse. *Brazil Demographic and Health Survey 1986: Preliminary Report.* Columbia: Westinghouse Institute for Research Development, 1986.

Bongaarts, John, and Mead Cain. "Demographic Responses to Famine," in Kenneth M. Cahill (ed.), *Famine.* New York: Orbis Books, 1982.

Boyer, Louis. "Dimensions Démographiques de la Crise Economique Mondiale." *Etudes en Développement* 12 (47-48), pp. 51–62, 1984.

Brasil, Ministério da Saúde. *Estatísticas da Mortalidade.* Brasília: Ministério da Saúde. Several Years.

Brenner, M. "Foetal, Infant and Maternal Mortality During Periods of Economic Instability." *International Journal of Health Services,* 3 (2), 1973.

Carr, Barry. "The Mexican Left, the Popular Movements, and the Politics of Austerity, 1982–1985," in Barry Carr and Ricardo A. Montoya (eds.), *The Mexican Left, the Popular Movements, and the Politics of Austerity.* San Diego: Center for U.S.-Mexican Studies, University of California, 1986.

Carrón, Juan M. "Shifting Patterns in Migration from Bordering Countries to Argentina: 1914–1970." *International Migration Review* 13, pp. 475–487, 1979.

CCRP/Westinghouse. *Tercera Encuesta Nacional de Prevalencia de Uso de Anticonceptivos, Demografía y Salud: Informe Preliminar.* Bogotá: Corporación Centro Regional de Población, 1986.

Céspedes, V. *Costa Rica: Recuperación sin Reactivación.* San José: UNED, Academía de Centroamérica, 1985.

Charbonneau, Hubert, and Larosse André (eds.). *The Great Mortalities: Methodological Studies of Demographic Crises in the Past.* Dolhain, Belgium: Ordina Editions, 1979.

Chen, Lincoln C., and Alauddin Chowdhury. "The Dynamics of Contemporary Famine," in *Proceedings of the International Union for the Scientific Study of Population, Population Conference, Mexico.* Liège: Ordina, 1977.

Collver, O. Andrew. *Birth Rates in Latin America: New Estimates of Historical Trends and Fluctuations.* Berkeley: Institute of International Studies Research Series No. 7, University of California, 1965.

Cornia, G. Andrea. "A Survey of Cross-Sectional and Time-Series Literature on Factors Affecting Child Welfare." *World Development* 12 (3), pp. 187–202, 1984.

Cortázar, R. "Chile: Resultados Distributivos, 1973–1982." *Notas Técnicas* 57. Santiago: CIEPLAN, 1983.

Dias, L., M. R. Camarano and Aaron Lechtig. "A Drought Recession and Prevalance of Low Birth-Weight in Poor Urban Populations of the Northeast of Brazil," in James P. Grant (ed.), *Situação mundial da infância 1986.* Brasília: UNICEF, 1985.

Easterlin, Richard A. *The American Baby-Boom in Historical Perspective.* New York: National Bureau of Economic Research, 1962.

Estado de Minas. "DIEESE Acha Pequeno Novo Piso Salarial." Belo Horizonte: *Estado de Minas,* November 1, 1987.

Eyer, J., and P. Sterling. "Stress-Related Mortality and Social Organization." *Review of Radical Political Economy* 9 (1), 1977.

FAISA (Fundação de Assistência à Infância de Santo André). *Relatório anual..* Santo André: FAISA. Several Years.

FIBGE (Fundação Instituto Brasileiro de Geografia e Estatística). *Perfil Estatístico ade Criânças e Mães no Brasil: 1974–75*. Rio de Janeiro: Fundação IBGE, 1982.

────. *Perfil Estatístico de Crianças e Mães no Brasil: Aspectos Sócio-econômicos da Mortalidade Infantil em Áreas Urbanas*. Rio de Janeiro: Fundação IBGE, 1986.

────. *Anuário Estatístico do Brasil, 1986*. Rio de Janeiro: Fundaçâo IBGE, 1987.

────. *Pesquisa Nacional por Amostra de Domicílios (PNAD)*. Rio de Janeiro: Fundação IBGE, several years.

Figallo, Daniel, and Mariano Valderrama. "Pobreza y Supervivencia en el Perú." Paper presented at the XIVth General Assembly of CLACSO, Recife, November 15–20, 1987.

Foxley, A., and Dagmar Raczynski. "Vulnerable Groups in Recessionary Situations: The Case of Children and the Young in Chile." *World Development* 12 (3), 1984.

García, Norberto E., and Victor E. Tokman. *Acumulación, Empleo y Crisis*. Santiago, Chile: PREALC, Investigaciones Sobre Empleo (Number 25), 1985.

Glass, David V. "Marriage Frequency and Economic Fluctuations in England and Wales, 1851–1934," in L. Hogben (ed.), *Political Arithmetic*. London: 1938.

Haignere, Clara S. "The Application of the Free-Market Economic Model in Chile and the Effects on the Population's Health Status." *International Journal of Health Services* 13 (3), pp. 389–405, 1983.

Hakkert, Ralph. *Trends and Differentials of Mortality in Brazil, 1950 to 1975*. Ph.D. Thesis, Cornell University. Ithaca, New York: 1984a.

────. "Conseqüências da Crise nas Tendências Demográficas de São Paulo," in ABEP, *Anais do IVo Encontro Nacional de Estudos de População, Águas de São Pedro* 3, pp. 1433–47, 1984b.

Higobassi, Darci. "Migração Está em Debate." *Folha de São Paulo*, July 12, 1987.

Hogan, Daniel J. "Demografia e Conjuntura: Reflexões Metodológicas." *Revista Brasileira de Estudos de População* 2 (1), Jan./June, 1–7, 1985.

Hojman, David E. "Free-Market Economic Policies and Infant and Child Mortality in Chile: Multiple Regression, Principal Components and Simultaneous Equation Models." Liverpool: University of Liverpool, Centre for Latin American Studies Occasional Paper 6, 1985.

Hugo, Graeme J. "The Demographic Impact of Famine: A Review," in Graeme J. Hugo and Bruce Currey, *Famine as a Geographical Phenomenon*. Dordrecht: Reidel, pp. 7–31, 1984.

IMAS (Instituto Mesclado de Ayuda Social). *Resumen General a Nivel Nacional de los Asentamientos de Tugurios Analizados por Regiones Programáticas del IMAS*. San José, Costa Rica: IMAS, 1984.

INDEC (Instituto Nacional de Estadística y Censos) (Argentina). *Censo de Población y Vivienda 1980. Serie B, Características Generales*. Buenos Aires: INDEC, 1981.

Infante, Ricardo. "Brasil: Características Estruturais dos Mercados de Trabalho Urbanos," in *Anais do XIII Encontro Nacional de Economia*. Rio de Janeiro: ANPEC (Associação National dos Centros de Pós-Graduação em Economia), vol. 2, pp. 399–430, 1985.

Kane, Penny. "The Demography of Famine." *Genus* 43 (1-2), pp. 43–58, 1987.

Kirk, Dudley. "The Influence of Business Cycles on Marriage and Birth Rates," in *Demographic and Economic Change in Developed Countries*. Princeton: Princeton University Press, 1960.

Klein, Emilio, and José Wurgaft. *La Creación de Empleo en Períodos de Crisis*. Santiago, Chile: PREALC, Investigaciones sobre Empleo (Number 24), 1985.

Leser, Walter. "Crescimento da População da Cidade de São Paulo entre 1950–1970 e seu Reflexo nas Condições de Saúde Pública," in M. C. Andrade et al., *Meio Ambiente, Desenvolvimento e Subdesenvolvimento*. São Paulo: HUCITEC, pp. 15–44, 1975.

Lessa, Ricardo. "Malas Prontas." *Istoé* 551, pp. 43–46, 1987.

Macedo, Roberto. "Brazilian Children and the Economic Crisis: Evidence from the State of São Paulo." *World Development* 12 (3), pp. 2003–21, 1984.

Macmahon, B. and S. Yen. "Unrecognised Epidemic of Anencephaly and Spina Bifida." *Lancet*, pp. 31–33, 1971.

Martine, George, Ivany C. Neiva, and Marle Macedo. "Migração, Crise e Outras Agruras." Paper Presented at the IVth National Meeting of ABEP, Águas de São Pedro, 1984.

Mata, L., et al. *Health and Social Development in Costa Rica: Intersectorial Action*. San José: Universidad de Costa Rica, INISA, 1984.

Monteiro, Carlos A. "Contribuição para o Estudo do Significado da Evolução do Coeficiente de Mortalidade Infantil no Município de São Paulo, SP (Brasil) nas Três Últimas Décadas (1950–1979)." *Revista de Saúde Pública* 16 (1), 1982.

MTSS (Ministerio de Trabajo y Servicios Sociales) y DGEC (Dirección General de Estadística y Censos). *Encuesta Nacional de Hogares, Empleo y Desempleo*. San José, Costa Rica: MTSS, 1977–1986.

Nitrini, Dácio. "Desemprego Provoca Aumento dos Favelados." *Folha de São Paulo*. August 24, 1981.

Paoletti, Ricardo. "Enclave Brasileiro." *Istoé* 560, pp. 58–59, 1987.

Pollack, M., and J. Uthoff. *Costa Rica: Evolución Macroeconómica, 1976–1983*. Santiago, Chile: PREALC, Monografías Sobre Empleo (Number 50), 1985.

PREALC. *Household Behavior and Economic Crisis. Costa Rica 1979–1982*. Santiago: PREALC, Documento de Trabajo (Number 270), 1985a.

——— . *Más Allá de la Crisis*. Santiago: PREALC, 1985b.

Pressat, Roland. "Interprétation des Variations à Court Terme des Taux de la Natalité." United Nations, Annals of the World Population Conference, Belgrade, 1969.

Raczynski, Dagmar. "Condiciones Sócio-económicas Recesivas y Morbi-Mortalidad Infantil," in *População e Saúde: Anais do Seminário Latino-Americano*, UNICAMP, vol. 2, pp. 303–75, 1985.

Raczynski, Dagmar, and César Oyarzo. "¿Por qué Cae la Tasa de Mortalidad Infantil en Chile?" *Estudios CIEPLAN* 6, pp. 45–84, 1981.

Riveros, L., and F. Labbé. "Situación Distributiva y el Impacto del Desempleo: un Análisis de Largo Plazo." *Revista de Economía*. Universidad de Chile, 1984.

Roett, Riordan. "Brazil and the Debt: Will the Cost be Too High?" Paper presented at the Conference on the Latin American Debt: Problems and Policies. Stanford: Stanford University, September 17–19, 1987.

Rosero, Luiz. "Social and Economic Policies and their Effects on Mortality: The Costa Rican Case." Paris: IUSSP-INED, 1983.

Sabóia, João. "Tranformações no Mercado de Trabalho no Brasil Durante a Crise: 1980–1983." Revista de Economia Política 6, pp. 82–106, 1986.

Sachs, Jeffrey. "A Verdade sobre o Modelo Asiático." Senhor 342, pp. 5–17, 1987.

SEADE (Fundação Sistema Estadual de Análise de Dados). Pesquisa de Emprego e Desemprego, Principais Resultados, Vol. 34. São Paulo: SEADE, 1987.

Sen, A. Poverty and Famines: An Essay on Entitlement and Deprivation. Oxford: Clarendon Press, 1981.

SEPLAN (Secretaria de Estado do Planajamento e Coordenação Geral) (Rondônia). Boletim de Migração, Ano VI. Pôrto Velho: SEPLAN, 1986.

Silva, Alberto C. da. "Malnutrition in Brazil after 1975." Washington, D.C.: World Bank, mimeo., 1986.

Sogner, Sølvi. "Nature and Dynamics of Crises (Including Crises in Developing Countries)," in Hubert Charbonneau and André Larosse (eds.). The Great Mortalities: Methodological Studies of Demographic Crises in the Past. Dolhain, Belgium: Ordina Editions, pp. 311–31, 1979.

Solimano, Giorgio, and Clara S. Haignere. "Free-Market Politics and Nutrition in Chile: a Grim Failure after a Short-Lived Success." New York: Center for Population and Family Health Working Paper 7, Columbia University, 1984.

Torrealba, Ricardo. "Mercado de Trabajo y Migraciones Laborales entre Colombia y Venezuela en el Contexto de la Crisis Venezolana: 1980–1986," in Gabriel Bidegain Greising (ed.). Las Migraciones Laborales Colombo–Venezolanas. Carácas: ILDIS/Nueva Sociedad/UCAB, pp. 125–147, 1987.

Trussell, T. James, and Anne R. Pebley. The Potential Impact of Changes in Fertility on Infant, Child, and Maternal Mortality. Washington, D.C.: World Bank Staff Working Paper 698, 1984.

UNICEF. Ajuste com Dimensão Humana, Parte II da Edição Completa, Situação Mundial da Infância. Brasília: Ideal, 1987.

United Nations. Socio-Economic Development and Fertility Decline in Costa Rica. New York: United Nations, Dept. of International Economic and Social Affairs, 1985.

_____ . Economic Recession and Specific Population Groups. New York: United Nations, Dept. of International Economic and Social Affairs, 1986.

United States Department of Justice. Immigration and Naturalization Annual Report. Washington, D.C.: United States Department of Justice, 1985.

Van Roy, Ralph. "Undocumented Migration to Venezuela." International Migration Review 18, pp. 541–557, 1984,

Vetter, David M. "A Evolução das Condições de Saneamento Básico da População Urbana Durante a Década de 70: uma Análise Preliminar." Revista Brasileira de Estatística 44 (173–4), pp. 181–98, 1983.

Villar, Juan Manuel. "Argentine Experience in the Field of Illegal Immigration." International Migration Review 18, pp. 453–473, 1984.

Wood, Charles H. "Infant Mortality Trends and Capitalist Development in Brazil: The Case of São Paulo and Belo Horizonte." *Latin American Perspectives* 4 (4), pp. 56–65, 1977.

World Bank. *Poverty in Latin America: The Impact of Depression.* Washington, D.C.: World Bank, 1986.

Zurron Ócio, Domingo. "Salários em queda." *Folha de São Paulo.* September 17, 1987.

5

Austerity and Regional Development Strategy in Argentina and Latin America

Alejandro Rofman

The Crisis of Accumulation in the Argentine Economy

Between 1974 and 1985 Argentina traversed a decade of stagnation. Per capita production declined nearly 15 percent. Investment rates, which had traditionally hovered around 20 percent of gross domestic product (GDP), stood at roughly 12 percent. Capital flight, financial speculation, depressed internal markets, sluggish external markets, and the constriction of state expenditures combined to reduce the overall accumulation process. The economy's autonomy and the state's economic policies were severely limited by payments on foreign debt service. These payments decreased a savings rate already eroded by stagnation, while economic policy aimed at stabilizing the current balance of payments inhibited the possibility of growth and conditioned the direction of that which did occur.

Argentina's employment structure was affected. Historically high unemployment of 6 percent, underemployment at 7 percent, and rising levels of informal employment and self-employment were evidence of the job market's increasing orientation toward tertiary activities. In 1970 skilled labor represented 40 percent of the economically active population (EAP). By 1980 the EAP was only 25 percent, whereas self-employment increased by 5 percent and tertiary sector workers increased to 50 percent of EAP. In sum, the Argentine state's situation was as follows:

1. Poor organizational coordination, reduced economic and social programs, and low capacity for mobilization
2. Increased state payments on the foreign debt

Table 5.1   The Public Sector in Argentina
            (as percent of GDP)

	Total Expenditures	Capital Expenditures	Deficit
1970	32.9	8.5	1.1
1971	32.1	8.2	3.8
1972	31.0	8.6	4.6
1973	33.7	7.5	6.6
1974	37.6	8.7	6.9
1975	37.8	8.7	14.0
1976	37.7	13.1	9.8
1977	36.1	13.4	3.2
1978	41.11	13.0	3.8
1979	38.2	10.7	3.5
1980	41.3	9.6	4.3
1981	41.9	9.8	7.1
1982	48.6	8.1	14.1
1983	49.9	8.8	15.7
1984	35.0	7.8	12.0
1985*	32.8	7.7	5.5*
1986*	31.2	8.2	2.9*

* Budgeted
Source: Secretaria de Hacienda, Argentina

3. Curtailed productive functions and increased regulatory functions
4. Reduced investment capability
5. Fiscal constraint due to scarce disposable resources
6. Regressive tax system
7. Restrictive credit and monetary policies

The military regime's conception of the state, privatization, and decentralization, giving political responsibility to the provinces, but not authority to mobilize resources, has led to a deteriorization of the state. The Argentine state's adoption of the external debt, as well as the transfer of private debt to the state, had a profound impact on state expenditures (see Tables 5.1 and 5.2). Debt interest remained around 15 percent of expenditures, requiring a reduction of other programs. Three of four double-digit state deficits in the sixteen years shown have been linked to financing the foreign debt (1982, 1983, and 1984). The decline in deficits (1985 and 1986) only emphasized the paucity of public resources and derived from restrictions on expenditures related to external debt payments. In sum, the Argentine economy's accumulation capability has seriously deteriorated. The state's fundamental role in development has been hampered by stagnation and external debt.

Table 5.2   Net Deficit and Gross Deficit (as percent of GDP)

	Gross Deficit (1)	Debt Interest (2)	Net Deficit (1-2)	Debt Interest as % of Total Public Expenditure
1981-83	12.6	7.7	4.9	16.5
1984	12.0	4.9	7.1	14.0
1985*	5.5	5.6	-0.1	17.1
1986*	2.9	4.1	-1.2	13.1

* Budgeted
Source: Calculations based on information from the Secretaria de Hacienda.

The other source of capital for Argentine economic growth has been foreign investments. International capital markets have been greatly perturbed in the 1980s. As the U.S. Treasury absorbed funds from throughout the Western financial system, investment in Latin America rapidly declined. Multinational corporations reduced their risk investments from pre-1975 levels. In addition, the fall in petroleum prices reduced significantly the availability of petrodollars, a major factor motivating Western banks' lending initiatives in Latin America in the 1970s. Given this scenario, multilateral financial institutions have provided the only remaining supply of international credits. The IMF, however, imposes strict conditions on domestic policy and the World Bank often provides funding for enterprises that do not represent productive investments.

In sum, Argentina faces grave constraints on state economic policy. One possibility is a significant stimulation of domestic markets, which could reinvigorate the productive sector and increase state revenues. However, this solution appears elusive, given restraints imposed by external debt interest payments and faithful compliance with the conditions of IMF standby accords. Indeed, there appears to be only a narrow margin available to the Argentine government to negotiate advantageously with the IMF. Unilateral reduction of interest payments—as in Peru—could free certain resources, but Argentina would face the international banking system's response. Assuming that interest payments were stopped, however, the structural conditions of the Argentine economy do not guarantee a rapid rebuilding of external savings levels. Given the possibility of aggravated capital flight or instability in domestic capital markets resulting from confrontations with foreign lenders, the short-term outlook would not foresee substantial improvement in capital accumulation. Finally, the demand for interest payments on foreign debt requires that the trade surplus be increased as much as possible. Given the high inelasticity of exports on current international markets, the only viable alternative is reduced imports. This further hinders the increase of production because import levels are closely related to the dynamic of growth. If imports are not allowed to expand, then economic expansion will be restricted.

In short, the Argentine economy's crisis seems unlikely to be resolved in either the short- or mid-term. My analysis proceeds from this fundamental premise: For now and for the foreseeable future, economic growth will be limited, and the domestic market will operate under conditions of acutely restricted internal and external savings.

The situation throughout the rest of Latin America exhibits the same outlines of heavy indebtedness, net flight of financial resources from Latin America to the developed economies, and serious accumulation difficulties. The weakening of Latin American economies and their manifest incapacity to expand rest precisely on the fact that they have become providers of resources to core nations in a movement of financial flows that is totally perverse. Argentina, in particular, and Latin America, in general, are mired in a structural crisis (see Table 5.3).

Traditional Approaches to
Regional Development Planning in Argentina
and Latin America

In Latin America, the first regional planning programs were developed in the 1940s and 1950s. They were founded on academic research from and the experiences of Western developed nations. Their primary aim was to further develop exploitation of natural resources. Numerous Latin American regional development programs attempted to increase use of water resources by imitating the Tennessee Valley Authority (TVA) model. Similarly, regional programs were implemented to assist areas devastated by natural disasters, especially earthquakes.

By the late 1950s and 1960s, regional development plans were even more structured by core nations' experiences. In Argentina, the growth pole model quickly emerged as a solution to regional inequalities. This model assumed that the possibilities of growth in a depressed or underdeveloped region are positive if resources available to produce economic expansion were concentrated in a specific locale, which could then generate multiplier effects across the entire region. However, neither the magnitude nor the availability of required investment was considered. Presumably, external savings would be available. Of course, without extensive investment levels, this developmentalist model was impractical.

Table 5.3   Latin America: Net Capital Income and Resource
             Transfers (U.S. $billions)

Year	Net Capital Income (1)	Net Payments on Utilities & Interest (2)	Resource Transfers (3)=(1)-(2)
1973	7.9	4.2	3.7
1974	11.4	5.0	6.4
1975	14.3	5.6	8.7
1976	17.9	6.8	11.1
1977	17.2	8.2	9.0
1978	26.2	10.2	16.0
1979	29.1	13.6	15.5
1980	29.4	17.9	11.5
1981	37.5	27.1	10.4
1982	20.0	38.7	-18.7
1983	3.2	34.3	-31.1
1984	9.2	36.2	-27.0
1985	2.4	35.3	-32.9
1986	8.6	30.7	-22.1

Source: CEPAL "Preliminary balance of the Latin American economy,
1986" in Notes on the Economy and Development. Santiago de
Chile, 1986, p.22.

In 1958, Argentina passed its first law regulating investment in order
to stimulate relatively underdeveloped regions. Succeeding development
plans in 1963 and 1974—the last—called for regional plans using both
public and private investments. Public investment incentive programs
were to supplement low regional savings. These programs assured
attractive returns to private investors.[1] The "growth centers" model
assumed that private investors would conform to the state's selection of
urban areas and provision of infrastructures. From 1958 to 1975 this
assumption was based on the premise that foreign investment would
flow uninterruptedly and that domestic investors would be willing to
respond to these incentives. Indeed, state subsidies for private borrowing
produced negative interest rates. This internal transfer of funds was
aimed primarily at manufacturing firms and the housing industry.

Over the twenty years, then, the apparently unshakable foundation
of economic growth sustained an intense developmentalism. Foreign
investment, domestic private savings and public savings, and subsidized
financing constituted the sources for a relatively active investment process.
The promotion of industry became the regional development mechanism
to accompany the global model of import substitution industrialization
(ISI). This model typified the Latin American developmentalist style,
which was firmly grounded on the uninterrupted expansion of industrial
activity. And, indeed, during this period it found decisive support in
the behavior of investment rates.

Even though a regional planning system linked to the national development plans was never instituted, it is possible to identify the basic characteristics of local-regional development planning experiences and the manner in which regional strategies figured in the national plans. In both cases the technical and organizational structures that developed were devoid of input from the regional sectors involved. The plans were based on proposals for spatial transformation designed entirely within the centralized planning agencies. The Central Planning Office, manned by technicians hired to draft the plans, received certain guidelines from the political administration. Goals, objectives, strategies, and program models were discussed within the technocratic bureaucracy at the central planning agency. Ultimately, the final document containing the national plan and corresponding regional strategies assembled the opinions of the technocratic bureaucracy without any grass roots social input or control.

The 1974 plan, for the first time, diverged somewhat from this pattern. Some forms of participation were encouraged through business and labor summits, which sought to elaborate certain general outlines of the plan. Nevertheless, the technocratic component remained in place and the theoretical-ideological bases for the plan were never subjected to popular debate.

The local-regional development plans exhibited characteristics and strategies similar to those of the national plans. Practically without exception, the organization of local planning systems displayed a hierarchical structure where goals, objectives, and models were discussed and selected at the top without participation of those social groups who were to be directly affected. This top-down organization was replicated even in instances involving small geographic areas. For example, numerous irrigation projects were subcontracted to private companies with virtually no sociopolitical control and/or evaluation.

Thus the planning process was based on the developmentalist style and sought the concentration of investments in growth centers capable of diffusing development geographically. Although improvement of the spatial distribution of capital was discussed, the problematic level of distribution was not. State agencies responsible for managing these processes proved to be totally isolated from regional societies that they aimed to transform.

Traditional Regional Planning Models, Economic Crisis, and Austerity

In the 1980s, deterioration in the capital accumulation process exposed serious contradictions within the basic assumptions of regional planning models popularized during the developmentalist phase of Argentine and Latin American socioeconomic expansion. The fundamental inconsistency originated in the impossibility of sustaining the viability of selected growth centers. This problem stemmed from the lack of savings rates adequate to finance the large-scale public and private investments required by the model. The state could not generate the revenues or obtain the loans necessary for infrastructural investments that would attract private capital. Local capital was scarce and foreign capital was unwilling to wager on the long run promise of profits from slowly maturing developmental projects. Thus the growth centers model of regional development was not a cause of the accumulation crisis facing Latin America, in general, and Argentina, in particular, but has reinforced that crisis.[2]

The design and implementation processes associated with developmentalist regional plans have proven inadequate to the realities of reduced foreign investment, low domestic savings, and IMF-enforced reorientation of state policies to enhance exports and debt payments. Vertically structured planning processes with little input from state political actors or local groups emphasized centralized control over the content and objectives of regional plans. In an era of sustained foreign investment, credit, and a growing international economy, information flows from the bottom up, and consultation with political officials could be minimized without catastrophic consequences. Facing capital outflows, reduced foreign markets, and IMF constraints on state intervention, these design and implementation processes could not be sustained.

Regional plans, which were conceived as finished documents and never subjected to internal evaluation or modification, were unable to cope with a dynamic and changing reality. Economic crisis and austerity have forced such plans and their projected time frames to crumble and have invalidated much of the process of regional development planning. In particular, econometric planning models emphasizing long-term quantitative goals exclusive of other planning instruments have frequently been derailed as the productive relations, processes of state investment, and other "exogenous" factors have disrupted the regional system.

These characteristics of the Latin American (and Argentine) state became strongly entrenched during the long period of authoritarian administration that typified much of the 1970s. In fact, it was in these regimes that the technocratic focus peaked and formal, but ineffective, regional planning had its widest diffusion. The essential character of authoritarian systems of government appeared to make the possibility of close interaction between political structures and those expected to serve them through the articulation of planning proposals more viable than in the complex and decentralized decisionmaking framework of democratic regimes. This was not the case. The absence of authentic popular representation under authoritarian governments and the global policies of these periods impeded subordination of planning systems to political structures. Planning structures were always better defined and less autonomous during periods of constitutional government. Nevertheless, democratic governments as well were unable to control planning agencies effectively.

In Argentina, for example, regional planning has completely ignored all forms of effective popular participation. The neediest social sectors, and those areas that showed evidence of relative underdevelopment, were repeatedly the object of special attention in regional development programs. Yet these programs were designed and implemented without the participation of those who would be directly affected. Their exclusion was a principal cause of these plans' inefficacy. Divorced from their social base and disconnected from the aspirations and the material support of those who would be the actual recipients of their implementation, these plans were empty shells without the drive or capacity to effect social transformation.

Profound modifications in the general processes of accumulation undermined, during the late 1970s and early 1980s, the developmentalist approach. At the same time, the weaknesses of these plans and planning processes have led to a concern in the late 1980s with democratization of decisionmaking processes as a means to formulate and enact regional development in an era of austerity.

Regional Development Strategy in an
Era of Austerity: A Propositional Inventory

The above assessment of new socioeconomic realities in Argentina and Latin America rests on the following contemporary reality:[3]

1. The accumulation crisis facing Argentina is deeply rooted in the current external debt phenomenon, the reduction of internal consumption, and the aggravated process of de-industrialization during the 1980s.

2. The resolution of this crisis cannot be accomplished in the short run. The reversal of structural tendencies discussed above would require, even under favorable circumstances, a number of years.

3. The easing of capital drains imposed by foreign debt interest payments will not lead to a return to satisfactory savings levels since other factors will continue to play a significant role in economic processes. However, a new focus on the issue of the external debt, resulting in the reduction or elimination of interest payments without the agreement of foreign lenders, will entail costs that cannot be accurately estimated but that very likely impinge on savings capacities of Latin American

nations. The new external context of this hypothetical case will doubtlessly impose a diversion of resources from investment to consumption, especially of goods and inputs whose purchase on credit will be made more difficult.

4. Planning in general and regional planning in particular demand improvement. Traditional models favoring large public and private investments within the context of the dominant "development centers" theories are totally lacking in validity. These models had already been subjected to serious criticisms by analysts arguing that Argentine and Latin American conditions, more disarticulated than those existing in the developed countries where these models originate, are not conducive to the successful implementation of these regional planning strategies.

5. Finally, it is necessary to focus on another important criticism of regional development plans designed and executed in Argentina. This criticism centers on the structures that historically nourished these models, structures characterized by bureaucratization, the absence of social control over their proposals, and top-down proposal design processes. This same bureaucratic structure designs and adopts strategies elaborated within the very state apparatus, in the form of the *plan book*, without feedback or supervision.

The general principles of an alternative regional planning strategy for Latin American nations are as follows:

1. Regional planning must include popular input through a process that incorporates grass roots groups from the target region as participants.

2. State involvement must provide direction and general program guidelines such that each local-regional plan will be compatible with those of other regions. In an era of low investment, the state must guide this process toward strategic enterprises with rapid capital maturation and with strong emphasis on those projects that can supply the infrastructural equipment needed to satisfy basic social needs. The plans must set global priorities for investment. Beyond this, there must be an intensive effort to launch programs with low capital/labor ratios, programs that mobilize the productive capacities of the labor force in targeted regions.

3. Given the low capacity for state involvement and the prior experience of grass roots organizations, popular institutions, and religious organizations, regional planning processes should incorporate these entities at all stages of regional planning. Of course, even here the state will provide decisive support in its provision of public savings, institutional structures, and a general frame of reference for such programs.

4. Regional planning models cannot be used unless they are based on the premise that planning is a dynamic and continuing process, flexible, and open to revision. Given the likelihood of continuing fiscal

restraints and global uncertainties, rigid plan book models lack relevance and will be invalidated by the very socioeconomic contexts they aim to transform.[4] Enacted regional plans must be evaluated and modified in response to new situations. Long-term objectives must be set and linked to social action strategies that bring together "the real situation" and that elaborated in an ideal model. Planning thereby ceases to be a simple technocratic action and becomes an instrument of political transformation.

Implementation of regional programs leads to emergent frameworks of power relations. The planning process must take into account this power framework in order to determine those forces resistant or conducive to the implementation of proposed strategies. The mission of the planning process is political rather than technical, since it recognizes that the likelihood of enacting policies is directly linked to the existing social structure and the new power relations that emerge. The decisionmaking model incorporates an analysis of the interests, resources, and organizational capacities of those groups affected by regional plans and seeks to incorporate them. This is done not to co-opt segments that might resist a plan. Indeed, it is quite possible that this process will allow political organization to influence and resist or transform the plan. This failure, however, will not derive from technical deficiencies but from the accumulation of forces in the body politic favorable to those resisting the proposed strategies.

5. Planning organizations must be open to popular and political control. Highly technocratic agencies lack the flexible, efficient, open structure required for effective regional planning in an era of uncertainty and austerity. The aim of planning is to integrate the state—as a policy director—and the civil society that is the object of policies into an active, dynamic, and flexible structure exercising sharp critical capacities and receptive to majority opinions in the selection of action strategies.

In Latin America, in general, and Argentina, in particular, the state has been incapable of organizing its planning structure along these lines.[5] Regional plans have been designed but seldom implemented. They remain grounded in an approach devoid of any theoretical or methodological innovation and popular participation. Thus they are relegated to the vertical bureaucratic structures of the state.

6. Given Latin America's position in the international division of labor, the limits on state intervention mandated by capital markets and institutions and the high level of instability and uncertainty confronting any program of regional planning, a major priority must be the identification of activities that appear more valid and urgent in the short run and, at the regional level, more likely to be successfully implemented with or without state support. The development of employment based on

self-sufficient community action, cooperatives, and small-scale enterprises seems to be the most adequate strategy.

In relatively less developed regions, especially in their rural sectors and in those urban areas where low-income households and unemployment or underemployment are predominant, the stimulation of new employment must be coordinated with the direct participation of the affected population. In low-income rural areas regional planning must necessarily involve the progressive elimination of the *minifundio* (extremely small-scale subsistence oriented family farms) as an inefficient production model and a socioeconomic framework that generates conditions of abject poverty and squalor.

7. The state cannot renounce responsibility for formulating a global regional development strategy that harmonizes activities throughout the nation and that is consistent with a development style that realizes profound social transformations democratically. The highly centralized organization of Latin American states is incapable of enacting a national strategy while retaining a unified vision of national interest. Decentralization must generate a genuine rapprochement of the state and civil society. Such national and regional development programs, within a decentralized state, are indispensable for Argentina and Latin America to effect necessary structural changes and consolidate democratic social and political institutions.[6] If, because it is uninterested or unable, the state does not furnish these general requirements, civil society must act to find partial solutions with clearly defined objectives. The participative strategy proposed here will be appropriate in both instances. In the first case it will integrate and complement the state's directive actions. In the second, it will substitute for it.

The state must stimulate private investments sufficient to reactivate Latin American economies and sustain their development in the current international economy. However, this should not inhibit, but rather should encourage, regional and local actions directed toward structural transformations that would raise the standard of living of the neediest rural and urban social sectors. State involvement is essential when local social actors are unable to enact needed transformations, for example, in the case of landownership systems in rural areas. Nevertheless, local and regional groups cannot abdicate responsibility and wait for state intervention. Participative planning presents a formal structure for articulating the interests of the neediest sectors and matching them to the planning and policy implementation process.

This vision of regional planning processes is being debated not only in Argentina but also throughout Latin America. The contingencies of socioeconomic development, the failure of the traditional models, and the need for a planning strategy that incorporates the input of the social sectors affected are subjects of interest in various academic centers and decisionmaking institutions throughout the hemisphere. The most fruitful experiences have been those of countries where concrete circumstances have forced this reformulation. Two interesting cases are Peru and Chile. In Peru, decentralization, made possible by the constitutional reforms of 1979, has been the subject of deliberations since the establishment of the new democratic government. In Chile, where civil society has been subjected to an authoritarian regime, the search for a concerted and innovative model to be implemented after the return to representative democracy has resulted in an intense debate in written documents, seminars, and congresses where the topics of national transformation and popular participation have been paramount.

Notes

This chapter represents the initial results of research carried out since 1986 by the Center for Urban and Regional Studies (CEUR), with partial financial support from the Consejo Nacional de Investigaciones Laborales (CONICET). Marcos Gerber participated in the material and theoretical development of this chapter.

1. These inducements were visible in several concurrent actions: (1) The economies of scale and urbanization of the large metropolitan areas continued to attract productive investment. It was therefore necessary to provide significant monetary benefits in the form of tax exemptions and customs reforms as incentives for investment in new regions. In this manner the profit rates for businesses willing to set up operations outside of the already developed zones would defray the additional transport costs deriving from increased distances between the location of the business, the areas providing raw materials, and the market. (2) The state had to act positively in the development of infrastructures related to external economies within selected regions. The provision of such basic social capital allowed the state to guide investment into those areas it chose as the most appropriate for stimulation. It was assumed that the inferior capacity of such areas to generate external economies is responsible for the high territorial concentration of investment. (3) The selection of target areas was made in strict accordance with the theory of growth centers. The various development plans have explicitly stated these criteria. The best example was, perhaps, that of the 1971–1975 plan. Formulation of regional development policy was based on a listing of urban centers inside the country considered capable of generating multiplier effects from productive investments.

2. If the social system lacks sufficient resources to invest massively, and if disarticulated accumulation short-circuits multiplier effects from concentrated large-scale investments, then the model ends in total collapse.

3. Fernando Ordoñez presented two papers on this topic at the Regional Recycling Seminar, University of São Paulo, São Paulo, Brazil, in May 1986. These were "El desarrollo regional en el contexto de los procesos de ajuste

macroecónomicos" and "La planificación regional y ajuste con crecimiento en América Latina."

4. Some observers have characterized planning as a game of changing strategies that succeed one another in response to new situations produced by the historical development of a society.

5. There have been isolated efforts that appeared to direct certain strata within the state toward the revision of traditional agencies and models. In this context, efforts made in 1985 and 1986 by the Secretaría de Promoción Social through its urban development agencies should be noted. The experiences of various municipalities around the country in the implementation of such local socioeconomic development policies have been valuable. The Consejos de Gestión Democráticos of the City of Buenos Aires initiated a planning process that incorporates ample popular participation and seeks to alter the decisionmaking model in the most important Argentine municipality.

6. In relation to this, see also Alejandro Rofman, "Descentralización y democracia," Funcación Ebert, Buenos Aires, Argentina, 1986. Translated from the Spanish by Danilo Levi, Department of Sociology, Tulane University.

6

The Polarization of Class and Space in the Contemporary Latin American City

Alejandro Portes and Michael Johns

Introduction

The basic contours of urbanization as it occurs in the periphery of the world economy have changed little in the 1980s. If there is any noticeable trend, it is toward the accentuation of phenomena that first attracted notice in the 1960s. Urban primacy, accelerated rural–urban migration, the growth of unregulated settlements in the outskirts of the major cities, income disparities, and the absorption of a vast proportion of the urban labor force by the informal sectors are still defining features of Third World urbanization. The overaccumulation crisis that had emerged in the advanced countries by the late 1960s worked—somewhat paradoxically—to offer the Third World massive developmental possibilities in the form of the export of capital, namely, the entry of multinational corporations and loans by international finance capital. Beginning around 1980, however, the paradox of capital's uneven development emerged once again, but this time severing the flow of the foreign capital on which Latin America so urgently depended for its economic development.

Consequently, the burdensome foreign debts contracted during the years of easy global credit have forced many countries into drastic austerity programs and deep recessions. In Latin America, economic conditions deteriorated to a level comparable only with that following the 1929 depression. The regional GNP declined for the first time in forty years, a weighted average of −4.1 in 1981–1982; but with individual

An earlier version of this chapter was published in the *Journal of Economic and Social Geography* (Netherlands) 77, 1986: 378–388.

country figures that, like those of Mexico and Peru, reached truly catastrophic levels.[1]

As a result, hopes for overcoming the contradictions of peripheral development, dim even during times of economic growth, have all but disappeared in the minds of many. The cities, which concentrate and reflect in heightened form the distortions of this pattern of development, have also been sites where responses to the new conditions have been felt with unique force. These responses have ranged from widespread violence and mass militance to an increasing popular withdrawal into reconstituted urban subsistence enclaves, each trend defying the already precarious hold of states in the course of national events.

In this paper, we review those major trends characteristic of peripheral urbanization with an emphasis on the contemporary Latin American experience. Such trends include: urban primacy and the relative absence of secondary-city systems, the character and dynamics of the informal sector, housing deficiencies and state housing policy, and the recent rise of popular organizations oriented toward self-sufficiency or militant demand making. These trends are important because they represent the form in which continuity and change of peripheral class structures are reflected in space, at both the national and the local levels.

Resilient Primacy

Urban primacy continues to be the center of much controversy. Some argue that primacy blocks development and urge the construction of secondary-city systems to enhance economic progress and growth.[2] To be sure, primacy causes urban ecological problems, diseconomies of scale, and spatially concentrated growth. The idea of grafting the North American urban spatial pattern onto peripheral urban landscapes, however, ignores the fact that space is a social process. Primacy is deeply entrenched, and although some secondary cities are growing and indications of reverse polarization exist, the pattern of high urban concentration in most countries of the Third World remains the dominant theme of population distribution in space.[3]

The Latin American experience of urban dominance over the countryside and dominance of the major city over the entire nation dates back to events in colonial times but was heavily reinforced with the full incorporation of the region into the British-dominated commercial circles during the nineteenth century.[4] Agro-export and mineral enclave production worked, at the time, as archetypical examples of the logic of disarticulated accumulation. Markets were abroad; thus labor was not relevant as a source of demand for domestic production and represented, instead, a necessary cost. Whenever possible, owners of the export enclaves—foreign and national—strove to reduce labor costs through various devices as a means to increase absolute profits. The export of raw materials, which underwent little processing in the countries of origin, coupled with the import of capital and consumer goods from the centers, severely circumscribed multiplier effects in these incipient capitalist economies.[5]

The old colonial towns, which had existed as political-administrative centers for the extraction of rural surplus, embodied use values (ports, transport infrastructure, locational advantage, markets, housing, and so forth) and class interests that worked to further attract new economic activities. The acceleration of the primate spatial patterns under conditions of classic dependency thus evolved as the urban-based owning classes maintained control of the import-export trade and captured any spin-offs from agro-export and mineral production.[6]

The production of foodstuffs and raw materials for the world market only partially proletarianizes the labor force that it employs. In Latin America, during the nineteenth century, the typical pattern was non- or semiproletarianization under which peasants bound by debt peonage or *inquilinaje* (leasehold), sharecroppers, and slaves worked the mines and the coffee, cotton, tobacco, henequen, and sugar plantations. Many laborers who worked in the export enclaves had plots of land from which they drew most of their livelihood and that of other household members, a pattern also reported frequently in export production in Africa.[7]

This partial proletarianization limits worker consumption demands, thereby circumscribing local multiplier effects. Moreover, employers of this labor force are not bound by the need for its close spatial concentration. Because the rural production-consumption (work-home) unity is not completely broken, laborers can migrate both seasonally and daily. The low-cost and abundant rural labor power dampens, in turn, the incentive to innovate technologically, again hindering the generation of multiplier effects. Around the agro-export areas, then, except for the concentration of small storage, processing, service, and retailing facilities, little urbanization could occur.[8]

The dearth of regional integration also helps explain the paltry secondary-city development in most peripheral countries. The rural production of commodities found markets in advanced capitalist countries. These products were syphoned out via the line of least resistance, undergoing little processing along the way. What little local demand (machinery, consumer commodities) emerged was usually met by imported commodities that retraced the geographical channels of product outflow toward the centers. Third World regions thus typically entered capitalist exchange at the behest of a foreign power that had productive forces sufficiently developed to both capture their products and dominate their consumption of technology, commodities, and money capital.[9]

The "take-off" of urban primacy during the classic agro-export phase of external dependency then, results from: (1) the old colonial cities' ability to control the circulation of agro-export commodities and trade in general because of favorable location, historically developed bundles of urban use values, and class forces that continued to exercise spatial control; (2) the partial proletarianization of labor power, which limited consumption, technological advancement, and therefore the possibility of secondary-city growth; and (3) poor regional integration, a result of localities being linked to international markets rather than regional-national markets that would have forged intranational links via multiplier effects.

The next phase of economic development, known as import substitution industrialization (ISI), began in the larger countries of Latin America, such as Brazil, Mexico, and Argentina, during the 1930s and extended gradually to smaller ones and to peripheral countries elsewhere. In the major Latin countries, ISI was propelled by a relatively well developed network of national industries constructed during the late nineteenth century, as well as by the collapse of the central economies after 1929. A second phase of the process commenced in the 1950s, this time tightly tied to international finance and global markets. During the entire ISI period, national consumer commodity production increased dramatically, but that of capital goods grew at a slower pace and was confined, for the most part, to the larger countries. The market for consumer durables, however—the point around which pivoted the entire industrial "deepening" project—remained circumscribed by the accumulation pattern that was disarticulated despite strategies of income concentration and state subsidies to producers and upper-class consumers.[10]

Although it was in the interest of nascent industry to expand the market, effective demand remained limited to the elite, an emerging professional-bureaucratic "middle" class, and, to a much more limited extent, an incipient formal proletariat. Since ISI industries required imported technologies and inputs and since these could only be acquired with foreign exchange, the need to maintain the profitability of the agro-export sector remained; this need reinforced in turn, as a key factor in the defense of profits, the continuing downward pressure on wages.[11] The use of turnkey plants, which generated few local linkages and employed only small numbers, worked to further shrink final wage demand. ISI did create an urban proletariat and strengthened the bureaucratic middle class employed in the public and private sectors. At the same time, it stole markets away from many petty commodity producers, who were either ruined or forced to search for other niches in the economy.[12]

Import substitution industrialization, combined with foreign investment and increased capital penetration of the countryside, worked to produce a rapidly urbanized space. In Latin America, the rural labor force dropped from 54.7 percent to 32.1 percent of the total EAP between 1950 and 1980, and industrial growth and productivity far surpassed those in the agrarian sector. Latin American urban dwellers as a proportion of total population rose from 50 percent to 65 percent during the same period.[13]

The urbanization accentuated the primate city system orientation. ISI establishments located in the large cities to capture the bundles of urban use values that these cities afford. These include a large labor force, transportation facilities, market availability, and access to private and state institutions. Manifold service activities proliferate around the demand created by wages, profits, and rents, all arising from concentrated industrial development. These employment opportunities act, in turn, like a magnet for a peasantry gradually displaced by agricultural mechanization and demographic pressure on the remaining subsistence enclaves. The absence of similar opportunities in secondary cities and the frequent resistance of local elites to accelerated inbound migration functioned to channel the flow toward the larger centers, thus reinforcing their primacy.[14]

Secondary cities with few exceptions have remained weak. The integration of production processes and markets across regional space has not been forthcoming. With the partial exception of the large Latin American and the newly industrialized Asian countries, most peripheral economies remain dependent on the export of a few basic products, and their industrial establishments lack backward linkages that would tie secondary centers into an integrated and dynamic urban system. Except for secondary-city growth around certain place-specific resources areas and planned growth poles (most of which have proven unsuccessful),[15] the urban landscape of the Third World continues to be dominated by the major politico-administrative and commercial centers established during the colonial period.

Capital does not flow easily to the secondary cities of peripheral nations. The colonial and agro-export phases of economic organization produced secondary towns and cities with impoverished social and physical infrastructure, paltry markets, inexperienced labor power, and only skeletons of state institutions. The highly developed productive forces (especially transport and communications) and credit system from the centers shaped agro-export production's outward orientation via the peripheral countries' main cities and ports. Places were plucked out of their regional context and garnered for production and commercialization of export commodities. Such practices retarded any "organic" development of domestic capitalist social relations and prevented the emergence of a balanced urban distribution.

In synthesis, we note that the urban landscape of peripheral nations is a faithful reflection of a class structure conditioned by the subordinate incorporation of these countries in the international division of labor and by the interests of domestic owning classes, first based on the countryside and now securely ensconced in urban industry and finance. At the other extreme, only a minority of the labor force has been incorporated into fully capitalist relations of production, the rest remaining as an unprotected labor pool for agriculture and, subsequently, as the backbone of a burgeoning informal economy in the large cities. The development of informality, paralleling the growth of a modern industrial-commercial complex, gives to contemporary Third World cities their distinct physiognomy. Its principal features are described below.

The Underside of Economic Growth: Informality and Rural-Urban Migration

The informal sector can be tentatively defined as the sum aggregate of income-earning activities, excluding those which are contractual and legally regulated.[16] Although this definition encompasses criminal activities, the concept is customarily applied to commodities—like food, clothing, and housing—that are not intrinsically illegal but whose production and exchange take place outside legal regulation. Even after excluding criminal activities, the definition of informality has been subject to much debate. Controversies center around whether it represents a sector of the economy, of the population, or of the labor market.[17]

Much of this discussion is really over semantics and can be resolved by labeling "informal" all relationships of production characterized by the *absence* of: (1) a clear separation between capital and labor; (2) a contractual relationship between both; and (3) a wage labor force whose conditions of work and pay are legally regulated. Thus defined, the informal sector is structurally heterogenous and comprises activities such as direct subsistence, petty production and trade, homework, and putting-out arrangements.

For many years, economists believed that these activities were interstitial and destined to disappear with the advance of industrialization. The reason is that informality was believed to be a consequence of the imperfect penetration of capitalism in the periphery of the system; with the advance of capitalist relations, precapitalist ones would fall by the wayside.[18] It is difficult to continue to voice these predictions in the face of mounting evidence that points precisely in the opposite direction. Informality is a resilient part of social and economic reality that has not gone away despite rapid industrialization in a number of peripheral countries.

Between 1950 and 1975, the gross Latin American investment coefficient hovered around 20 percent of GDP per year, a figure comparable to those recorded during the industrializing drives of the now-developed countries. While the Latin American GDP grew at a healthy 5.5 percent per year during this period, the rates of growth for industrially related commodities such as steel, electricity, and cement were much higher. In 1975, for example, steel production was approximately twenty times what it had been twenty-five years earlier.[19]

The response of labor markets to this accelerated process of industrialization was not what standard theories had predicted. Informal employment, as defined by the United Nations (UN) Employment Programme for Latin America (PREALC), declined only from 46 to 42 percent of the Latin American labor force. In 1950, the informal sector occupied 30 percent of the urban EAP; in 1980, with an industrial plant four times larger, informal employment still stood at 30 percent. The self-employed represented 22 percent of total manufacturing employment at the beginning of this period; by 1980, they were still 21 percent, indicating no decline in the number of those employed in petty artisan and informal manufacturing shops.[20]

There is reason to believe, however, that even these estimates are overoptimistic. PREALC defines informally employed as the total number of the self-employed—excluding professionals—unremunerated family workers, and domestic servants. Excluded are informal wageworkers, that is, those hired casually and who lack social security protection. This exclusion leads to a significant underestimate of the informally employed in most countries and cities. In Bogotá, for example, informal workers according to the PREALC definition represented about a third of the under-EAP in 1984; if a more appropriate definition based on exclusion from social security coverage is employed, the figure increases drastically to over half of the urban EAP.[21] In general, whenever unprotected workers are added to the definition of informal employment, its relative size increases from about a third to half or more of the urban EAP. For Latin America as a whole, informal employment can be estimated to represent about 60 percent of the total EAP.

Regardless of how the informal sector is measured, it is clear that the predicted secular trend toward its disappearance with the advance of capitalist industrialization has not materialized in Latin America. Similar results in other Third World regions[22] have led to a search for a plausible explanation of why the experience of labor absorption of the now-industrialized countries has not been repeated in the periphery. The best-known explanations are those that attribute this pattern to excess demographic growth in Third World countries, coupled with imported industrial technologies that tend to absorb capital rather than labor. Excess population growth plus its displacement to cities outstrip the capacity of modern industry to create employment; labor-saving machinery and technology, brought from the advanced countries, reduce this capacity still further.

There is much truth in this argument, especially in terms of the impact of massive migration on urban labor markets. However, the argument also assumes that the informal sector functions exclusively as a refuge from destitution for those deprived from access to modern employment. In orthodox circles, the informal economy has been equated with an "abnormally swollen" tertiary sector of minimal productivity; international agencies thus routinely label workers employed in these activities as "underutilized."[23] If informality were exclusively a refuge from destitution, two facts would logically follow: First, income levels among the informally employed would be significantly lower than among regular workers; second, those who found employment in formal activities would never leave them voluntarily. However, the available empirical evidence questions both predictions.

Labor surveys in cities in Colombia, Brazil, Peru, and Chile indicate that average income levels of those employed in informal activities are not necessarily inferior to incomes of formal sector workers and can, at times, be higher. Similarly, income disparities tend to be as high or higher in the informal economy, which indicates the presence of a group with substantial earnings. An analysis of the entire labor force in Lima, for example, produced a Gini coefficient of inequality of .40 for the modern sector and .51 for the informal.[24] Similar results obtained elsewhere negate the conventional description of the informal sector as a last-resort alternative to unemployment.

The existence of remunerative opportunities in the informal economy also helps explain a second relevant finding, namely the number of formal workers who voluntarily abandon their protected employment in order to become informal artisans and entrepreneurs. In her study of the footwear industry in Colombia, Lisa Peattie found, for example, that the vast majority of enterprises in this sector were informal shops catering to both the popular and high-priced segments of the market. Most informal entrepreneurs were former workers of the large factories who learned the necessary skills during their periods of formal employment and used their severance pay as working capital. Similar findings have been reported by studies of informal enterprise in Mexico, Uruguay, and Peru.[25]

We thus have evidence that the resilience of the informal sector even after accelerated processes of industrialization is not due exclusively to its serving as a cushion to low labor absorption by modern industry. Clearly, much informal activity, including subsistence initiatives such as the self-construction of shelter, is of a "survival" type, but this is by no means the whole story. Another explanation must exist. The central implication of the available research literature is that informal relations of production are functional simultaneously for those involved in them and for large firms in the formal sector.

Modern enterprises often absorb more labor than appears in the official statistics, but they do so through disguised mechanisms that bypass state regulation. There is a generalized resistance among large firms to increasing a contractually hired and legally protected labor force, which raises costs and decreases managerial flexibility, and there is a concomitant tendency to make use of the highly elastic labor supply offered by informal workers. The latter are accessible through two principal channels: (1) direct hiring on a casual basis; and (2) subcontracting of production or marketing to smaller informal concerns. Clearly, not all modern economic activities can be conducted with casual workers or subcontracted. There are many tasks, however, that can be organized in this manner.

Such practices play a role primarily in the industrial sectors subject to a high degree of seasonal fluctuation and/or that employ large proportions of semi- and unskilled workers, for example, in textile and apparel manufacturing, where the problem of adjusting the size of the work force is compounded by the need to make continual changes in production processes in order to accommodate shifts in fashion. The situation encourages product differentiation according to firm size. In Argentina, for example, both large and small firms make heavy use of subcontracting to informal workshops and seamstresses working at home in order to meet sudden shifts in demand. These practices do not represent "lags" from the earlier history of the Argentine textile industry but in fact reemerged and grew in response to increased regulation of factory production.[26]

Construction is another industry where flexibility of labor use is a primary concern. In this case, systems of multiple subcontracting have been devised to recruit temporary workers. Major construction firms generally retain small supervisory staffs and then subcontract. Multiple layers of subcontracting have been reported by studies in Dakar, Bogotá, and Mexico City.[27] Although the proportions of informal labor may be higher in volatile, labor-intensive industries, practices linking formal and informal sectors are also prominent in industries not having these characteristics. In a now-classic study, Birbeck found that garbage pickers at the public dump in Cali, Colombia, end up supplying one of the largest industries in the city with significant quantities of raw materials at a fraction of the import equivalent. The pickers are, in effect, industrial outworkers who are employed by a modern firm on a regular basis but who nevertheless must absorb all risks and health costs associated with their jobs. The case is a particularly poignant illustration of disguised employment practices: The workers not only labor under the illusion of self-employment but are commonly seen as symbols of underemployment and marginality.[28]

Street traders represent another group assigned the same "marginal" status and also appearing to be self-employed. Studies in several Latin American cities have indicated, however, that these activities are generally part of well-organized commercial networks controlled, ultimately, by modern firms. Through chains such as these, the work of humble and poorly paid workers is incorporated into the production and marketing strategies of large corporations. Although well concealed from public view, such arrangements represent an important element underlying the profitability of many firms.[29]

Reasons why the informal sector has persisted over time and why its activities have not been confined to survival at the margin should now be apparent. Instead of a "lag" from precapitalist times, informal activities are an integral part of national economies and contribute to the development of their lead sectors. As Bryan Roberts noted, informal production has been seldom limited to traditional crafts but has been itself continuously modernized to accompany the development of the formal economy.[30] This conclusion suggested in turn that the description of peripheral economies as "dual" is inappropriate. Instead, these are unified economies under the hegemony of a modern capitalist sector that relies, in turn, on the continuing vitality of precapitalist modes of labor incorporation.

The severe contraction of economic growth during the 1980s has served to further highlight the interconnectedness of the modern capitalist and informal sectors and to expose the vulnerability of the latter. An important feature of the new situation is the punishment absorbed by once-stable formal sector workers, punishment in the form of either reduction of wages or widespread unemployment. Effects of the crisis on the informal economy have been contradictory. On the one hand, armies of the informally employed have swelled as released formal sector workers seek other income-earning opportunities and as family members of retained workers who have suffered pay cuts attempt to balance family budgets. On the other hand, the very opportunities sought by new entrants in informal activities shrink with the decline in formal wages, as the latter constitute the core of demand for a range of informally produced goods and services. Moreover, the decline in operations of both local and international capitalist enterprises further reduces irregular work opportunities, previously available through subcontracting.[31]

The slowdown in capitalist sector production, then, has simultaneously increased the size of the informal economy in many countries and limited its ability to maneuver into and around the formal circuits of capital on which it ultimately depends. In the most extreme cases, this has resulted in a shift of informal workers toward urban subsistence activities, a pushing of the poor out of the money economy.[32]

Seeking Shelter:
Shantytowns and the Established City

In most large cities of the Third World, the housing needs of the poor are generally met outside the regulated market. Contrary to what happens in the developed countries, large segments of the peripheral cities have been self-constructed by their inhabitants as a response to the absence of alternatives: the lack of sufficient private or state-produced housing units or the means to acquire them. As Anthony Leeds noted years ago, squatter settlements occur only under capitalism and, in particular, under the conditions of dependent capitalist development outlined above.[33] This is not to say that mass urban housing in the self-labeled "socialist" countries is necessarily superior, but that the manifold popular initiatives giving rise to squatter and other unregulated settlements occur primarily as a response to the constraints of peripheral capitalist urbanization.

Exceptions exist, to be sure, particularly in the more advanced Third World countries with a better income distribution. In cities like Montevideo and, until recently, Buenos Aires, squatter settlements were the exception rather than the rule. The resistance displayed by low-income groups in these cities to be displaced to the urban periphery in response to central-city urban renewal and rent increases shows clearly that, for them, the distant "squatment" is an alternative of last resort.[34] However, this alternative has become the norm for the urban poor throughout most Third World countries. Numerous studies have reported on the proportion of the urban population and of urban space occupied by the self-built city. Figures tend to range from one-fourth to two-thirds of inhabitants and up to 75 percent of the urban area in cities of Latin America, Africa, and Southeast Asia.[35]

The naive view of things associated with the earlier school of marginality studies equated the precarious housing condition of squatters with their occupational situation. Peripheral settlements, according to this view, were the abode of the most recent migrants, the most unskilled workers, the unemployed, and the destitute; they also housed a good share of "lumpen" elements such as thieves, beggars, and prostitutes. An important contribution of recent empirical research has been to disabuse people of this notion by showing the social heterogeneity of the settlements. Research in cities throughout the Third World has produced three consistent findings: first, that unemployment levels in these areas are not significantly higher than in the rest of their respective cities; second, that workers of all kinds—from teachers and other white-collar employees to laborers in informal shops—are found living in the settlements; and third, that this occupational heterogeneity not only is settlement-wide but also extends to individual households as their members alternate between various forms of employment in formal and informal sectors.[36]

As many have noted, unemployment is an unaffordable luxury in the economic context of peripheral cities. The state takes little responsibility for individual survival and thus the poor must find some kind of income-generating activity, no matter how precarious. Squatter settlements and related phenomena are thus not generally the consequence of unemployment but of poverty in employment, as the compensation to labor is much lower than that required to gain access to commercial or state-provided housing. Wages, even those paid to formal sector workers, are generally out of line with prices in the "normal" housing markets, a situation that forces all kinds of people to seek alternative solutions. Some resolve their shelter problem by doubling up with relatives, whereas others endure high rents in dilapidated central-city quarters. However, neither of these alternatives offers a permanent solution. The peripheral settlement does, and it is for this reason that wide segments of the urban population—from established factory workers to informal laborers, from new migrants to the city-born—are found among the peripheral settlements' promoters and inhabitants.[37]

The relationship between working-class wages and shelter may be seen, however, from another angle. Whereas from the point of view of workers, unregulated housing is the way to make ends meet, from the point of view of employers, it is a means to keep wage levels at a fraction of what they would otherwise have to be. The fact that returns to labor in these economies are computed independently of the market cost of shelter constitutes a significant boon to formal capitalist firms. A corollary is that workers of modern enterprises, although apparently fully incorporated into capitalist relations, are in reality semiproletarianized to the extent that the informal economy absorbs a significant share of the cost of their reproduction. This absorption occurs through the self-construction of shelter—a subsistence activity—and through land and rent transactions at the margins of the regulated economy.[38]

Links between the modern economy and squatter settlements are not limited, however, to the self-construction of shelter. The heterogeneity of the settlements' population goes beyond occupational diversity to encompass a variety of class positions. In particular, three social classes are well represented in these areas: the informal proletariat, the informal entrepreneurs, and the formal proletariat. Informal shops abound in the settlements, while informal middlemen often live in or near them in order to gain ready access to their labor pool. These areas thus provide the necessary space for the materialization of the subcontracting relationship linking informal and formal enterprises. The absence or near absence of rents for the space employed in production, added to the low costs of their labor power, goes a long way toward explaining the competitive edge of informal enterprises despite their low levels of capitalization.

Finally, the settlements are the sites where the two segments of the urban proletariat—formal and informal—meet on a regular basis and in significant numbers. They meet in the shantytown streets, shops, and shacks. They meet within each household, as different family members become employed in one or another segment of the urban economy. The consequences of these encounters are multiple, but the most significant one, on a regular basis, is its impact on the reproduction costs and hence wage levels of the formally employed. Life in a "modern" sector in a peripheral city is conditioned, at every step, by its relationship with the informal sector.

Repairs of any sort; merchandise sold on credit and in minimal quantities; secondhand clothing, furniture, and appliances; food items produced and sold through clandestine channels; access to unlicensed electricity, water, and transportation, these are components of the routine struggle for survival in the settlements. They furnish a livelihood to their purveyors while simultaneously lowering costs and facilitating access to consumption to the clients.[39] It is this articulation between the modern and the informal, enacted daily and in manifold ways in the settlements, that allows factory workers and office employees to survive and even save within the constraints of a meager wage. It is also, needless to say, another way through which returns to labor in the modern sector can remain indefinitely lower than the formal market costs of subsistence.

Governmental plans to deal with peripheral settlements often proceed in blissful ignorance of these realities of the urban economy and, for this reason, either fail or are derailed from their original goals. In the 1980s, state policies have alternated between eradication and in situ improvement of settlements, on the one hand, and between housing project construction and the provision of sites with services, on the other.[40] Rightist governments and, in particular, the brand of military authoritarian regime common in Latin America until recently have leaned toward the first of each pair of alternatives. Eradication of settlements, particularly those near the central city, and removal of their inhabitants to remote government housing projects are the means to accomplish three goals: first, to beautify the city and give it the semblance of spatial "order"; second, to provide work to the urban construction industry—often in the hands of friends of the regime; and third, to shift the costs of the entire package onto the shoulders of the "beneficiaries" through rentals or mortgage payments.[41]

The problem is that urban wage levels, both formal and informal, are generally insufficient to support this new burden. Thus, the beautification-and-order policy of conservative authorities comes into conflict with the interest of their own class allies in the preservation of an abundant and low-cost labor force. As seen above, the informal economy—centered in the unregulated settlements—makes possible the in situ reproduction of this labor pool. Since employers are generally reluctant to adjust wages in order to compensate for the cost of government housing and long-distance public transport and since workers are unable to afford them, the outcome of these policies takes two predicable forms: a return to the status quo ante as settlers find ways to colonize other areas of the central city or the transformation of the projects into de facto settlements through massive defaults, along with the provision, by a chastised government, of subsidized public services. These outcomes have been documented at length in several instances.[42]

In situ improvement and site-and-services projects are generally more acceptable to the urban working class and, not coincidentally, to the long-term interests of its employers. The problem is that government resources are generally too meager to meet more than a small proportion of the demand. In the 1980s, the crisis and cutoff of international capital, which has restored to the IMF the economic enforcement power that had been weakened somewhat in the years of easy credit, has only reinforced the fiscal conservatism that already characterized most Latin American countries since the 1970s. The result, of course, is a further exacerbation of collective consumption problems and new limits on the state's intervention into the housing problem. More than ever before, the effective solution to the urban housing crisis continues to be left to the initiative of the affected population.

One final point: Although the interest of capital owners and, to a lesser extent, of the bureaucratic-professional class continues to be the reproduction of an abundant and easily accessible labor pool, the owners are also interested in preserving as much physical distance as possible between their own residential space and that of the self-built city. Their reasons have to do with aesthetics, fears of political mobilization and violence by the poor, and the general desire to forget about how the real economy functions in these cities. The private automobile has enabled the residential spaces of the well-to-do to be located farther and farther away from the city center. In Latin America, at least, the strong imitative pattern of upper-class consumption has led to residential developments that, complete with shopping centers and other amenities, are faithful copies of the standard North American suburb.

The Santiago of the 1980s offers perhaps the most poignant example. Toward the foot of the Andes, there is an area of luxurious housing, fine apartment buildings, and quiet, tree-lined streets. The shantytowns of the poor have been forcefully removed from these areas in order to avoid any discordant note to their image of peace and prosperity. Toward the east and south, however, most of the real city grows in endless stretches of crowded tenements, housing projects, and shantytowns. A recent administrative reform subdivided the city of Santiago into thirty-two small municipalities in order to consolidate legally the separation between the rich and the poor. Responsibility for public services such as education, health, and parks and the funds to administer them have been transferred from the central government to these local units. According to a government economist, the richest municipality of Santiago spent approximately U.S. $2,130 per capita in public services in 1986; the poorest spent U.S. $12 or about 0.5 percent of its wealthier counterpart.

Bogotá is perhaps the typical peripheral capital, having been selected as such for studies by the World Bank and other international agencies. Even there, the process of spatial polarization of the classes has evolved to such an extent that it is possible to speak, not of one, but of three separate cities. Central Bogotá houses the administrative centers of government and headquarters of the major companies; it also preserves some of the architectural jewels of the city's colonial past. The center is the point where the different classes meet, at least during the working day.[43]

At dusk, there begins an exodus that, like that of North American cities, removes the middle and upper classes from the center and toward the northern suburbs: Chapinero—an older and stable middle-class area—and, past it, the exclusive suburbs of Antiguo Country and El Chicó. Luxurious shopping malls like Unicentro complete the illusion of being in a city of the developed world. Although there are differences in residential design, including those stemming from the pervasive fear of crime in Bogotá, the overall pattern of secluded and ample residences, good roads and parks, and automobiles everywhere fits well the model of North American suburban areas.

As the workday ends, the working-class population heads in the opposite direction: toward the modest but established neighborhoods in the south and, past them, the endless proliferation of pirate subdivisions stretching toward the Andes.[44] As in most other major peripheral cities, this spatial polarization of the classes creates the illusion among the well-to-do that "theirs" is the only city. In fact, the real growth of Bogotá takes place in the opposite direction, under precarious conditions, and is spurred on by the greed of some and the need and will of the many.

Confronting the System

Polarization of the residential space is the most important but not the only physical reflection of the pattern of uneven development and unbalanced distribution of the economic rewards. The contemporary central-city space also reflects this pattern in heightened form. The juxtaposition of ornate colonial government palaces, modern rectilinear skyscrapers, U.S.-style shopping malls, dilapidated tenements, instant shanties in the empty lots, all side by side, offers a poignant visual image of the social structure underneath. The image also conveys the sense that this structure has been and will continue to be shaped by the interests of the few. Indeed, the contradictory peripheral city does function to maximize gain for those in control of the modern sector, but this is not the whole story. Time and again, the apparently atomized urban masses have mobilized to defend their conditions of material survival and even their political beliefs.

The consensus during the 1970s among Third World urban specialists was, however, that political movements of the poor were seldom revolutionary and were oriented, for the most part, to measured demand making within the existing political order.[45] Even such widely publicized manifestations of urban radicalism as the *campamento* (politically organized squatters) settlements in Salvador Allende's Chile turned out, on closer inspection, to be orchestrated under government acquiescence. According to one observer, most settlers in the highly visible and militant *campamento* Nueva Habana were more interested in securing land titles and improving their living quarters than in subverting the social order. Similarly, in Brazil, a highly organized *favela* movement quickly reverted to political quiescence when outside conditions turned adverse after the 1964 military coup.[46]

Although popular mobilizations for narrowly circumscribed goals were the norm during the 1960s and 1970s, the situation may be changing during the 1980s. Throughout most of Latin America, negative economic growth during the early 1980s and IMF-inspired recessionary programs have expelled significant numbers from regular protected employment and have swelled the army of the informally employed. The fact that costs of these adjustment policies have been disproportionately borne by the poor, even though the policies have thus far not yielded any tangible improvement to the lot of the poor, has further inflamed popular resentment.

There have been three types of reactions to these conditions:

Spontaneous Riots. They have usually followed either governmental attempts to increase the price of public goods such as transportation or a severe decline in the quality of services provided. In São Paulo, for example, "the majority . . . are poorly paid and ill-fed workers who live under precarious conditions and spend many hours each day on expensive and extremely tiring public transportation to reach work."[47] When the trains and buses are delayed or break down—a frequent occurrence—employers fine their workers for late arrival. In response, a series of outbreaks of popular furor has led to the destruction of train stations and other equipment over a period of several years. These spontaneous movements then extended to other Brazilian cities, in particular, Rio de Janeiro. Similarly, in Santo Domingo, the suppression of public services and government subsidies to basic consumption items as part of an IMF-style adjustment policy led to three days of citywide riots in 1984. Subsequent research showed that the most violent confrontations occurred in or around the poorest settlements.[48]

Community-based Militance. Organized on the basis of place of residence rather than place of employment, a number of popular groups have emerged in peripheral cities to defend community interests or pressure the authorities for needed improvements. Although apparently "apolitical" and focused on narrow neighborhood demands, these community-based groups can mobilize quickly in support of broad political causes when the opportunity presents itself. Military governments that attempted to organize the "inert" urban masses for political support have learned this lesson to their chagrin. The Argentine military junta of the late 1970s, for example, attempted this strategy by supporting the neighborhood councils, mothers' centers, and other seemingly innocuous associations in the *villas* of greater Buenos Aires. When the situation turned propitious, after the military defeat in the Falklands, these areas, led by the same community organizations, erupted in opposition to the regime. These movements, known as *vecinazos*, played an important role in the demise of the military government.[49]

Disengagement. Economic crisis has reached such extremes in other countries that popular organizations, especially in the peripheral settlements, have veered away from political demand making and toward a search for self-sufficiency. Residents have devised new survival strategies, which include collective purchase, preparation, and consumption of food; collective house improvements; collective child care; and cooperative organization for the production of consumer goods to be sold in the city streets. The entire population of some settlements, including women and children, have been mobilized in the effort at economic survival.

Disengagement from the surrounding economy is obviously not complete, as the effort to produce and sell goods in the market indicates. There have been instances, however, of a concerted attempt to evolve an alternative grass roots economy, separate from the officially sponsored one. This has been the case in Chile, where popular economic organizations of the *poblaciones* (permanent housing settlements that resulting from the emergency housing programs during the late 1960s) surrounding Santiago and other large cities have struggled with the worst employment crisis and the most repressive regime experienced by the country in this century. Although still the exception rather than the rule, disengagement and economic self-reliance in some areas have reached such development that leaders view them as the model for the future organization of the country's economy.[50]

Similar experiences have been reported in São Paulo, Monterrey, and Mexico City. In the latter city, the aftermath of the 1985 earthquake saw government relief trucks turned back at the entrance of El Tepito, a working-class neighborhood. Leaders of this highly organized community refused all official assistance unless the goods were entrusted to their own organizations. Otherwise, they argued, the reconstruction effort would become bogged down in the corruption and inefficiency prevalent elsewhere.[51]

Research on Third World urban movements during the 1960s did anticipate one of the major causes of the widening scope of popular struggles. The structural reinterpretation of social and economic inequality that has given rise to many of the new movements did not emerge spontaneously but came initially from the outside. Parties and movements and, in particular, the Catholic church's "Option for the Poor" program provided the personnel and organizational capability for the start of self-help popular associations. The church's *comunidades de base* are thus found at the core of most recent successful mobilizations for political struggle or self-sufficiency in Argentina, Brazil, Chile, and other South and Central American countries.[52] Once initiated, however, the new contestatory organizations of the poor tend to acquire a life of their own based on an economic and political environment that increasingly justifies their existence.

To conclude, the political economy of Latin American cities is one where the resolution of the plight of underdevelopment promised by accelerated capitalist industrialization has not materialized. Instead, the process has produced a more complex and more contradictory social fabric. External inequality of power between nations and the internal one between the classes are the major factors ultimately responsible for the direction that peripheral industrialization and urbanization have taken. This is reflected in growing spatial polarization, the expansion of the self-built city, and the self-serving use of labor outside the modern economy by those inside it. In Latin America, the reaction to the exacerbation of these trends during the recent crisis has been an apparent shift of popular movements from narrow reinvindicational pursuits to more militant and wide-ranging forms of protest.

There are, no doubt, multiple variations in this landscape, conditioned by the history and unique circumstances of each city and country. Still, in the trends toward polarization and confrontation common throughout urban centers of the Third World, one discerns the seeds of major processes of social change. It may well be that, as Maurice Dobb said of late feudalism, for a social order based on the relentless exploitation of its weakest members, history will have its own particular reckoning.[53]

Notes

1. Enrique Iglesias, "The Latin American Economy During 1984: A Preliminary Overview," *CEPAL Review* 25 (1985), pp. 7–44.

2. See E. Johnson, *The Organization of Space in Developing Countries* (Cambridge, Mass.: Harvard University Press, 1970); D. Rondinelli, "Towns and Small Cities in Developing Countries," *The Geographical Review* 11 (1983) pp. 14–28.

3. Christopher Chase-Dunn, "The Coming of Urban Primacy in Latin America," *Comparative Urban Research* 11 (1985), pp. 14–28.

4. Alejandro Portes and John Walton, *Urban Latin America* (Austin: University of Texas Press, 1976).

5. See Albert Hirschman, *A Bias for Hope* (New Haven: Yale University Press, 1971).

6. William Glade, *The Latin American Economies* (New York: American Books, 1969).

7. See Claude Meillassoux, "From Reproduction to Production," *Economy and Society* 1 (1972), pp. 93–105; Harold Wolpe, "The Theory of International Colonialism: The South African Case," in Ivan Oxal, Tony Barnett, and David Booth (eds.), *Beyond the Sociology of Development. Economy and Society in Latin America and Africa* (London: Routledge and Kegan Paul, 1975), pp. 229–252.

8. The U.S. South's antebellum urban landscape was also very weakly developed, a pattern generally explicable in these terms. See G. Wright, *Old South, New South* (New York: Basic Books, 1986).

9. A typical example is Mendoza, the major urban center of the Argentine wine-producing region. According to Balán, local production was originally organized around small family-owned enterprises. In addition, Mendoza, by the

turn of the century, was a service center linked to an already populated and integrated rural area. However, this provincial export economy created a two-way link: manufactured goods exchanged for wine. The limited size of the local markets and the competitiveness of national and especially international industry blocked the emergence of a local industry sector and regional integration. See Jorge Balán, "Regional Urbanization Under Primary-Sector Expansion in New-Colonial Countries," in Alejandro Portes and Harley Browning (eds.), *Current Perspectives in Latin American Urban Research* (Austin: Special Publications Series of the Institute of Latin American Studies, University of Texas at Austin, 1975), pp. 151–179.

10. See Celso Furtado, *The Economic Development of Latin America* (New York: Cambridge University Press, 1970); Glade, op. cit.; Anibal Pinto, "The Opening Up on Latin America to the Exterior," *CEPAL Review* 11 (1980), pp. 313–356; Carlos Anglade and Carlos Fortin, *The State and Capital Accumulation in Latin America* (Pittsburgh: University of Pittsburgh Press, 1985).

11. Alain de Janvry, "Material Determinants of the World Food Crisis," *Berkeley Journal of Sociology* 21 (1976), pp. 2–26. Alain de Janvry and Carlos Garramón, "Laws of Motion of Capital in the Center–Periphery Structure," *Review of Radical Political Economics* 9 (1977), pp. 29–38. Alain de Janvry and Carlos Garrmón, "The Dynamics of Rural Poverty in Latin America," *Journal of Peasant Studies* 5 (1977), pp. 206–216.

12. See E. Lizzano, *La Integración Economica Centroamericana* (Mexico: Fondo de Cultura Economica, 1975).

13. See Norberto Garcia and Victor Tokman, "Changes in Employment and the Crisis," *CEPAL Review*, 1984, pp. 103–115.

14. Jorge E. Hardoy, *Las Ciudades en América Latina* (Buenos Aires: Paidos, 1972); Jorge E. Hardoy, "Two Thousand Years of Latin American Urbanization," in J. E. Hardoy (ed.), *Urbanization in Latin America: Approaches and Issues* (Garden City, New York: Anchor Books, 1975), pp. 3–56.

15. Jose L. Corraggio, "Hacia una Revisión de la Teoría de los Polos de Desarrollo," *EURE* 11 (1972), pp. 39–62.

16. This section reproduces passages of two previous papers: Alejandro Portes and Lauren Benton, "Industrial Development and Labor Absorption," *Population and Development Review* 10, no. 4 (1984), pp. 589–611 (reprinted with the permission of the Population Council); and Alejandro Portes, "Latin American Class Structures: Their Composition and Change During the Last Decades," *Latin American Research Review* 20, no. 3 (1985), pp. 7–39 (reprinted with permission).

17. See Dagmar Raczynski, "El Sector Informal: Controversias e Interrogantes," *Estudios CIEPLAN* 13 (1977).

18. For an example of this literature see S. V. Sethuraman, *The Urban Informal Sector in Developing Countries* (Geneva: International Labour Office, 1981); and D. Mazumdar, "The Urban Informal Sector" (Washington, D.C.: World Bank Staff Working Paper #211).

19. Enrique Iglesias, "Development and Equity: The Challenge of the 1980s," *CEPAL Review* 15 (1981), pp. 7–46; Norberto Garcia, "Growing Labour Absorption with Persistent Underemployment," *CEPAL Review* 18 (1982), pp. 45–64.

20. Ibid. PREALC, *Dinámica del Subempleo en America Latina* (Santiago de Chile: International Labour Office, 1981); Victor Tokman, "Development Strategy and Employment in the 1980s," *CEPAL Review* 15 (1981), pp. 133–141.

21. Hugo Lopez Castaño, Marta L. Henao, and Oliva Sierra, "El Empleo en el Sector Informal: El Caso de Colombia" (Working Paper, Center for Economic Research, University of Antioquia, Medellin, 1982).

22. On African cities see Chris Gerry, "Petty Production and Capitalist Production in Dakar: The Crisis of the Self-Employed," *World Development* 6 (1978), pp. 1147–1160; David Webster, "The Political Economy of Survival," *Work in Progress* (University of Witwatersrand, 1979), pp. 57–64; Janet McGaffey, "Fending for Yourself: The Organization of the Second Economy of Zaire," in Nzongola-Ntalaja (ed.), *The Crisis in Zaire: Myths and Realities* (Trenton, N.J.: Africa World Press, 1986), pp. 141–151. On Southeast Asia, Terry McGee, *The Southeast Asian City* (London: G. Bell, 1967); Terry McGee, *Hawkers in Hong Kong: A Study of Planning and Policy in a Third World City* (Hong Kong: Centre for Asian Studies, University of Hong Kong, 1973); Manuel Castells, "Small Business in a World Economy: The Hong Kong Model, Myth and Reality," in *The Urban Informal Sector: Recent Trends in Research and Theory* (Proceedings of the Seminar on the Informal Sector in Center and Periphery, Johns Hopkins University, June 1984).

23. See, for example, Paul Bairoch, *Urban Unemployment in Developing Countries: The Nature of the Problem and Proposals for Its Solution* (Geneva: International Labour Office, 1973); Elsa Chaney, "The World Economy and Contemporary Migration," *International Migration Review* 13 (1985), pp. 204–212.

24. Daniel Carbonetto, Jenny Hoyle, and Mario Tueros, "Sector Informal Urbano en Lima Metropolitana" (Lima: Special Report, Center for Development Research (CEDEP), January 1985).

25. See Lisa Peattie, "What Is to Be Done with the 'Informal Sector': A Case Study of Shoe Manufacturers in Colombia" (Department of City and Regional Planning, MIT, Manuscript, 1981); Bryan R. Roberts, "The Provincial Urban System and the Process of Dependency," in A. Portes and H. Browning (eds.), *Current Perspectives in Latin American Urban Research* (Austin: Institute of Latin American Studies and The University of Texas Press, 1976), pp. 99–132; Patricia Arias and Bryan Roberts, "The City in Permanent Transition: The Consequences of a National System of Industrial Specialization," in J. Walton (ed.), *Capital and Labor in the Urbanized World* (Beverly Hills: Sage, 1985) pp. 149–175.

26. Beatriz Schmukler, "Diversidad de Formas Capitalistas en la Industria Argentina," in V. Tokman and E. Klein (eds.), *El Subempleo en América Latina* (Buenos Aries: El Cid Editores, 1979).

27. Gerry, op. cit. See also Gabriel Murillo and Monica Lanzetta, *Articulación entre el Sector Informal y el Sector Formal de la Economia de Bogotá* (Bogota: Final Report to the International Development Research Centre, Universidad de los Andes, 1985); Larissa Lomnitz, "Mechanisms of Articulation between Shantytown Settlers and the Urban System" *Urban Anthropology* 7 (1978), pp. 185–205.

28. Chris Birbeck, "Self-Employed Proletarians in an Informal Factory: The Case of Cali's Garbage Dump" *World Development* 6 (1978), pp. 1173–1185.

29. Ray Bromley, "Organization, Regulation, and Exploitation in the So-called 'Urban Informal Sector': The Street Traders of Cali, Colombia" *World Development* 6 (1978), pp. 1161–1171; Lourdes Beneria, "Gender, Skill, and the Dynamics of Women's Employment" (Washington, D.C.: Paper presented at the Conference on Gender in the Work Place; The Brookings Institute, May, 1984); Alois Moller, "Los Vendedores Ambulantes en Lima," in V. Tokman and E. Klein (eds.) *El Subempleo en América Latina* (Buenos Aries: El Cid Editores, 1979); Isis Duarte, "Marginalidad Urbana en Santo Domingo" (Santo Domingo: Paper presented at the First Congress of Dominican Sociology, November 1978).

30. Bryan R. Roberts, *Cities of Peasants: The Political Economy of Urbanization in the Third World* (London: Edward Arnold, 1978), ch. 5.

31. Carbonetto et al., op. cit. See also Alejandro Portes, Silvia Blitzer, and John Curtis, "The Urban Informal Sector in Uruguay: Its Internal Structure, Characteristics, and Effects" *World Development* 14 (1986).

32. Victor Tokman, "Wages and Employment in International Recessions: Recent Latin American Experiences" *CEPAL Review* 20 (1983), pp. 113–126; Isis Duarte, "Fuerza Laboral Urbana en Santo Domingo, 1980–1983" *Estudios Sociales* 16 (1983), pp. 31–53; Clarissa Hardy, *Hambre más Dignidad: Ollas Comunes* (Santiago de Chile: PET, 1986).

33. Anthony Leeds, "The Significant Variables Determining the Character of Squatter Settlements" *América Latina* 12 (1969), pp. 44–86.

34. See Lauren A. Benton, "Reshaping the Urban Core: The Politics of Housing in Authoritarian Uruguay" *Latin American Research Review* 21 (1986), pp. 33–52.

35. For summary estimates see Portes and Walton, op. cit., ch. 2, and Manuel Castells, *The City and the Grassroots* (Berkeley: University of California Press, 1983), ch. 16.

36. Ibid.; Benton, op. cit. For a more detailed statement of these conclusions, see Alejandro Portes, "Urbanization, Migration, and Models of Development in Latin America," in John Walton (ed.), *Capital and Labor in the Urbanized World* (Beverly Hills: Sage, 1985), pp. 109–125.

37. Ibid.; Roberts (1978) op. cit., ch. 6; Castells, op. cit.; Benton, op. cit.

38. For a more detailed statement and evidence see Alejandro Portes and John Walton, *Labor, Class, and the International System* (New York: Academic Press, 1981), ch. 3; see also David Collier, *Squatters and Oligarchs: Authoritarian Rule and Policy Change in Peru* (Baltimore: The Johns Hopkins University Press, 1976).

39. Duarte, op. cit.; Fortuna and Prates, op. cit.; Larissa Lomnitz, *Networks and Marginality, Life in a Mexican Shantytown* (New York: Academic Press, 1977).

40. Alan Gilbert, "Urban and Regional Development Programs in Colombia Since 1951," in W. Cornelius and F. Trueblood (eds.), *Latin American Urban Research*, Vol. 5 (Beverly Hills: Sage, 1975), pp. 241–275. See also Alejandro Portes, "Housing Policy, Urban Poverty, and the State," *Latin American Research Review* 14 (1979), pp. 3–24; and Janice E. Perlman, *The Myth of Marginality, Urban Poverty and Politics in Rio de Janeiro* (Berkeley: University of California Press, 1976).

41. Benton, op. cit.

42. Portes, op. cit. (1979); Collier, op. cit.; Wayne A. Cornelius, *Politics and the Migrant Poor in Mexico City* (Stanford: Stanford University Press, 1975).

43. See Eduardo Morales and Sergio Rojas, "Relocalización Espacial de la Pobreza, Politica Estatal y Presión Popular, 1979–1985," in *Espacio y Poder: Los Pobladores* (Santiago de Chile: FLACSO, 1987), pp. 75–121.

44. Gabriel Murillo and Elizabeth Ungar, *Politica, Vivenda Popular y el Processo de Toma de Decisiones en Colombia* (Bogotá: Universidad de los Andes, 1979); Gilbert, op. cit.; Portes and Walton, op. cit. (1976), ch. 2.

45. See Portes and Walton, op. cit. (1976), ch. 3; Cornelius, op. cit.; Collier, op. cit.; Castells, op. cit.

46. Anthony Leeds and Elizabeth Leeds, "Accounting for Behavioral Differences: Three Political Systems and the Responses of Squatters in Brazil, Peru, and Chile," in John Walton and L. H. Masoti (eds.), *The City in Comparative Perspective: Cross National Research and New Directions in Theory* (Beverly Hills: Sage Publications-Halsted Press, 1976), pp. 193–248.

47. L. Kowarick and M. Campinaro, "São Paulo: The Price of World City Status" *Development and Change* 17 (1986), pp. 159–174.

48. Jose A. Moises and Verena M. Alier, "A Revolta Dos Suburbanos," in CEDEC (ed.), *Contadicões Urbanas e Movimentos Socialis* (São Paulo: Co-edicões CEDEC/Paz e Terra, 1977), pp. 13–63; Carlos Doré y Cabral, "Distribución Espacial de la Protesta Popular en Santo Domingo" (Santo Domingo: Working paper, INTEC, 1985).

49. Jorge Balán and associates, "Estudio Comparativo de Organizaciones en *Villas* del Gran Buenos Aires" (Buenos Aires: Research in progress, CEDES, 1985); Elizabeth Jelin, *Los Nuevos Movimientos Sociales* (Buenos Aires: Centro Editor de America Latina, 1985). See also Ruth C. L. Cardoso, "Movimentos Sociais no Brasil Pós 64: Balanco Critico," in B. Sorj and M. H. Tavares de Almeida (eds.), *Sociedade e Politica no Brasil Pós—64.* (São Paulo: Brasiliense, 1983).

50. The "staying power" of these subsistence-oriented organizations is questionable, however. There seems no doubt that they are last resort, survival responses to conditions of intense adversity. The fluctuating enrollment and the "cook together but eat apart" format of the popular soup kitchens, coupled with the rather limited active participation of members, calls for a cautious assessment of their political consciousness. The question is to what extent these survival responses can be translated into a larger social vision and organization. See Hardy, op. cit.; Mariana Schkolnik, *Sobrevivir en la Población Jose M. Caro y en Lo Hermida* (Santiago de Chile: PET, 1986); and Clarissa Hardy and Luis Razeto, "Los Nuevos Actores y Practicas Populares: Desafios a la Concertación" (Santiago: Working Paper #42, Centro de Economia Humana, 1984).

51. *Newsweek*, 30 September 1985. Personal reports of site observers interviewed by the authors.

52. Hardy and Razeto, op. cit.; A. Douglas Kincaid, "Agrarian Development, Peasant Mobilization, and Social Change in Central America" (Doctoral dissertation, Department of Sociology, The Johns Hopkins University, 1987).

53. Maurice Dobb, *Studies in the Development of Capitalism* (New York: International Publishers, 1981).

References

Arias, P., and B. Roberts. "The City in Permanent Transition: The Consequences of a National System of Industrial Specialization," in J. Walton (ed.), *Capital and Labor in the Urbanized World*. Beverly Hills: Sage, pp. 149–175, 1985.

Bairoch, P. *Urban Unemployment in Developing Countries: The Nature of the Problem and Proposals for its Solution*. Geneva: International Labour Office, 1973.

Balán, J., et al. "Estudio Comparativo de Organizaciones en *Villas* del Gran Buenos Aires." Research in progress. Buenos Aires: CEDES, 1985.

Beneria, L. "Gender, Skill, and the Dynamics of Women's Employment. Paper presented at the Conference on Gender in the Work Place, The Brookings Institute, Washington, D.C., 1984.

Benton, L. A. "Reshaping the Urban Core: The Politics of Housing in Authoritarian Uruguay." *Latin American Review* 21, pp. 33–52, 1986.

Birbeck, C. "Self-Employed Proletarians in an Informal Factory: The Case of Cali's Garbage Dump." *World Development* 6, pp. 1173–1185, 1978.

Bromley, R. "Organization, Regulation, and Exploitation in the So-Called 'Urban Informal Sector': The Street Traders of Cali, Colombia." *World Development* 6, pp. 1161–1171, 1978.

Carbonetto, D., J. Hoyle, and M. Tueros. "Sector Informal Urbano en Lima Metropolitana." Special Report, Center for Development Research. Lima: CEDEP, 1985.

Cardona, R. *Dos Barrios de Invasión*. Boletin No. 21. Bogatá: Associación Colombiana de Facultades de Medicina, 1968.

Cardoso, R.C.L. "Movimentos Sociais no Brasil Pós 64: Balanco Critico," in B. Sorj and M. H. Tavares de Almeida (eds.), *Sociedade e Politica no Brasil Pós— 64*. São Paulo: Brasiliense, 1983.

Castells, M. *The City and the Grassroots*. Berkeley: University of California Press, 1983.

Castellis, M. "Small Business in a World Economy: The Hong Kong Model, Myth and Reality," in *The Urban Informal Sector: Recent Trends in Research and Theory*. Johns Hopkins University: Proceedings of the Seminar on the Informal Sector in Center and Periphery, 1984.

Chaney, E. "The World Economy and Contemporary Migration." *International Migration Review* 13, pp. 204–212, 1985.

Chase-Dunn, C. "The Coming of Urban Primacy in Latin America." *Comparative Urban Research* 11, pp. 14–28, 1985.

Collier, D. *Squatters and Oligarchs: Authoritarian Rule and Policy Change in Peru*. Baltimore: The Johns Hopkins University Press, 1976.

Cornelius, W. A. *Politics and the Migrant Poor in Mexico City*. Stanford: Stanford University Press, 1975.

Corraggio, J. L. "Hacia una Revisión de la Teoría de los Polos de Desarrollo. *EURE* 11, pp. 39–62, 1972.

Dobb, M. *Studies in the Development of Capitalism.* New York: International Publishers, 1981.

Doré y Cabral, C. "Distribución Espacial de la Protesta Popular en Santo Domingo. Working Paper. Santo Domingo: INTEC, 1985.

Duarte, I. "Marginalidad Urbana en Santo Domingo." Paper presented at the First Congress of Dominican Sociology. Santo Domingo, 1978.

Fortuna, J. C., and S. Prates. *Sector Informal o Relaciones Informales: El Caso de Montevideo.* Montevideo: CIESU, 1986.

Garcia, N. "Growing Labour Absorption with Persistent Underemployment." *CEPAL Review* 18, pp. 45–64, 1982.

Garcia, N., and V. Tokman. "Changes in Employment and the Crisis." *CEPAL Review*, pp. 103–115, 1984.

Gerry, C. "Petty Production and Capitalist Production in Dakar: The Crisis of the Self-Employed." *World Development* 6, pp. 1147–1160, 1978.

Gilbert, A. "Urban and Regional Development Programs in Colombia Since 1951," in W. Cornelius and F. Trueblood (eds.), *Latin American Urban Research* vol. 5, Beverly Hills: Sage, pp. 241–275, 1975.

Glade, W. *The Latin American Economies.* New York: American Books, 1969.

Hardoy, J. E. *Las Ciudades en América Latina.* Buenos Aires: Paidos, 1972.

———. "Two Thousand Years of Latin American Urbanization," in J. E. Hardoy (ed.), *Urbanization in Latin America: Approaches and Issues.* Garden City, New York: Anchor Books, pp. 3–56, 1975.

Hardy, C., and L. Razeto. "Los Nuevos Actores y Practicas Populares: Desafios a la Concertación." Working Paper #42. Santiago: Centro de Economica Humana, 1984.

Hirschman, A. *A Bias for Hope.* New Haven: Yale University Press, 1971.

Iglesias, E. "Development and Equity: The Challenge of the 1980s." *CEPAL Review* 15, pp. 7–46, 1981.

———. "The Latin American Economy During 1984: A Preliminary Overview." *CEPAL Review* 25, pp. 7–44, 1985.

Johnson, E. *The Organization of Space in Developing Countries.* Cambridge, Mass.: Harvard University Press, 1970.

Kowarick, L., and M. Campinaro. "São Paulo: The Price of World City Status." *Development and Change* 17, pp. 159–174, 1986.

Leeds, A. "The Significant Variables Determining the Character of Squatter Settlements." *América Latina* 12, pp. 44–86, 1969.

Leeds, A., and E. Leeds. "Accounting for Behavioral Differences: Three Political Systems and the Responses of Squatters in Brazil, Peru, and Chile," in J. Walton and L. H. Masotti (eds.), *The City in Comparative Perspective: Cross National Research and New Directions in Theory.* Beverly Hills: Sage Publications-Halsted Press, pp. 193–284, 1976.

Lomnitz, L. *Networks and Marginality, Life in a Mexican Shantytown.* New York: Academic Press, 1977.

———. "Mechanisms of Articulation between Shantytown Settlers and the Urban System." *Urban Anthropology* 7, pp. 185–205, 1978.

136   *Alejandro Portes and Michael Johns*

Lopez Castãno, H., M. Henao, and O. Sierra. "El Empleo en el Sector Informal: El Caso de Colombia." Working Paper. Medillin: Center for Economic Research, University of Antioquia, 1982.

McGaffey, J. "Fending for Yourself: The Organization of the Second Economy of Zaire," in Nxpmhps-Ntalaja (ed.), *The Crisis in Zaire: Myths and Realities.* Trenton, N.J.: Africa World Press, pp. 141–151, 1986.

McGee, T. *The Southeast Asian City.* London: G. Bell, 1967.

———. *Hawkers in Hong Kong: A Study of Planning and Policy in a Third World City.* Hong Kong: Centre for Asian Studies, University of Hong Kong, 1973.

Mazumdar, D. "The Urban Informal Sector." Staff Working Paper #211. Washington, D.C.: World Bank.

Moises, J. A., and V. Martinez Alier. "A Revolta Dos Suburbanos," in CEDEC (ed.), *Contradicões Urbanas e Movimentos Sociais.* São Paulo: Co-edicões CEDEC/ Paz e Terra, 1977.

Moller, A. "Los Vendedores Ambulantes en Lima," in V. Tokman and E. Klein (eds.), *El Subempleo en América Latina.* Buenos Aires: El Cid Editores, 1979.

Murillo, G., and M. Lanzetta. *Articulación entre el Sector Informal y el Sector Formal de la Economia de Bogotá.* Final Report to the International Development Research Centre. Bogotá: Universidad de los Andes, 1985.

Murillo, G., and E. Ungar. *Politica, Vivenda Popular y el Processo de Toma de Decisiones en Colombia.* Bogotá: Universidad de los Andes, 1979.

Peattie, L. "What is to be Done With the 'Informal Sector': A Case Study of Shoe Manufacturers in Colombia," MIT: Department of City and Regional Planning, Manuscript, 1981.

Perlman, J. E. *The Myth of Marginality, Urban Poverty and Politics in Rio de Janeiro.* Berkeley: University of California Press, 1976.

Portes, A. "Housing Policy, Urban Poverty, and the State." *Latin American Research Review* 14, pp. 3–24, 1979.

———. "Urbanization, Migration, and Models of Development in Latin America," in J. Walton (ed.), *Capital and Labor in the Urbanized World.* Beverly Hills: Sage, pp. 109–125, 1985.

Portes, A., and L. Benton. "Industrial Development and Labor Absorption." *Population and Development Review* 10, no. 4, pp. 589–611, 1984.

Portes, A., S. Blitzer, and J. Curtis. "The Urban Informal Sector in Uruguay: Its Internal Structure, Characteristics, and Effects." *World Development* 14, 1986.

Portes, A., and S. Sassen-Koob. "Making it Underground: Comparative Material on the Informal Sector in Western Market Economies." *American Journal of Sociology* 93, pp. 30–61, 1986.

Portes, A., and J. Walton. *Urban Latin America.* Austin: University of Texas Press, 1976.

———. *Labor, Class, and the International System.* New York: Academic Press, 1981.

Raczynski, D. "El Sector Informal: Controversias e Interrogantes." *Estudios CIEPLAN* 13, 1977.

Roberts, B. R. "The Provincial Urban System and the Process of Dependency," in A. Portes and H. Browning (eds.), *Current Perspectives in Latin American*

Urban Research. Austin: Institute of Latin American Studies and The University of Texas Press, 1976.

———. *Cities of Peasants. The Political Economy of Urbanization in the Third World.* London: Edward Arnold, 1978.

Rondinelli, D. "Towns and Small Cities in Developing Countries." *The Geographical Review* 11, pp. 14–28, 1983.

Schmukler, B. "Diversidad de Formas Capitalistas en la Industria Argentina," in V. Tokman and E. Klein (eds.), *El Subempleo in América Latina.* Buenos Aires: el Cid Editores, 1979.

Sethuraman, S. V. *The Urban Informal Sector in Developing Countries.* Geneva: International Labour Office, 1981.

Souza, P. R., and V. Tokman. "Distrución del Ingreso Pobreaza, y Empleo en Areas Urbanas," in PREALC (ed.), *Sector Informal Runcionamento y Politicas.* Santiago de Chile: International Labor Office, 1978.

Tokman, V. "Development Strategy and Employment in the 1980s." *CEPAL Review* 15, pp. 133–141, 1981.

———. "Wages and Employment in International Recessions: Recent Latin American Experiences." *CEPAL Review* 20, pp. 113–126, 1983.

Webster, D. "The Political Economy of Survival." *Work in Progress.* University of Witwatersrand, pp. 57–64, 1979.

7

Heterodox Shocks and the Political Economy of Democratic Transition in Argentina and Brazil

William C. Smith

Introduction

The politics of economic stabilization in capitalist societies has long been a polemical topic in the study of international political economy. In particular, orthodox stabilization programs associated with the International Monetary Fund (IMF) have received much attention from analysts of differing theoretical persuasions. Debates have centered on the impact of IMF-style orthodox programs on both democratic and authoritarian regimes, focusing specifically on political factors such as executive administrative capability, elite cohesion, and the role of political legitimacy.[1]

Conspicuously absent from this debate have been analyses of the possible alternatives to IMF-style orthodox stabilization. The transition from authoritarianism to civilian government with the inaugurations of Raúl Alfonsín in Argentina in December 1983 and José Sarney in Brazil in March 1985 thus offers an opportunity to reexamine rival paradigms of structural adjustment and economic stabilization and their implications for democracy in Latin America.

The new civilian governments in Argentina and Brazil rejected the orthodox adjustment policies espoused by the IMF and, instead, implemented stabilization programs of "heterodox shock." These novel stabilization plans promised to strengthen democratic rule by bringing inflation under control without recession and politically dangerous reductions in living standards. Many analysts have in effect suggested an elective affinity between heterodox shock policies and the new democratic governments. As Albert Hirschman put it:

To be sure, the new democratic governments, especially when they take over from greatly detested or despised authoritarian regimes, will have to cope with a burst of combativeness of social groups. But at the same time they can call upon a special reserve of good will and trust which stands to their credit as a result of the political liberties and human rights they have restored or established. It is this considerable asset of the new Argentinian and Brazilian governments that was a basic factor in the success of the monetary reforms, for if the inflationary tug-of-war, in which the various social groups have engaged for so long, is suddenly to be replaced by cooperation and willingness to believe in the success of the new policy, some basic trust must exist in the government that is enunciating the new program.[2]

This chapter will examine this apparently serendipitous affinity between heterodox policies and democracy in Argentina and Brazil. Can self-directed economic stabilization succeed where externally imposed IMF conditionality has failed? Will home-brewed austerity capture the domestic political support that failed to materialize in support of IMF economic adjustment programs? Or will initial successes give way to the familiar cycle of inflation, crisis in the external sector, and foreign borrowing? In addition to analyzing the Austral and Cruzado Plans, as these heterodox programs were baptized in Argentina and Brazil respectively, I will also discuss "social and economic pacts," their role in policy implementation, and their contribution to democratic consolidation.

Orthodoxy, Heterodoxy, and the Logic of Collective Action

Orthodox stabilization programs have been implemented in many different countries at various times with or without formal recourse to the IMF. Despite this diversity, it is still possible to speak of a general orthodox paradigm. In addition to a commitment to market-based solutions and the rolling back of "excessive" state intervention in the economy, IMF adjustment programs have three basic goals: (1) the correction of the external trade deficit and stabilization of international reserves at safe levels; (2) the elimination of the public sector deficit; and (3) the reduction of inflation.[3]

Since the onset of the debt crisis in 1982, orthodox IMF programs have failed in Mexico, Bolivia, and Peru, as well as in Argentina and Brazil. Colombia and Venezuela have negotiated successfully with their bank creditors, but the two countries have refused to submit to IMF-directed austerity programs. Generally, orthodox policies have had far more success in meeting the external payments objective than in reducing inflation. Some critics have argued, in fact, that guaranteeing external solvency is really the only objective pursued by orthodox programs.[4]

Conventional stabilization programs have failed to curb inflation for a variety of technical reasons,[5] but sharply heightened social and distributional conflicts are equally crucial. These conflicts illustrate several basic coordination problems in the logic of collective action. Theoretical discussions of the "prisoners' dilemma" in situations of high inflation in which labor and capital are in strategic interdependence suggest that the structure of payoffs probably will resemble a negative-sum game. Regardless of labor's strategy (acceptance of wage restraint or, conversely, militant struggle to raise wages), the best strategy for individual capitalists will be to raise prices as high and as rapidly as possible, thereby reducing real wages and increasing real profits. This increases sociopolitical conflict in which both labor and capital will end up worse off than if they had agreed to maintain wages and profits constant, but with a lower rate of inflation.[6]

Similarly, because of the pronounced asymmetry between receiving the benefits and sharing the costs, stabilization programs are extremely susceptible to breakdown due to "free-rider" effects. There are strong incentives for all actors—capital, labor, and the state—to refuse to share the burden of austerity. Since the benefits of reduced inflation are inherently collective, "attempts to transfer the costs of stabilization onto others will be the norm rather than the exception."[7]

This perspective underscores the rationality of the actors' refusal to share in the costs of austerity, but it reveals little of the class content of distributional struggles that lead to the breakdown of stabilization programs. The privileged position of business is rooted in the control entrepreneurs exercise over wealth, production, and investment decisions and capital's indispensable role in the process of accumulation.[8] Workers and unions, in contrast, do not control productive assets and consequently cannot exercise the same leverage in distributional conflicts. Labor, therefore, usually suffers a disproportionate decline in real income during periods of high inflation, while sustaining a disproportionate burden of the sacrifices imposed by anti-inflationary programs.

This asymmetry in costs explains why organized labor is almost always more opposed to stabilization efforts than is business. Austerity and recession, while hurting individual capitalists and firms, often play a functional role for capital as a whole by recreating the conditions (via Joseph Schumpeter's "creative destruction") for a new cycle of accumulation. In addition, because of their superior material resources, entrepreneurs wield immense leverage vis-à-vis state elites in shaping stabilization policies in accord with business interests.[9]

Are there alternatives to orthodoxy that are both compatible with fragile democracies and less prone to collapse because of domestic political consequences? The theorists of the Austral and Cruzado Plans asserted that sharp distributional conflicts, in which capital gains the upper hand (and authoritarian solutions become more probable), are less likely to occur if heterodox policies are implemented. Heterodox policies are designed to combat inflation without the regressive income distribution associated with conventional stabilization. The *heterodoxos* do not reject the necessity of external adjustment or the efficacy of tight control over monetary variables in curbing runaway inflation. They do, however, object to the high social costs involved and deny that a sharp recession is needed to cure inflation. In this regard, the *heterodoxos* interpret the economic debacle of the military-sponsored "Process of National Reorganization" in Argentina as a particularly striking example of the ineffectiveness and perverse social impacts of the orthodox paradigm. The architects of the Cruzado Plan drew similar lessons from the failure of the orthodox gradualism practiced in Brazil by the IMF-sponsored stabilization programs of 1981 to 1983.[10]

Argentine and Brazilian *heterodoxos* based their policy prescriptions on a key characteristic of both economies: the pervasive indexation of virtually all types of monetary contracts, rents, wages, and bonds to official price indexes. In a highly inflationary environment, formal indexation, or "monetary correction," enables economic agents (particularly capital) to partially avoid the erosion of their wages and rents. Indexation, in effect, creates a built-in "memory system" perpetuating inflation indefinitely: Future inflation is simply a function of past inflation.[11]

The *heterodoxos* make this memory system the cornerstone of their critique of and alternative to IMF-style stabilization. They argue that there is a significant, and frequently overlooked, "inertial" component in inflations of 100 percent, 200 percent, and higher. Inertial inflation in indexed economies is the reason that orthodox policies designed to reduce aggregate demand have little impact on inflation. Orthodox shocks as well as orthodox gradualism are, therefore, doomed to failure; effective stabilization mandates the sudden elimination of the effects of past inflation. The "heterodox shock" programs designed to eradicate this memory system generally contain the wholesale deindexation of public and private sector prices and a sweeping monetary reform, including the creation of a new currency with a fixed parity in relation to the U.S. dollar. A temporary freeze on wages and prices is the sine qua non of the heterodox paradigm.[12]

The *heterodoxos* are neither socialists nor naive Keynesian interventionists. They favor temporary controls to cool off distributional struggles and to help avoid the negative-sum payoffs common to conventional stabilization programs. Moreover, some *heterodoxos* have argued that temporary wage and price controls will help to bolster liberal democratic politics. Why?

The *heterodoxos* respect the role of price mechanisms in competitive markets and argue that stringent controls are necessary to assure price stability only until the inertial component of inflation has been eliminated. Unlike the negative-sum game under hyperinflation, once price equilibrium has been attained and inertial factors purged, continued state intervention in markets should be unnecessary. The "visible hand" of the state moves the economy from a high-inflation equilibrium to a low-inflation equilibrium. Then, barring external shocks, and if the government (through social pacts, for example) can maintain a moderate wage policy, competition and the self-interest of individual capitalists should allow the market's "invisible hand" to reproduce low-inflation equilibrium. If transitory coordination of labor and capital through wage and price controls is combined with a concerted attack on the "deep" structural causes of inflation stressed by conventional orthodoxy (protectionism, subsidies, overvalued exchange rates, and so forth), then price stability and renewed economic growth will be possible, even without authoritarianism.

The Austral and the Cruzado Plans: Heterodox Theory in Action

The Argentine and Brazilian economies contrasted sharply on the eve of their respective heterodox experiments.[13] Argentina's relations with the IMF, the U.S. Treasury, and creditor banks were at an impasse. Foreign exchange reserves were depleted, and the domestic manufacturing sector was still reeling from the de-industrialization promoted by the preceding regime's neoliberal economic policies. Brazil also had major problems. The economic authorities were once again out of compliance with the seventh set of economic objectives agreed to with the IMF. But Brazil was enjoying a strong cyclical recovery, with growth rates of 4.5 percent and 8.3 percent in 1984 and 1985, respectively, and with very comfortable foreign exchange reserves (see Tables 7.1 and 7.2).

Despite these differences, the catalyst in both countries for the dramatic policy change was identical: extremely high inflation that threatened a "crisis of confidence" and a disruption of capital accumulation. Monthly inflation in Argentina by June 1985 surpassed 30 percent, shooting for a 2,300 percent annual rate, while GDP growth for the first semester of 1985 was 9 percent below that for the same period the previous year. In Brazil on the eve of the Cruzado Plan, domestic and foreign investment

Table 7.1   Argentina: Principal Economic Indicators, 1981-1986

	1981	1982	1983	1984	1985	1986[a]
I. Production, inflation, Public sector finances		Annual Growth Rates (%)				
Gross domestic product (GDP)	-6.5	-5.2	3.4	2.4	-4.4	5.0
Industrial production	-16.0	-4.7	10.8	4.0	-10.4	
Consumer price index	104.5	164.8	343.8	626.7	672.2	80.0
Expansion of money supply	68.5	176.3	362.0	546.7	697.9	
Federal budget deficit (% of GDP)	15.9	16.7	15.6	12.5	4.0	6.0
II. Wages and employment						
Real wages in industry	-10.7	-10.5	29.3	16.0	-14.5	-7.5
Unemployment rate (%)		6.0	4.9	4.6	6.0	5.0
III. Balance of payments		Billions of U.S. Dollars				
Current account balance	-4.6	-2.2	-2.4	-2.5	-1.3	-1.6
Merchandise balance	.8	2.6	3.7	3.9	4.6	4.4
Exports	9.2	7.2	7.8	8.1	8.4	7.8
Imports	8.4	4.6	4.1	4.1	3.8	4.4
Net services	-5.4	-4.9	-6.2	-6.5	-5.9	
Capital account (net)	1.8	1.4	.1	3.3	.6	
Disbursed foreign debt	35.7	43.6	46.0	47.8	49.3	
Debt service ratio (interest/exports in %)	35.2	56.8	58.2	52.7	50.6	51.0

a Preliminary estimates.
Sources: 1981-1985 data from the IDB, Economic and Social Progress in Latin America,
1986 Report (Washington, D.C.: Inter-American Development Bank, 1986).

Table 7.2 Brazil: Principal Economic Indicators, 1981-1986

	1981	1982	1983	1984	1985	1986
I. Production, inflation, Public sector finances		Annual Growth Rates (%)				
Gross domestic product (GDP)	-1.6	0.9	-3.2	4.5	8.3	8.2
Industrial production	-5.5	0.6	-6.8	6.0	9.0	12.1[a]
General price index (GPI)	95.2	99.7	211.0	223.8	235.1	104.1[a]
GDP per capita	-4.0	-1.5	-5.6	2.1	5.9	4.4[a]
Expansion of money supply	87.2	65.0	95.0	203.5	312.1	500.0+[a]
Federal budget deficit (% of GDP)	7.1	6.2	3.0	1.6	3.2	
II. Wages and employment index[b]						
Minimum wage	99.0	100.0	88.0	83.0	86.0	
Industrial wages	102.9	109.8	92.0	106.8	141.1	
Industrial employment	92.6	87.7	80.3	80.1	87.5	
III. Balance of payments		Billions of U.S. Dollars				
Current account balance	-11.8	-15.4	-6.8	0.1	-0.1	-1.9
Merchandise balance	1.2	0.7	6.5	13.1	12.5	10.5
Exports	23.3	19.0	21.9	27.1	25.6	23.3
Imports	22.1	18.3	15.4	13.9	13.2	12.8
Net services	-13.2	-16.1	-13.4	-13.2	-13.3	-12.5
Capital Account (net)	12.8	10.8	5.5	5.0	1.0	-0.9
Disbursed foreign debt	71.9	83.2	91.6	99.8	99.7	
Debt service ratio (interest/exports in %)	40.2	60.5	43.4	39.5	41.9	39.9

a Preliminary estimates.
b 1980=100

Sources: 1981-1985 data in items I and II are from the Central Bank's Conjuntura Economica and Boletim, various numbers; preliminary estimates for 1986 from Latin American Economic Report, 31 December 1987. Data for 1981-1985 in item III from the Economic and Social Progress in Latin America: 1986 Report (Washington, D.C.: Inter-American Development Bank, 1986); 1986 data are from CACEX.

had declined sharply and monthly inflation was over 16 percent and headed for an annual rate of 400–500 percent in 1986.

The threat of hyperinflation in both countries spurred Juan Sourrouille, the Argentine economy minister, and Dilson Funaro, the Brazilian finance minister, to implement untried emergency measures. Sourrouille unveiled the Austral Plan on June 14, 1985, and President Sarney announced the Cruzado Plan on February 28, 1986.

The Austral Plan's chief policy instruments consisted of: (1) a new currency—the austral—to replace the peso at a rate of 1 austral per 1,000 pesos, with the exchange rate devalued 18 percent in terms of the U.S. dollar; (2) the imposition of a wage and price freeze, with citizens urged to denounce violators; (3) a combination of policies to reduce the budget deficit, including large increases in charges for government-produced services (such as electricity, petroleum products, transportation); and (4) a pledge not to print inflationary quantities of money—this commitment to be carried out by separating the Central Bank's acquisition of domestic assets from the financing needs of the Treasury.

Initial reactions to the Austral Plan exceeded expectations. Wage and price controls succeeded in bringing down inflation from 30 percent in June to approximately 3 percent per month by the end of 1985, and industrial output rebounded a strong 13 percent in the last quarter of 1985 (see Figure 7.1).

Despite these triumphs, the private sector became increasingly critical of Alfonsín's policies. Agricultural producers, led by the Sociedad Rural Argentina (Argentine Rural Society, or SRA), complained of low prices and protested against taxes on commodity exports. Manufacturers responded with capital strikes, and shortages of consumer goods and industrial inputs became widespread. Organized labor, led by the Confederación General-de-Trabajo (General Labor Confederation, or CGT), became more militant in demanding wage increases. By February 1986, there were powerful political forces pushing for a revision of the Austral's freeze on wages and prices.

Reacting to these pressures, in March and April 1986 Sourrouille announced a second phase of the Austral Plan. Along with moderate wage increases, Sourrouille replaced the system of rigid price controls with a new scheme of "administered prices" designed to satisfy entrepreneurs' demands for price hikes to accompany the increased costs of inputs.

The loosening of controls immediately sparked an acceleration of inflation. By the third quarter of 1986, the average of consumer and wholesale price indexes grew at a monthly rate of 7.2 percent. Much of the blame for this was attributed to the Central Bank, which had resisted the tight monetary policies insisted on by the IMF. Economy

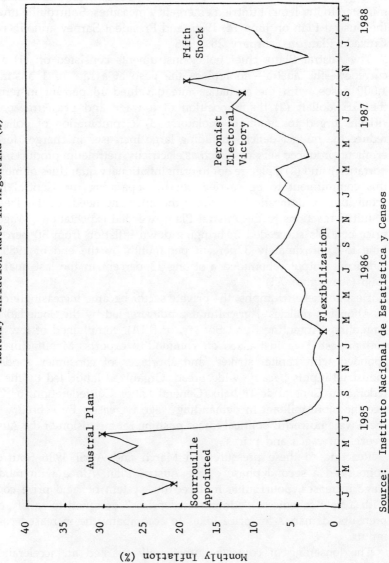

Figure 7.1

Monthly Inflation Rate in Argentina (%)

Source: Instituto Nacional de Estatistica y Censos

Minister Sourrouille and the Central Bank also fought over the pace and scope of reforms of the financial system. These disputes reveal the political constraints that made it virtually impossible to mount a frontal attack on the underlying causes of inflation. The resulting impasse placed an enormous, and increasingly unsustainable, burden on wage and price controls.

Having consolidated control over economic policymaking in September 1986, Sourrouille embarked on a more restrictive monetary policy and reintroduced direct control over wages and prices. An attempt was made to maintain purchasing power by allowing wages to rise in line with inflation.

Despite the stops and starts, reliance on flexible controls scored some successes: Following a period of stagnation, GDP expanded by 11 percent and industrial output by over 26 percent in the twelve months ending September 1986, while investment in machinery and equipment jumped nearly 35 percent in the same period. At 86.8 percent, inflation in 1986 was the lowest in twelve years. But these figures are misleading because the Alfonsín administration failed to control the inflationary pressures generated by this expansion.

In January 1987, inflation jumped 7.6 percent, the second-highest increase since the Austral's inception, forcing Sourrouille to announce yet another round of heterodox shocks, including another "temporary" freeze on wages and prices. When the reimposition of controls failed to stem the resurgence of inflation, the economic team was obliged to give ground in response to IMF pressure for more structural adjustment. Official discourse shifted to a greater emphasis on intensified fiscal restraint, tight monetary policy, deregulation of markets, and privatization of public enterprises.

Alfonsín and Sourrouille adopted steadily more orthodox measures, including extremely high positive interest rates, which rekindled inflationary pressures while simultaneously threatening recession and higher unemployment. In July 1987 a fourth shock was administered, but labor and entrepreneurial resistance torpedoed wage and price controls, leading to an inflation rate of about 180 percent for 1987.

A palpable loss of credibility in the government's management of the economy, plus a general sense of *desencanto* (disenchantment), led to the Radicals' defeat in the September 1987 elections, in which the Peronists staged an impressive political comeback. The government responded with a fifth shock designed to reduce the budget deficit through large increases in tax revenues and higher charges for public services, which produced a sharp decline in real wages and strengthened already strong recessionary tendencies—growth for 1987 was a meager 2.0 percent.

The virtual exhaustion of foreign exchange reserves (interest payments on the foreign debt totaled U.S. $4.4 billion in 1987, with a trade surplus of only U.S. $1.5 billion), together with the Peronists' demands for new policies, forced Alfonsín and Sourrouille to adopt a tougher line vis-à-vis the IMF and creditor banks. Still, by early 1988 there was little to distinguish Argentina's stabilization policies from conventional IMF orthodoxy.

Brazil's experience with heterodox policies paralleled Argentina's. The measures announced by President Sarney in February 1986 were broadly similar to the Austral Plan. The Cruzado Plan included: (1) the creation of a new monetary unit, the cruzado (one cruzado replaced 1,000 cruzeiros), fixed at a rate of 13.8 to the U.S. dollar; (2) the total deindexation of the economy through abolition of monetary correction on almost all financial assets; (3) a temporary freeze on prices, wages, and salaries (which were first raised 8 percent, including a 15 percent hike in the minimum wage), with the population exhorted to monitor prices; and (4) a formula for converting wages and salaries into cruzados that yielded a modest, but significant, redistribution of income in favor of many workers and the middle class.[14]

The Cruzado Plan's immediate impact was little short of miraculous. Inflation fell sharply to a monthly rate of less than 1 percent, with accumulated inflation for the March–October period of less than 10 percent (see Figure 7.2). These results appeared to validate Finance Minister Funaro's promise of "Swiss inflation with Japanese growth." But trouble soon appeared in the form of black markets, illegal price gouging, and shortages of many foodstuffs and basic consumer items. Also, official plans for sweeping administrative reform floundered badly, and government ministries and state enterprises strongly resisted mandated budget cuts. Despite the boom in consumption, businesses complained of reduced profit margins and held back from making new investments even though the economy was operating dangerously close to installed capacity.

Key advisers pressed urgently for loosening of controls, but the Funaro team's response was a classic case of "too little, too late." The first, relatively minor, modifications—dubbed the Cruzadinho—were made in July 1986. Sarney refused to consider more basic reforms. Instead, the president defended the Cruzado Plan as the means to construct a "Brazil with a standard of living for all the population equal to that of Mediterranean Europe."[15]

Major modifications were postponed until after the November 1986 elections, which the leading government party, the Brazilian Democratic Movement party (PMDB), won handily thanks to the Cruzado Plan's popularity and the consumption boom it generated. Immediately tagged

Figure 7.2

Monthly Inflation Rate in Brazil (%)

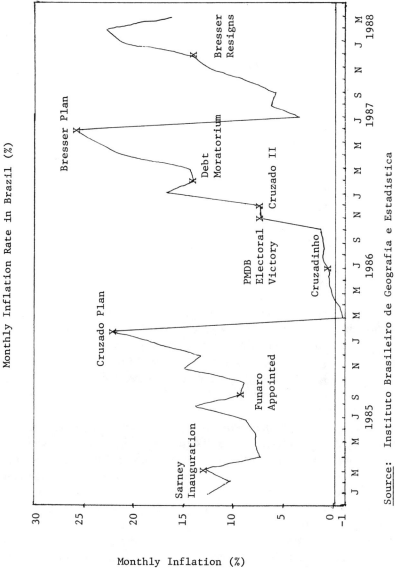

Monthly Inflation (%)

Source: Instituto Brasileiro de Geografia e Estadistica

as the Cruzado II, the package of economic adjustments attempted to correct growing distortions in the structure of relative prices. The principal objective was to force a reduction in middle-class demand by means of a return to minidevaluations of the currency and price increases ranging from 30 to 100 percent on items such as automobiles, gasoline, alcohol fuel, electricity, telephone and postal services, liquor, and cigarettes.

Although welcomed by the business community as necessary to restore eroded profit margins, these measures dramatically accelerated inflation. In the first quarter of 1987 the official price index soared 14–15 percent per month. The Cruzado Plan collapsed suddenly. With its international reserves virtually exhausted, Brazil was forced in February to declare a moratorium on interest payments on U.S. $67 billion of its debt to commercial banks. Finance Minister Funaro's position was untenable, and he was replaced in April by well-known economist Luiz Carlos Bresser Pereira.[16]

In June 1987 Bresser announced the ambitious Plan for Macroeconomic Consistency to remedy the "mistakes" of the original Cruzado Plan.[17] Bresser's policies momentarily succeeded in bringing inflation down to the 3–6 percent range (see Figure 7.2), but prices soon soared once again to double-digit levels. Unemployment increased, real wages nose-dived, and production declined, with GDP growth for 1987 at only 3.0 percent.

In less than eighteen months Brazil had experienced three shock treatments. As in Argentina, each successive shock was progressively more "orthodox" in both objectives and policies. Brazil had lost the game of "chicken" over the debt moratorium with the IMF and its creditor banks.[18] Consequently, the Sarney government reluctantly agreed to a compromise settlement on U.S. $4.5 billion of interest arrears owed creditor banks.

Finally, in December 1987, when President Sarney rejected tough fiscal measures, Bresser Pereira resigned. His successor, Mailson Ferreira da Nóbrega, a bland technocrat with links to the previous military regimes, promised fiscal austerity, wage cuts, and the reestablishment of good relations with the IMF and the banks. The return to the failed nostrums of the past only highlighted the extent to which Brazil's deepening political paralysis had blocked effective management of the country's gargantuan economic problems. Inflation, which had risen nearly 340 percent in 1987, continued to soar at monthly rates above 20 percent; in 1988 price increases could easily surpass 600 percent or more. The illusion of painless stabilization and "zero inflation" had been shattered irrevocably.

Social Pacts and Stabilization

A comprehensive review of macroeconomic policy under the Austral and the Cruzado Plans must incorporate the political initiatives of the Alfonsín and Sarney administrations as well as transformations in state-society interactions in the process of democratization.

Having accomplished the "first transition" to democracy with the installation of civilian governments, Argentina and Brazil entered a "second transition" in which the chief task became the creation and consolidation of a democratic regime. The consolidation of fragile democracies gave a particular urgency to the search for new mechanisms by which the relevant collective actors could be brought into the decisionmaking process. In a crisis context, proposals for *concertación* through "social and economic pacts" gained considerable cachet.[19]

Concertación is essentially a neocorporatist institutional arrangement to facilitate bargaining among labor organizations, business groups, and state elites. However, the objectives of *concertación* go beyond the regulation of distributive conflicts to proposals for the establishment of rules or norms to guide the functioning of the global economic system. In Western Europe, where it has been practiced for decades in a number of countries, *concertación* has served to consolidate representative democracy by contributing to the emergence of more sharply crystallized collective identities of key societal actors. In the European context, *concertación* has not replaced parliament and the party system as the principal means of interest mediation. Rather it has been an additional arena contributing to a pluralist order by redefining the mode of action of the principal protagonists in society and in the polity.[20]

The allure of stabilization via pact making in Latin America lies in the possibility of counteracting negative-sum payoffs in situations of high inflation and low institutionalization of sociopolitical conflict. Through pact making, relevant social and economic actors are called upon to cooperate actively in making stabilization work, rather than shifting the burdens of austerity onto other groups in pursuit of short-term advantages. Many politicians and social scientists have believed that in addition to facilitating a more equitable sharing of the costs of stabilization, macroeconomic policymaking through social pacts would foster a more democratic political culture in which confrontation and veto politics are replaced by a new logic of positive-sum outcomes based upon compromise and bargaining. Theoretically, all groups and sectors would be better off in this "democratic class struggle."

Frankly, in the Latin American context, this description of the virtues of social pacts appears somewhat utopian. For example, how can social actors be induced to forgo the advantages of free riding? If positive-sum solutions are so readily available, why did earlier attempts to form social pacts collapse?[21] Finally, given weak political parties and poorly institutionalized parliaments with scant powers, might not the corporatist bias of social pacts freeze, rather than expand, the scope of interest representation, thereby hindering democratization?

Several demanding conditions must be fulfilled for a social pact between business, organized labor, and the state to succeed. First, *concertación* requires that the government and the regime be accepted as legitimate by the relevant social actors. Second, there must be a reasonable convergence in the overall strategies followed by capital, labor, and the state. Third, notwithstanding their contradictory interests in a market economy, labor and capital must agree on a minimum agenda and there must be clear incentives to reach mutually satisfactory outcomes. Fourth, the state "must cede part of its decisional authority" on issues of economic policy to organized labor and associations representing en-trepreneurial interests, thereby attributing public status to private in-terests. Finally, in exchange for this attribution of public status, business and labor must "offer the state their political power, guaranteeing the state consensus and mobilizing their own resources to assure the legit-imation, efficiency and efficacy of state action."[22] In both Argentina and Brazil, fulfilling these conditions would prove no easy task.

Prior to the Austral Plan the Alfonsín government had frequently proclaimed its interest in forging a social pact, but no progress had been made. Neither entrepreneurs nor organized labor played a role in formulating the new heterodox policies. In fact, the first serious steps to organize tripartite commissions were not taken until after the Austral Plan was well under way. Two factors seemed to have moved the government to act: First, the Radicals' vote in the November 1985 congressional elections was significantly smaller than in 1983; and, second, as mentioned previously, labor militancy increased sharply in late 1985 and early 1986.

Negotiations among representatives of the government, business, and labor were acrimonious from the outset. The Peronist-dominated labor movement radicalized its opposition to Alfonsín's economic policies, as CGT leaders went beyond criticism of the government's wage policies to call for a fundamental revision of the Austral Plan, including suspension of negotiations with the IMF and a moratorium on debt payments. At the same time, direct bilateral discussions, without state participation, between the CGT and the representative organizations of industry, agriculture, and commerce, which had advanced in the pre-Austral period, broke down almost completely. Business, led by the Unión Industrial Argentina (Argentine Industrial Union, or UIA), generally supported the

Austral Plan's anti-inflation achievements and strongly opposed wage concessions to labor. After all, why agree to concessions in the context of *concertación* (negotiations) when the government's income policy guaranteed wage restraint? Why not let Alfonsín, Sourrouille, and the Radicals pay the political price of antagonizing labor?

The economic authorities had been able to get much of the Austral Plan implemented over the opposition of the CGT by winning the tacit acceptance of individual unions crucial to its policies. The government had taken advantage of, and had often promoted, serious divisions within the CGT between the more militant unions and the more conciliatory labor leaders belonging to the Grupo-de-los-15 and the large industrial unions affiliated with the 62-Organizaciones.[23] The more combative unions were hampered by their own divisions into an independent group of so-called renovating Peronists, known as the Comisión-de-los-25, and a faction led by CGT chief Saúl Ubaldini that advocated confrontation with the government.[24]

For Alfonsín and Sourrouille, deepening conflicts with organized labor did not mean cozy relations with the entrepreneurial class. The failure to incorporate the business community into an institutionalized social pact stemmed in part from capital's own political and organizational fragmentation. Contradictory interests pitted urban capital against rural producers. Industrial firms frequently had different interests from those of the commercial and financial sectors. In the key industrial sector, long-standing antagonisms also existed between smaller firms producing for the mass consumption market and large national and transnational firms producing for the affluent and for export to the world market.

Even though the *concertación* framework did not give capital a direct role in shaping macroeconomic policy, there existed an implicit pact between certain entrepreneurial groups and the Alfonsín regime. Unofficial contacts and negotiations between leading figures known as the "captains of industry" and Alfonsín and the economic authorities took place regularly. These "captains" included large private contractors dependent on public sector spending, powerful agro-business enterprises, and the elite of the most modern and dynamic manufacturing firms, many capable of competing in world markets.[25]

The Alfonsín government's project for industrial reconversion and reinsertion in the world economy, and the imperative to generate large trade surpluses to service the debt, essentially coincided with the interests of the largest and most dynamic firms, thereby making a formal social pact unnecessary. For Alfonsín and Sourrouille, it made better sense to avoid the cumbersome formalities of *concertación* and, instead, to try to gain private sector compliance by means of the special access to key policymakers granted to the top elite of the Argentine entrepreneurial class and specific transnational firms. It may be questioned, however, whether the privileged treatment accorded entrepreneurs who, in the past, had benefited handsomely from their support of military rule served the cause of democratic consolidation.

In the Brazilian case, the strong economic recovery and a freer atmosphere under civilian rule had strengthened the organized labor movement. Labor mobilization surpassed levels in the last years of military rule, with more than six million workers out on strike in both 1985 and 1986. Despite this capacity to mobilize the rank and file, the unions were still too weak to effectively defend labor's interests in direct collective bargaining with capital. Organized labor also seemed powerless to resist what some wags termed Sarney's "preferential option for the entrepreneurs." Organized labor's political vulnerability in the post-Cruzado period resulted not from its cooptation through a formal social pact but from its exclusion from effective participation in policymaking.

The Brazilian labor movement's weakness resulted largely from its fragmentation into two rival umbrella organizations, the Central Geral dos Trabalhadores (General Labor Confederation, or CGT) and the Central Unica-dos Trabalhadores (United Federation of Labor, or CUT), strongly linked to the Partido-dos-Trabalhadores (Workers' party, or PT) led by Luis Inácio "Lula" da Silva. Suspicious of the government's probusiness tilt, the CUT was openly hostile to Sarney's calls for tripartite negotiations, seeing proposals for a social pact as a trick to ensure wage restraint. The CGT, for its part, was inclined toward moderation and conciliation with business and the state but was afraid to make concessions for fear of losing support from member unions and rank-and-file workers. These organizational and ideological cleavages prevented labor from acting as an interlocutor able to negotiate on equal footing with the state and capital.[26]

The Sarney regime's willingness to resort to the use of draconian antilabor legislation negated its official discourse in favor of a pact and underscored the persistence of technobureaucratic modes of policymaking inherited from the authoritarian period. In practice, many key members of the Sarney government, including Finance Ministers Funaro and Bresser Pereira and their PMDB economists, demonstrated scant enthusiasm for incorporating organized labor and giving it an effective voice in macroeconomic policymaking. In this regard, at least, they did not differ fundamentally from their *ortodoxo* predecessors.[27]

The civilian government's relations with the business community, while much warmer than with labor, were far from tranquil. Entrepreneurs had enthusiastically welcomed Funaro's appointment to the finance ministry in 1985, correctly seeing him as one of their own. The Cruzado Plan had been greeted by the entrepreneurial class as little less than a plan of "national salvation." However, this enthusiasm did not imply political passivity. Businessmen in industry, finance, commerce, and agriculture adapted to the new openness of the political system by organizing to maximize their clout in the electoral arena and by lobbying the congress, the constituent assembly, and the executive agencies.[28]

Tensions emerged first between the government and rural producers angered by the government's plans for agrarian reform. Conflicts also involved the largest and most dynamic industrial firms. The government's failure to monitor prices effectively in the competitive sectors of the economy, comprised of thousands of small and medium-sized factories and retail outlets, made vigilance over large Brazilian companies, transnational firms, and state enterprises in the monopoly and oligopoly sectors all the more important. Consequently, a redistribution of the surplus in favor of competitive sector firms eroded the profitability of the larger companies, which, along with the banking sector, were saddled with the burden of the quest for price stability.[29]

Faced with the prospect of a disastrous recession and the threat that the moratorium on interest payments might touch off a full break with the international financial system, as well as by conflicts involving the drafting of a new constitution, state elites, entrepreneurs, and organized labor in Brazil, like their counterparts in Argentina, proved unable to defuse distributive conflicts through a social pact. And Brazilians, like Argentines, had to face the implications of the failure to create a policy consensus for future economic stability and the survival of democracy.

Too Much Democracy or Not Enough?

Argentina 5, Brazil 3. Unfortunately, this "score" is not the outcome of a soccer game between two traditional rivals, but the number of heterodox shocks each country has experienced, as of early 1988, since returning to democracy. Heterodox programs have helped to avoid disaster, but have they helped to produce economic stabilization and democratic consolidation?

The Austral and Cruzado Plans have shown that heterodox programs can successfully control high inflation. They have performed better than orthodox stabilization in curbing inflation and maintaining positive growth rates. They have also been moderately successful in cushioning the effects of austerity and in moderating regressive impacts on labor and the poor.[30]

Despite these achievements, the Argentine and Brazilian experiences demonstrate that heterodox programs face severe challenges when wage and price controls are loosened. Can the "invisible hand" of the market take over without the danger of reigniting inflation and renewing the distributive struggles that undermine fragile democracies? The answer, as orthodox critics correctly pointed out, depends in part on the audacity with which state elites take advantage of disinflation to attack the "deep" causes of endemic inflation. Paradoxically, success in reducing inertial inflation (and the "inflationary tax" charged by state and private agents such as banks and oligopoly price setters) may have actually exacerbated conflicts over income distribution. Moreover, in both countries, greater transparency in the functioning of the economy, combined with the ability to calculate costs more precisely, led labor and capital to act more aggressively to defend and, if possible, to increase their relative shares of national income.

Are heterodox policies more supportive of democracy than orthodox alternatives? A simple counterfactual example may be useful. What if IMF-style stabilization programs had been adopted by the Alfonsín and Sarney governments? Perhaps a positive trade balance would have been achieved, thus pleasing the IMF and creditor banks. However, conventional "external adjustment" would demand a high price: a deep recession made worse by rising inflation stemming from devaluation and high interest rates. Almost inexorably, this would lead to deepening social inequalities and worsening political tensions.

By postponing recession and ameliorating social conflict, heterodox policies bought time and badly needed maneuvering room for the beleaguered Alfonsín and Sarney governments. However, "semiloyal" military officers and conservative civilian sectors, who never liked heterodox policies in any event, frequently view the refusal to adopt tough (that is, orthodox) measures as tantamount to populism and a harbinger of uncontrollable unrest and economic collapse. This perception runs the risk of setting in motion a profoundly reactionary logic that demands authoritarian "restoration of order." In postauthoritarian situations, political legitimacy is very fragile and strongly contingent on material payoffs. A less equivocal loyalty to democratic institutions and norms requires time to develop. Heterodox policies alone cannot guarantee success, of course, but the Austral and Cruzado Plans did help these incipient democracies survive trying circumstances, giving democratic rulers the breathing space to defeat would-be authoritarians and to generate a more durable loyalty.

But there is a real danger. If heterodox stabilization merely attacks the inertial component of inflation, leaving underlying causes of high inflation and price disequilibrium untouched, policymakers will face a strong temptation to reimpose controls. But a succession of heterodox shocks will undermine the credibility of official policies, provoke a new eruption of runaway inflation, and seriously erode the legitimacy of democratic institutions. The frustration of popular expectations and the perception of incompetent economic management in fragile democracies frequently are the prelude to "ungovernability" and authoritarianism.

The use by policymakers of the heterodox breathing space raises additional questions about the interactions of democracy and stabilization. Heterodox policies acted on politicians and policymakers like a powerful aphrodisiac. A sense of euphoric complacency and easy popularity generated by the magical "quick fix" obscured the need to broaden and deepen the democratization process. At the outset of the transition from authoritarianism, social pacts in the framework of *concertación* were seen as ideal institutional arrangements for combating inflation while consolidating democracy. The evidence is ambiguous, but the Argentine and Brazilian experiences are not encouraging. For the most part, business and labor merely observed the unfolding of the Austral and Cruzado Plans from the sidelines. They protested vociferously when their interests were affected, but they had little or no say in policy implementation.

Several of the reasons for the marginal role played by *concertación* are evident. First, business associations and labor organizations, particularly the latter, were plagued by internecine struggles that made it difficult for them to mobilize the legitimacy and resources required of interlocutors in a workable social pact. Second, by pursuing particularistic strategies to maximize nominal wages or profits, labor and capital as collective actors operated as textbook examples of free riders bent on transferring the costs of stabilization onto each other or onto consumers and the state. Third, both the Alfonsín and the Sarney administrations were plagued by bureaucratic struggles within the policymaking apparatus. These intraregime struggles undercut state elites' ability to bargain and compromise with organized labor and business organizations. Rather than a willingness to cede part of their decisional authority to private groups, a prerequisite for successful macroeconomic policymaking through social pacts, state elites persisted in following familiar technobureaucratic modes of decisionmaking. In effect, the Alfonsín and Sarney governments demanded passive acquiescence to official policies at the same time as they refused effective consultation to the very parties on whose cooperation successful stabilization depended.

Heterodox policies today seem more a memory than a reality. Their audacity in setting forth new instruments to confront the economic crisis has been progressively diluted by moves toward more orthodox policies, including a greater opening to world markets, deregulation, privatization, and accommodation with external creditors.[31]

The initial popular enthusiasm for the Austral and Cruzado Plans has long since evaporated. The Alfonsín and Sarney governments failed to build new political institutions to channel popular support on behalf of a program of social and economic reform. Consequently, desperation, cynicism, and a retreat into civic privatism have become widespread in both Argentina and Brazil. Moreover, the initial successes of heterodox policies could not make up for a similar political timidity in reforming inefficient and unjust financial systems and revising fiscal and tax policies. A concerted effort attempting to parlay the initial euphoria produced by the Austral and Cruzado Plans into measures such as exchange reforms, elimination of public sector "sacred cows," and progressive taxation might have provided the underpinnings for long-term success.

Finally, the initial success in controlling inflation could not be sustained in view of the failure (shared by the IMF, international bankers, and advanced country policymakers) to resolve the debt crisis. These essentially political failures make sober judgments unavoidable. Alfonsín, Sarney, and their *heterodoxo* advisers not only hesitated to elicit support for their policies through *concertación*, they also shrank back from the politically unpalatable necessity of identifying clear winners and losers in what were unavoidable distributional conflicts.

The conundrum was a real one. In effect, rather than risk civilian rule (and their own power) by extending democratization beyond the politico-institutional sphere to address the transformation of the political economy, both the Alfonsín and the Sarney governments opted to manage the economy and structures of power remaining from the days of authoritarian rule. They probably felt they had no choice, and they may have been correct. But their chosen course was very dangerous because, by reaffirming the existing order, they lost popular support and legitimacy. Without active popular support, sustained by a belief in the government's commitment to fundamental changes, state elites in fragile democracies will face virtually irresistible pressures from powerful domestic interests and external actors to abandon alternative policies, like the Austral and the Cruzado Plans, in favor of unadorned IMF orthodoxy.

Are there any options? Economic mismanagement under authoritarianism left a disastrous legacy for the new democracies. In the late 1980s, after several years of civilian rule, the failures of the half-measures of the Austral and Cruzado Plans are also apparent. Perhaps the lesson to be learned is that if external adjustment programs are to succeed, the making of macroeconomic policy can no longer remain the exclusive preserve of technocratic elites, even those of a heterodox persuasion. Legitimation through elections is not sufficient to guarantee popular acceptance of painful stabilization policies. Stabilization must be negotiated directly through bargaining and compromise with relevant social and economic actors.

The evidence from Argentina and Brazil suggests that the negotiation process should not be limited to the confines of *concertación*. Social pacts may play a useful, but limited, role. There is a real danger that without the political will to extend representation—and real influence—to a broad array of collective actors, social pacts may actually undermine fragile democracies. The reliance on executive decree laws to implement heterodox stabilization is a clear brake on the democratization process. The rhetoric of social pacts serves to obscure the completely marginal role of political parties and parliamentary bodies in macroeconomic policymaking and implementation. Without this participation, social pacts are little more than a facade behind which the aggrandizement of executive prerogative and the privatization of state power continue undisturbed by accountability to elected representatives. The irony is that the centralization of power in the executive probably holds less promise for effective economic policies and democratic consolidation than a "riskier" strategy based on the empowerment of party politicians and other actors in civil society, long excluded from meaningful participation in national politics.

This is not the only possible interpretation. Others will no doubt feel that the full incorporation of the parties and major collective actors will only intensify an already contentious environment, thereby working against rational and consistent economic policymaking. Still, it is hard to escape the conclusion that heterodox policies have not fared better in Argentina and Brazil because democratization has not been carried far enough.

This preference for democracy is not merely a normative one; rather, it stems from practical concerns as well. Unfortunately, there is no easy recipe for economic stabilization with social justice and without authoritarianism. But if viable solutions are forthcoming, it is all but certain their implementation will require not less democracy, but more.

Notes

1. Robert R. Kaufman, "Democratic and Authoritarian Responses to the Debt Issue: Argentina, Brazil, and Mexico," *International Organization*, 39 (1985):473–503; Karen Remmer, "The Politics of Economic Stabilization: IMF Standby Programs in Latin America, 1954–1984," *Comparative Politics*, 19, 1 (1986):1–24; Harry Bienen and Mark Gersovitz, "Economic Stabilization, Conditionality, and Political Stability," *International Organization*, 39, 4 (1985):129–154; and Stephan Haggard, "The Politics of Adjustment: Lessons from the IMF's Extended Fund Facility," *International Organization*, 39, 3 (1985):505–534.

2. Albert Hirschman, "The Political Economy of Latin American Development: Seven Exercises in Retrospection," *Latin American Research Review*, 22, 3 (1987):28–29.

3. For an overview of IMF orthodoxy, see Tony Killick (editor), *The Quest for Economic Stabilization: The IMF and the Third World* (New York: St. Martin's

Press, 1982); William Cline and Sidney Weintraub (editors), *Economic Stabilization in Developing Countries* (Washington, D.C.: Brookings Institution, 1981); John Williamson (editor), *IMF Conditionality* (Washington, D.C.: Institute for International Economics, 1983); and Manuel Pastor, Jr., *The International Monetary Fund and Latin America: Economic Stabilization and Class Conflict* (Boulder, Colorado: Westview Press, 1987).

4. See Roberto Frenkel and Guillermo O'Donnell, "The Stabilization Programs of the International Monetary Fund and Their Internal Impacts," in Richard A. Fagen (editor), *Capitalism and the State in Latin America* (Stanford: Stanford University Press, 1979), 171–216.

5. For recent critiques of IMF conditionality and related monetarist approaches, see Cline and Weintraub (editors), *Economic Stabilization in Developing Countries*; Rudiger Dornbusch, "Stabilization Policies in Developing Countries: What Have We Learned?" *World Development*, 10, 9 (1982):701–708; Alejandro Foxley, *Latin American Experiments in Neoconservative Economics* (Berkeley and Los Angeles: University of California Press, 1983); and Joseph Ramos, *Neoconservative Economics in the Southern Cone of Latin America, 1973–1983* (Baltimore: The Johns Hopkins University Press, 1986).

6. Shlomo Maital and Y. Benjamini, "Inflation as a Prisoners' Dilemma," *Journal of Post-Keynesian Economics*, 2, 4 (1980):459–481. Also see Shlomo Maital and Irwin Lipnowski (editors), *Macroeconomics, Conflict, and Social Institutions* (Cambridge: Ballinger, 1985).

7. Kaufman, "Democratic and Authoritarian Responses to the Debt Issue," 479.

8. Charles Lindblom, *Politics and Markets: The World's Political Economic Systems* (New York: Harper and Row, 1977). Also see Fred Block, "The Ruling Class Does Not Rule: Notes on the Marxist Theory of the State," *Socialist Revolution*, 33, (1977):6–28.

9. Kaufman, "Democratic and Authoritarian Response," 480–481.

10. On Argentina, see Adolfo Canitrot, "Teoría y Práctica del Liberalismo. Política Antiinflacionaria y Apertura Económica en la Argentina, 1976–1981," *Desarrollo Económico*, 21, 82 (1981):131–190; Daniel Heymann, "La Inflación Argentina de los Ochenta y el Plan Austral," *Pensamiento Iberoamericano*, 9 (January-June 1986):89–128; Juan V. Sourrouille, Bernardo P. Kosacoff, and Jorge Lucangeli, *Transnacionalización y Política Económica en la Argentina* (Buenos Aires: Centro de Economía Transnaciónal/Grupo Editor Latinoamericano, 1985); Roberto Frenkel, José Maria Fanelli, and Carlos Winograd, "Stabilization and Adjustment Programmes and Policies in Argentina" (Buenos Aires: CEDES, December 1986); and Jorge Schvarzer, *La Política Económica de Martínez de Hoz* (Buenos Aires: Hyspamérica, 1986). On Brazil, see Pérsio Arida and André Lara-Resende, "Inflação Inercial e Reforma Monetária: Brasil," in Pérsio Arida (editor), *Inflação Zero: Brasil, Argentina, Israel* (Rio de Janeiro: Paz e Terra, 1986):9–37; Francisco Lopes, *O Choque Heterodoxo: Combate à Inflaçâyao e Reforma Monetária* (Rio de Janeiro: Editora Campus, 1986); Eduardo Modiano, *Da Inflação ao Cruzado: A Política Econômica no Primeiro Ano da Nova República* (Rio de Janeiro: Editora Campus, 1986); and William G. Tyler, "Stabilization, External Adjustment, and

Recession in Brazil: Perspectives on the Mid-1980s," *Studies in Comparative International Development*, 21, 2 (1986):5–33.

11. See Lopes, *O Choque Heterodoxo*, 124, for the clearest explication of the operation of the "memory system." Also see Luiz Bresser Pereira and Yoshiaki Nakano, *The Theory of Inertial Inflation: The Foundation of Economic Reform in Brazil and Argentina* (Boulder, Colorado: Lynne Rienner, 1987), Chapter 3.

12. Rudiger Dornbusch, "A New Chance for Argentina," *Challenge* (January-February 1986):15–20; Eliana A. Cardoso, "What Policymakers Can Learn From Brazil and Mexico," *Challenge* (September-October 1986):19–26.

13. Brazilian statistics in this section are found in *Conjuntura Econômica* (Fundação Gétulio Vargas), various numbers; Argentina data are found in *Informe Económico de Coyuntura* (Consejo Profesional de Ciencias Económicas), various numbers, and in Frenkel, Fanelli, and Winograd, "Stabilization and Adjustment Programmes and Policies in Argentina." This section and the next also draw upon the following journalistic sources: for Argentina, the weekly airmail editions of *La Nación*, *Clarín*, and *Clarín Económico*; for Brazil, the weekly news magazines *Senhor* and *Veja*, supplemented by the daily newspapers *Folha de São Paulo* and *Jornal do Brasil*. During July and August 1987 interviews were conducted with academics, businessmen, and public officials in Rio de Janeiro and Buenos Aires.

14. SEPLAN, *Brasil: Programa de Estabilização Económica* (Brasília, D.F.: Secretariat of Planning of the Presidency, 1986).

15. For fascinating "insider" accounts of the disputes and personalities involved, see Alex Solnik, *Os Pais do Cruzado Contam Por Que Não Deu Certo* (Porto Alegre: L and PM, 1987); and Carlos Alberto Sardemberg, *Aventura e Agónia: Nos Bastidores do Cruzado* (São Paulo: Companhia das Letras, 1987). See Paul Singer, *O Dia da Lagarta: Democratização e Conflito Distributivo no Brasil do Cruzado* (São Paulo: Brasiliense, 1987) for a scathing critique of the Cruzado Plan.

16. For the context of Funaro's fall, see William C. Smith, "The Travail of Brazilian Democracy in the New Republic," *Journal of Interamerican Studies and World Affairs*, 28, 4 (Winter 1986–1987):56–57.

17. For the text of the "Plano de Consistência Macroeconômica," see *Folha de São Paulo*, (7 July 1987):20–23. The Interim Financing Agreement reached in November 1987 called for Brazil to put up $1.5 billion and its banks to contribute $3 billion.

18. Brazil's treatment by the cartel of creditor banks and the IMF is a reminder of the limited maneuvering room enjoyed by even the largest debtor countries. See Guillermo O'Donnell (1986 and 1987).

19. For useful comparative analyses, see Mario R. dos Santos (editor), *Concertación Político-Social y Democratización* (Buenos Aires: CLACSO, 1987), and Eli Diniz and Renato R. Boschi, "A Consolidação Democrática no Brasil: Processos Sociais, Intermediação de Interesses e Modernizaçãao do Estado," paper presented at a PNUD-UNESCO-CLASCO seminar in Lima, Peru, July 13–17, 1987.

20. *Concertación* is essentially a variant of social-democratic-style neocorporatism; on the compatibility between neocorporatist arrangements and pluralist democracy, see Claus Offe, "Societal Preconditions of Corporatism and Some

Current Dilemmas in Democratic Theory," Working Paper No. 14, Kellogg Institute, University of Notre Dame (1984). Liliana de Ris, Marcelo Cavarozzi, and Jorge Feldman, "El Contexto y los Dilemas de la Concertación en la Argentina Actual," in Dos Santos (editor), *Concertación Político-Social y Democratización.*

21. In 1973 and 1974 the Peronist regime failed in an attempt to implement a social pact. See Adolfo Canitrot, "La Viabilidad Económica de la Democracia: un Análls de la Experiencia Peronista, 1973–1976," *Estudios Sociales,* 11 (May 1978); and Robert Ayres, "The Social Pact as Anti-Inflationary Policy: The Argentine Case," *World Politics,* 4 (1976):473–501.

22. de Ris, Cavarozzi, and Feldman, "El Contexto y los Dilemas de la Concertación en la Argentina Actual," 192–193 and passim. The delegation of public status and political power to labor and capital is a prerequisite to securing their cooperation; see Claus Offe, "The Attribution of Public Status to Interest Groups," in Susan Berger (editor), *Organizing Interests in Western Europe* (Cambridge: Cambridge University Press, 1981):123–158.

23. A representative of Los 15 held the post of labor minister from April to September 1987.

24. See Héctor Palomino, "La Normalización de la CGT: ¿Diez Años no es Nada?" *El Bimestre Político y Económico,* 3 (1987):11–14, and "Los Conflictos Laborales Bajo el Gobierno Constitucional: Del Plan Austral al Ministro de Trabajo Carlos Alderete (1985–1987)," *Debate Sindical,* Fundación Friedrich Ebert, 1987.

25. Interviews with a high official of the UIA (Buenos Aires, 9 August 1987) and one of the so-called political operators (*operadores políticos*) of the "captains of industry" (Buenos Aires, 10 July 1987). For analysis of the entrepreneurial elite and relations with the state, see "El estado de los capitanes," *Crisis,* 30 (1987):21–25; Jorge Schvarzer and Ricardo Sidicaro, "Empresarios y Estado en la Reconstrución de la Democracía en la Argentina," *El Bimestre Político y Económico,* no. 5 (1987):5–14; and William Smith, "Reflections on the Political Economy of Authoritarian Rule and Capitalist Reorganization in Contemporary Argentina," in Philip O'Brien and Paul Cammack (editors), *Generals in Retreat: The Crisis of Military Rule in Latin America* (Manchester: Manchester University Press, 1985):37–88.

26. On the background of the labor movement, see Maria Herminia Tavares de Almeida, "Novo Sindicalismo and Politics in Brazil," in John D. Wirth, Edson de Oliveira Nunes, and Thomas Bogenschild (editors), *State and Society in Brazil: Continuity and Change* (Boulder, Colorado: Westview Press, 1987):147–178. For the more recent period see Maria Herminia Tavares, Silvia Magnani and Wilma Keller, "Sindicalismo Brasileño y Pacto Social," in Dos Santos (ed.), *Concertación Político-Social y Democratización,* 161–188; Singer, *O Dia da Lagarta,* 139–164; and Smith, "The Travail of Brazilian Democracy," 47–56.

27. It is striking that the "insider" accounts of the Cruzado Plan (cited in note 15) never mentioned negotiations or even discussions with labor representatives. For recent analyses of patterns of state-centric policymaking (that have changed remarkably little under civilian rule), see Olavo Brasil de Lima, Jr., and Sérgio Henrique Abranches (editors), *As Origens da Crise: Estado Autoritário e Planejamento no Brasil* (São Paulo: Editora Vértice, 1987).

28. On the role of entrepreneurs, see Eli Diniz, "O Empresariado e a Nova República," in *Cadernos de Conjuntura*, IUPERJ (May 1986) and "O Empresariado e o Momento Político: Entre a Nostalgia do Passado e o Temor do Futuro," *Ciñcias Sociais Hoje, 1986* (São Paulo: Cortez Editora, 1986).

29. Paul Singer, "Lo crucial del Plan Cruzado: Primer balance de la experiencia brasileña," *Nueva Sociedad*, 88 (1987):150–165.

30. For data on the impact of heterodox policies on wages and income distribution, see Chapters 2 and 3 in this volume. For a strong defense of the Austral Plan on precisely these points, see Frenkel, Fanelli, and Winograd, "Stabilization and Adjustment Programmes and Policies in Argentina."

31. All of these needed reforms are, of course, heavily conditioned by the drain of resources necessary to service the foreign debt. In Argentina, interest payments of about $4.5 billion on the $54 billion debt consume about 6 percent of GDP or about one-third of the central government's budgetary expenditures. In Brazil, interest payments of 4–5 percent of GDP on the $116 billion debt siphons off approximately 30 percent of domestic savings.

References

Arida, Pérsio, and André Lara-Resende. "Inflação Inercial e Reforma Monetária: Brasil," in Pérsio Arida (editor), *Inflação Zero: Brasil, Argentina, Israel*, Rio de Janeiro: Paz e Terra, 9–37, 1986.

Ayres, Robert. "The Social Pact as Anti-Inflationary Policy: The Argentine Case," *World Politics*, 4: 473–501, 1976.

Bienen, Harry, and Mark Gersovitz. "Economic Stabilization, Conditionality, and Political Stability," *International Organization*, 39(4): 129–154, 1985.

Block, Fred. "The Ruling Class Does Not Rule: Notes on the Marxist Theory of the State," *Socialist Revolution*, 33: 6–28, 1977.

Bresser Pereira, Luis, and Yoshiaki Nakano. *The Theory of Inertial Inflation: The Foundation of Economic Reform in Brazil and Argentina*, Boulder, Colorado: Lynne Rienner, 1987.

Canitrot, Adlofo. "Teoría y Práctica del Liberalismo. Politica Anti-inflacionaria y Apertura Económica en la Argentina, 1976–1981," *Desarrollo Económico*, 21(82): 131–190, 1981.

————. "La Viabilidad Económica de la Democracia: un Análisis de la Experiencia Peronista, 1973–1976," *Estudios Sociales*, 11 (May), 1978.

Cardoso, Eliana A. "What Policymakers Can Learn From Brazil and Mexico," *Challenger* (September-October): 19–26, 1986.

Cline, William, and Sidney Weintraub (editors). *Economic Stabilization in Developing Countries*, Washington, D.C.: Brookings Institution, 1981.

de Lima, Jr., Olavo Brasil, and Sérgio Henrique Abranches (editors). *As Origens da Crise: Estado Autoritario e Planejamento no Brasil*, São Paulo: Editora Vértice, 1987.

de Ris, Liliana, Marcelo Cavarozzi, and Jorge Feldman. "El Contexto y los Dilemas de la Concertación en la Argentina Actual," in Mariano R. dos

Santos (editor), *Concertación Político-Social y Democratización*, Buenos Aires: CLACSO, 1987.

Diniz, Eli. "O Empresariado e a Nova República," in *Cadernos de Coyuntura*, IUPERJ (May 1986) and "O Empresariado e o Momento Político: Entre a Nostalgia do Passado e o Temor do Futuro," *Ciências Sociais Hoje*, São Paulo: Cortez Editora, 1986.

Diniz, Eli, and Renato R. Boschi. "A Consolidação Democrática no Brasil: Procesos Sociais, Intermediação de Interesses e Modernização do Estado," Paper presented at a PNUD-UNESCO-CLACSO seminar, Lima, Peru, July 13–17, 1987.

Dornbusch, Rudiger. "Stabilization Policies in Developing Countries: What Have We Learned?" *World Development*, 10(9): 701–708, 1982.

———. "A New Chance for Argentina," *Challenge* (January-February): 15–20, 1986.

Foxley, Alejandro. *Latin American Experiments in Neoconservative Economics*, Berkeley and Los Angeles: University of California Press, 1983.

Frenkel, Roberto, José Maria Fanelli, and Carlos Wingograd. "Stabilization and Adjustment Programmes and Policies in Argentina," Buenos Aires: CEDES, December 1986.

Frenkel, Roberto, and Guillermo O'Donnell. "The Stabilization Programs of the International Monetary Fund and Their Internal Impacts," in Richard A. Fagen (editor), *Capitalism and the State in Latin America*, Stanford: Stanford University Press, 171–216, 1979.

Ground, Richard Lynn. "Orthodox Adjustment Programmes in Latin America," *CEPAL Review*, 23 (August): 46–81, 1984.

Haggard, Stephan. "The Politics of Adjustment: Lessons from the IMF's Extended Fund Facility," *International Organization*, 39(3): 505–534, 1985.

Hartlyn, Jonathan, and Samuel Morley. "Bureaucratic-Authoritarian Regimes in Comparative Perspective," *Latin American Political Economy: Financial Crisis and Political Change*, Boulder, Colorado: Westview Press, 38–52, 1986.

Heymann, Daniel. "La Inflación Argentina de los Ochenta y el Plan Austral," *Pensamiento Iberoamericano*, 9 (January-June): 89–128, 1986.

Hirschman, Albert. "The Political Economy of Latin American Development: Seven Exercises in Retrospection," *Latin American Research Review*, 22(3): 7–36, 1987.

Kaufman, Robert R. "Democratic and Authoritarian Responses to the Debt Issue: Argentina, Brazil and Mexico," *International Organization*, 39: 473–503, 1985.

Killick, Tony (editor). *The Quest for Economic Stabilization: The IMF and the Third World*, New York: St. Martin's Press, 1982.

Lindblom, Charles. *Politics and Markets: The World's Political Economic Systems*, New York: Harper and Row, 1977.

Lopes, Francisco. *O Choque Heterodoxo: Combate à Inflação e Reforma Monetária*, Rio de Janeiro: Editora Campus, 1986.

Maital, Shlomo, and Y. Benjamini. "Inflation as a Prisoners' Dilemma," *Journal of Post-Keynesian Economics*, 2(4): 459–481, 1980.

Maital, Shlomo, and Irwin Lipnowski (editors). *Macroeconomics, Conflict and Social Institutions*, Cambridge: Ballinger, 1985.

Modiano, Eduardo. *Da Inflação ao Cruzado: A Política Econômica no Primeiro Ano da Nova República*, Rio de Janeiro: Editora Campus, 1986.

O'Donnell, Guillermo. "Brazil's Failure: What Future for Debtors' Cartels?" *Third World Quarterly*, 9(4): 1157–1166, 1987.

_____. "External Debt: Why Don't Our Governments Do the Obvious?" *CEPAL Review*, 27: 27–33, 1986.

Offe, Claus. "The Attribution of Public Status to Interest Groups," in Susan Berger (editor), *Organizing Interests in Western Europe*, Cambridge: Cambridge University Press, 123–158, 1981.

_____. "Societal Preconditions of Corporatism and Some Current Dilemmas in Democratic Theory," *Working Paper No. 14*, Notre Dame, Indiana: Kellogg Institute, University of Notre Dame, 1984.

Palomino, Héctor. "Los Conflictos Laborales Bajo el Gobierno Constitucional: Del Plan Austral al Traba Carlos Alderete (1985–1987)," *Debata Sindical*, Fundación Frederich Ebert, 1987.

_____. "La Normalización de la CGT: ¿Diez años no es nada?" *El Bimestre Político y Económico*, 3: 11–14, 1987.

Pastor, Manuel Jr. *The International Monetary Fund and Latin America: Economic Stabilization and Class Conflict*, Boulder, Colorado: Westview Press, 1987.

Ramos, Joseph. *Neoconservative Economics in the Southern Cone of Latin America, 1973–1983*, Baltimore: The Johns Hopkins University Press, 1986.

Remmer, Karen. "The Politics of Economic Stabilization: IMF Standby Programs in Latin America, 1954–1984," *Comparative Politics*, 19(1): 1–24, 1986.

Santos, Mario R. dos. *Concertación Político-Social y Democratización*, Buenos Aires: CLACSO, 1987.

Sardemberg, Carlos Alberto. *Aventura e Agònia: Nos Bastidores do Cruzado*, São Paulo: Companhia das Letras, 1987.

Schvarzer, Jorge. *La Política Económica de Martinez de Hoz*, Buenos Aires: Hyspamérica, 1986.

Schvarzer, Jorge, and Ricardo Sidicaro. "Empresarios y Estado en la Reconstrución de la Democracía en la Argentina," *El Bimestre Político y Económico*, no. 5: 5–14, 1987.

SEPLAN. *Brasil: Programa de Estabilização Econômica*, Brasília, D.F.: Secretariat of Planning of the Presidency, 1986.

Singer, Paul. *O Dia da Lagarta, Democratização e Conflicto Distributivo no Brasil do Cruzado*, São Paulo: Brasiliense, 1987.

_____. "Lo Crucial de Plan Cruzado: Primer Balance de la Experiencia Brasileña," *Nueva Sociedad*, 88: 150–165, 1987.

Smith, William. "Reflections on the Political Economy of Authoritarian Rule and Capitalist Reorganization in Contemporary Argentina," in Philip O'Brien and Paul Cammack (editors), *Generals in Retreat: The Crisis of Military Rule in Latin America*, Manchester: Manchester University Press, 37–88, 1985.

_____. "The Travail of Brazilian Democracy in the New Republic," *Journal of Interamerican Studies and World Affairs*, 28(4): 47–56, 1986–1987.

Solnik, Alex. *Os Pais do Cruzado Contam Por Que Não Deu Certo*, Porto Alegre: L and PM, 1987.

Sourrouille, Juan V., Bernardo P. Kosacoff, and Jorge Lucangeli. *Transnacionalización y Política Económica en la Argentina*, Buenos Aires: Centro de Economía Transnaciónal/Grupo Editor Latinoamericano, 1985.

Tavares de Almeida, Maria Herminia. "Novo Sindicalismo and Politics in Brazil," in John D. Wirth, Edson de Oliveira Nunes, and Thomas Bogenschild (editors), *State and Society in Brazil: Continuity and Change*, Boulder, Colorado: Westview Press, 147–178, 1987.

Tavares, Maria Herminia, Silvia Magnani, and Wilma Keller. "Sindicalismo Brasileño y Pacto Social," in Mario R. dos Santos (editor), *Concertación Político-Social y Democratización*, Buenos Aires: CLACSO, 161–188, 1987.

Tyler, William G. "Stabilization, External Adjustment, and Recession in Brazil: Perspectives on the Mid-1980s," *Studies in Comparative International Development*, 21(2): 5–33, 1986.

Williamson, John (editor). *IMF Conditionality*, Washington, D.C.: Institute for International Economics, 1983.

Part 4
Responses to
Austerity Policies

8

Austerity and Trade Unions in Latin America

Edward C. Epstein

This chapter examines the response of organized labor to official austerity programs during the 1976–1984 period in seven Latin American countries—Argentina, Brazil, Chile, Colombia, Mexico, Peru, and Venezuela—where labor organization historically has been large and important. In the late 1980s, austerity policies express the accumulated effects of the energy price shocks of 1973 and 1979 on prices, the foreign debt crisis that emerged in the early 1980s, and the decline of export markets in the worldwide recession that followed (see Wionczek, 1985; Kim and Ruccio, 1985; Dornbusch, 1986; Thorp and Whitehead, 1987). For present purposes, austerity is measured by cuts in central government spending, as well as by the ensuing fall in worker real income and rising unemployment. Although a simplification of the range of trade union responses, the indicator used here will be strike activity (given its quantifiable nature). Unfortunately, the information on strikes and strikers used here is incomplete and available only by year rather than in monthly increments.

The austerity programs represented by reductions in spending for the case countries were present throughout the period studied, but especially in more recent years (see Table 8.1). The total magnitude of austerity has varied among the seven countries examined, from Argentina's average of 14.3 percent decline for each of the five years of central government spending cuts there to the 6.5 percent figure for the four Chilean years of reductions. Colombia has had only two austerity years (possibly three if the missing 1984 data were available), while Peru had almost continual austerity, a factor of some importance for the labor climate in Peru.

Because what trade unionists will be responding to are the effects of government austerity on their real income and the level of joblessness rather than the cutbacks themselves, data on such income and unem-

Table 8.1 % Change in Central Government Spending,* 1976–1984 (Underlined Figures Indicate Austerity Years)

	1976	1977	1978	1979	1980	1981	1982	1983	1984
Argentina	+05.6	−04.4	+10.3	+12.8	+22.7	−08.3	−29.6	−08.0	−21.3
Brazil	−11.0	+12.9	+11.0	−13.9	+15.6	−00.6	+05.4	−20.7	−01.1
Chile	+18.1	+42.4	+24.7	−02.9	+02.5	+19.4	−12.0	−05.8	−05.1
Colombia	−09.5	+14.3	+11.1	+03.5	+13.8	+04.7	+12.0	−04.9	na
Mexico	−06.6	+17.1	+11.7	+15.5	+18.7	+24.6	+12.2	−17.7	−05.7
Peru	−00.2	−04.6	−13.5	−00.8	+41.1	−00.1	+11.5	−14.7	−08.1
Venezuela	+10.7	+19.8	+04.6	−16.6	+05.7	+37.0	−06.7 /	−15.5 /	−10.6

* Government spending is that for the central government, deflated by the average of the December-to-December consumer and wholesale price indices. Wholesale prices for Brazil, Chile, Peru, and Venezuela refer only to manufacturing. Those for Mexico refer only to producer goods. Consumer prices for Colombia are for blue-collar workers only. Those for Peru reflect the difference between the annual averages.

/ Indicates a broken series where the information on either side of the sign is not strictly comparable.

na Not available.

Sources: Nominal government spending is from the IMF, Government Finance Statistics Yearbook, 1986 (Washington, D.C.: International Monetary Fund, 1986), 103, 223, 227, 257, 273, 728, 947; inflation figures are from ECLA, Economic Survey of Latin America, 1980 (Santiago, Chile: United Nations, 1982), 60, 126, 153, 337, 467, 537; and Economic Survey of Latin America and the Caribbean, 1984 (Santiago, Chile: United Nations, 1986), vol. 1., 81, 148, 176, 272, 428, 556, 608.

ployment during the 1976–1984 period for each of the seven countries are informative (see Table 8.2).

Whether measured by the total number of strikes or the number of strikers involved, strike activity also varied considerably in the period studied (see Table 8.3). Cases where strikes increased in number include Argentina between 1978 and 1984 (presuming that the existing trend continued for the missing years of 1980–1983), Brazil from 1980 to 1984, and Mexico from 1977 to 1982 (with the exception of 1980–1981). In contrast, strike frequency decreased for Chile in the years for which data are available between 1980 and 1984, and for Colombia and Venezuela in the 1980 to 1983 period. The Peruvian pattern is mixed, with strikes falling between 1981 and 1984, but rising steadily in the 1977–1981 period.

The examination of the number of strikers participating may be somewhat more illuminating than the number of strikes alone. Such numbers indicate the general mass support for strikes normally called by the union leadership. In the more recent years—themselves those most susceptible to occurrences of austerity—a general pattern of falling numbers can be discerned for all five cases where such participation figures exist. The number of strikers declined in Chile in the 1981–1984 period, in Mexico 1981–1982, in Peru 1980–1984 (except for 1981–1982), and in Venezuela between 1980 and 1984 (except for the small increase in 1982–1983).

My task is to offer some reasonable explanation for the observed pattern of trade union strike behavior. In what might be called the *economic hypothesis*, the frequency of strikes and number of strikers are seen primarily as a response to what is directly happening in the economy. Here union leadership is seen as pragmatic, calling strikes in times of an improving economy when employers might be more likely to grant wage increases, but yielding to economic realities during times of recession. As Scurrah and Esteves put it (1980: 13–14), "As conditions begin to worsen, existing unions fight to maintain their wage levels but increasing management resistance in the face of falling profits and the fear among workers of losing their jobs tends to lead to a fall-off in the number of strikes." Therefore, years of austerity with lower wages and higher unemployment should correspond to times of declining strike activity.

An alternative attempt at explanation focuses on the *political hypothesis*. In this scenario, union leaders have learned that the role of the state is as critical as that of the private sector. Although the state is usually an important employer in its own right, what is at stake here relates more to the political decision by those in control to use state power to intervene in the income-setting process or to suppress strikes. There are several

Table 8.2 Real Income Index (1976=100)[a] and % Unemployment,[b] 1976–1984

	1976	1977	1978	1979	1980	1981	1982	1983	1984
Argentina									
Income	100.0	98.5	96.7	111.1	124.2	111.1	99.2	128.3	162.8
Unemployment	4.5	2.8	2.8	2.0	2.3	4.5	4.8	4.2	3.8
Brazil									
Income	100.0	102.3	107.3	108.9	110.6	117.2	128.7	117.6	117.5
Unemployment	na	na	6.8	6.4	6.2	7.9	6.3	6.7	7.1
Chile									
Income	100.0	112.9	120.2	130.2	141.9	154.2	154/2	137.8	138.2
Unemployment	16.8	13.2	14.0	13.6	11.8	11.1	22.1	22.2	19.3
Colombia									
Income	100.0	94.4	105.3	112.2	113.0	114.4	118.3	124.2	133.5
Unemployment	10.61	9.0	9.0	8.9	9.7	8.2	9.3	11.8	13.5
Mexico									
Income	100.0	101.6	98.9	97.3	93.1	94.2	94.9	70.6	51.5
Unemployment	6.8	8.3	6.9	5.7	4.5	4.2	4.1	6.8	6.0
Peru									
Income	100.00	83.6	73.0	68.4	76.9	70.3	71.0	66.4	57.4
Unemployment	8.4	9.4	10.4	11.2	10.9	10.4	10.6	13.9	16.4
Venezuela									
Income	100.0	102.6	108.4	107.8	103.4	98.4	91.2	86.9	81.3
Unemployment	6.8	5.5	5.1	5.8	6.6	6.8	7.8	11.1	13.9

a All real income figures are index numbers where 1976 = 100. Those for Argentina and Colombia are based on wages of manual workers in manufacturing; that for Brazil refers to the average wage in all industry; that for Chile is for wages and salaries of workers and employees in the nonagricultural sector, excluding large-scale copper mining and the pulp and paper industries; that for Mexico is for the average wages in manufacturing, except that the figure for 1984 is based only on the January–October period as compared with the same period in 1983; that for Peru is for the wages of the private sector in metropolitan Lima; and that for Venezuela is for the urban worker salaries.

b Unemployment (with the exception of Peru) is for urban areas only. That for Argentina refers to metropolitan Buenos Aires; that for Brazil is the average of Rio de Janeiro, Sao Paulo, Belo Horizonte, Porto Alegre, Salvador, and Recife; that for Colombia is the average of Bogota, Barranquilla, Medellin, and Cali; that for Chile refers to metropolitan Santiago; and that for Mexico is the average of the metropolitan areas of Mexico City, Guadalajara, and Monterrey. That for Peru refers only to nonagricultural unemployment.

na Not available.

Sources: Real income for all countries except Venezuela is from ECLA, Economic Survey of Latin America and the Caribbean, 1984, vol. 1 (Santiago, Chile: United Nations, 1986), 33; that for Venezuela is from Hector Lucena, "Para conjurar la crisis economica," in CLACSO, El sindicalismo latinoamericano en los ochenta (Santiago, Chile: CLASCO, 1986), 183. Unemployment is from ECLA, Economic Survey of Latin America, 1980 (Santiago, Chile: United Nations, 1987), (1872), 44, 106, 136, 198, 450, 520; 1981 (1982), 557; and Balance preliminar de la economia latinoamericana, 1986.

Table 8.3 Strikes and Strikers, 1976–1984

	1976	1977	1978	1979	1980	1981	1982	1983	1984
Argentina									
Strikes	154	100	40	188	261	na	na	na	717
Brazil									
Strikes	na	na	137	224	81	79	126	312	626
Chile									
Strikes[a]	na	na	na	na	67	na	na	41	38
Strikers[b]	na	na	na	na	23	25	2	4	4
Colombia[c]									
Strikes[b]	na	na	266	137	261	219	149	147	147
Strikers[b]	na	na	23	30	31	23	60	54	31
Mexico									
Strikes[b]	654	604	845	936	1432	1174	2600	na	na
Strikers[b,e]	24	13	15	17	43	32	25	na	na
Peru									
Strikes[b]	440	234	364	653	739	871	809	643	509
Strikers[b]	258	1315	1398	841	481	857	572	786	697
Venezuela									
Strikes[b]	171	214	140	145	195	129	102	67	73
Strikers[b]	34	64	25	23	68	30	15	17	12

a The 1980 figures are estimates based on the monthly average of the entire September 1979–December 1980 period.

b,c 1.000s, while Alvaro Delgado (Politica y movimiento obrero, 1970–1983, Bogota: Editorial CEIS, 1984), 122, provides strike figures collected from press reports for the entire 1971–1980 decade, his are consistently lower (and probably less complete) than those cited here by the ILO from the Colombian government.

d These figures represent the total of both federal and local jurisdictions. Figures for 1983 and 1984 (of 230 and 221, respectively) were available only for the federal jurisdiction.

e Federal jurisdiction only.

na Figures are not available.

Sources: Argentine figures come from Elizabeth Jelin, Conflictos laborales en la Argentina, 1973–1976, Estudios Sociales 9, 46, for the first three months of 1976; from Ronaldo Munck et al., Argentina from Anarchism to Peronism (London: Zed, 1987), 229, for the rest of that year through 1980; and from El Bimestre (Buenos Aires), Nov.–Dec. 1984, p. 18, for 1984. Those on Brazil are from Maria Heminia Tavares de Almeida, O sindicalismo brasileiro entre a conservacao e a mudanca (Paper presented at the sixth meeting of the Associaco Nacional de Pos Graduaco e Pesquisa em Cienias Sociais, 1982), for 1978–1979; ILO, Yearbook of Labor Statistics (Geneva: United Nations, 1986), 924, for 1980–1983; and Margaret Keck, Labor and Politics in the Brazilian Transition (Paper presented at the meetings of the Latin American Studies Association, Albuquerque, N.M., 1985), footnote to Table 8, for 1984. All figures on Chile, Colombia, Peru and Venezuela, and for those on local jurisdiction strikes in Mexico from ILO, Yearbook of Labor Statistics, 1986, 924–927; those on federal jurisdiction strikes in Mexico from Ian Roxborough, Unions and Politics in Mexico (Cambridge: Cambridge University Press, 1984), 31, for 1976, and Miguel De La Madrid, Quinto informe de gobierno (Mexico, Government of Mexico, 1987), 243 for 1977–1984.

variants of this political hypothesis. In the populist regime version, the state seeks to expand popular sector earnings so as to build political support for itself and to create sufficient internal economic demand for an import substitution model of industrialization (Urrutia, 1969: 251–252; Wynia, 1978: 45–47). In the conservative bureaucratic-authoritarian version, the state restricts worker political involvement and income so as to attract the foreign investment seen as necessary to an export-oriented model of economic growth (O'Donnell, 1977: 57-58). Under the political hypothesis, what is critical to the number of strikes is the perceived response of the state to such action. Where those running the state have demonstrated their ability to use overwhelming coercion against strikers, such strike activity should decline. But where those in charge are thought to be politically weak and indecisive, strikes may escalate in frequency and scope, up to the point when unemployment reaches a high enough level to undercut such union militancy.

The next two sections, in turn, examine the explanatory power for each of the two hypotheses proposed.

The Economic Hypothesis

As a way of evaluating the economic hypothesis, I propose to compare separately the relationship of both real income and unemployment with each of the two measures of union behavior, the number of strikes and the amount of popular strike support in the 1976–1984 period. The ordinal-level statistic gamma will be used in all four cases. To facilitate the use of this statistic (and to maximize the number of cases in each table cell), each of the variables has been collapsed into the three categories of low, medium, and high. The procedure for such transformations has been to measure the range of each variable and then categorize the data on the basis of the distribution of cases within that range. Again, falling income for workers and rising unemployment are hypothesized, at least in part, as the direct result of the government austerity programs so common to Latin America in the early 1980s. The expectation is that strike behavior should be *positively* correlated with income (falling income should mean fewer strikes and strikers, and the converse should be true as well) and *negatively* correlated with unemployment (more unemployment leads to less strike activity by the unions).

I have addressed this issue in Tables 8.4 and 8.5. In Table 8.4, the weakness (+.06 and +.07) of the coefficients suggests that *no clear statistical relation exists between income and strikes* in the seven countries examined. Closer examination of the data for individual cases reveals a

Table 8.4   Real Income and Strike Behavior, 1976–1984

	Number of Strikes[a]			Number of Strikers[b]		
	Low	Medium	High	Low	Medium	High
Income						
Low	14	5	6	9	6	2
Medium	7	2	2	3	0	3
High	6	2	4	8	2	4

[a] Gamma = +.06.
[b] Gamma = +.07.
Source: Tables 8.2 and 8.3

Table 8.5   Unemployment and Strike Behavior, 1976–1984

	Number of Strikes[a]			Number of Strikers[b]		
	Low	Medium	High	Low	Medium	High
Unemployment						
Low	14	5	10	11	4	8
Medium	5	1	2	2	2	1
High	8	2	0	7	2	0

[a] Gamma = −.48.
[b] Gamma = −.44.
Source: Tables 8.2 and 8.3

contradictory pattern: Using correlational coefficients, the variables are positively related for Argentina, Chile, and Venezuela, negatively linked for Peru and Mexico, inconsistent for Colombia, and statistically insignificant for Brazil. In contrast, the reasonably strong gammas (−.48 and −.44) in Table 8.5 between unemployment and strike activity suggests that the opposite is true here. As other researchers have found, *rising joblessness clearly does have a measurable effect in discouraging strikes.* Thus the economic hypothesis as it relates to the effect of unemployment merits consideration.

The Political Hypothesis

As outlined earlier, the central issue here is union leaders' perception of state responses to future strikes. Where there is a high likelihood of coercion, prudent leaders may avoid calling strikes for fear of undermining their own credibility. The possibility of coercion's being used against strikers, in turn, relates to the nature of the regime in power.[1]

Four regime types are listed, ranked from low to high in terms of a proclivity toward violence:

1. Populist democratic
2. Conservative democratic
3. Inclusionary or populist authoritarian
4. Exclusionary or bureaucratic authoritarian

The term *populist* is meant to suggest a political linkage between key regime actors and lower status groups, usually including organized labor, where favorable policy treatment is used as an inducement for political support from the popular sector. In the case of nonpopulist regime types, such a sense of mutual interest is absent; instead of being seen as a potential ally, organized elements of the popular sector, such as unions, are viewed as a probable enemy. The democratic/authoritarian dichotomy is also relevant where public officials in a democratic environment are more likely to be constrained in their behavior toward the general public by formal constitutional limitations and the realities of electoral politics.

Although the identification of a particular regime type is rather subjective, given the ambiguity of regime categories, Table 8.6 represents my effort to assign each of the seven countries to one of the four regime types during the overall 1976–1984 period.

An additional factor related to the likelihood of regime-generated violence against strikers might be called the coercion capability of any regime. Such capability is seen as derived from the degree of internal unity each regime possesses. This is a measure of the ratio of the regime's support to the opposition the regime encounters from key interest groups. Even a regime prone to the use of coercion may be unable to effectively respond to a challenge to its authority in cases in which the regime is thoroughly fragmented. Such internally weak regimes are likely to be forced to make concessions in cases in which they are unable to mobilize sufficient violence to intimidate their opponents. The ultimate concession, of course, may be the yielding of power and the end of the regime.

In the absence of a reliable index of regime coercion that could be applied to the labor movement in individual countries,[2] I constructed one from the data available on each of the seven cases studied here. Several considerations influenced this process. First, where such new indices might run from no coercion to strong coercion on a one-to-seven scale, a presumption was made that each of the regime types would differ from the others due to its basic nature. Except when in advanced decomposition prior to their replacement, populist democracies

Table 8.6   Political Regimes in Seven Countries, 1976-1984

Regime Type	Government
Populist democratic	
Argentina[a] 1983-1984	Alfonsin
Venezuela 1976-1984	Perez, Herrera Campins, Lusinchi
Conservative democratic	
Colombia 1976-1984	Lopez Michelsen, Turbay, Betancur
Peru 1976-1984	Belaunde
Populist authoritarian	
Mexico[a] 1976-1984	Echeverria, Lopez Portillo, de la Madrid
Peru 1976-1983	Morales Bermudez
Bureaucratic authoritarian	
Argentina 1976-1983	Videla, Viola, Galtieri, Bignone
Brazil 1976-1984	Geisel, Figueiredo
Chile 1976-1984	Pinochet

[a] Cases of special difficulty in categorization include an example of populist democracy--the Alfonsin government in Argentina--given the tenuousness of links to organized labor, and several cases of inclusionary authoritarianism--Morales Bermudez in Peru, and Lopez Portillo and de la Madrid in Mexico--given the highly conservative nature of the most of the policies encountered.

were assumed to lie toward the low coercion end of the scale (1–4); bureaucratic authoritarian regimes were assumed to fall toward the high end (4–7); and both conservative democracies and populist authoritarian regimes were assumed to fall in the middle of the scale (3–5). A major regime crisis initially might increase the coercion score, while a decision to yield power, as with a shift from an authoritarian to a democratic form via elections, might lower the level of coercion below the normal range for a specific regime type. How do the country cases fit these expectations?

The three cases of the military-run bureaucratic authoritarian regimes— Argentina under Videla, Brazil under Ernesto Geisel and João Baptista de Oliveira Figueiredo, and Chile under Augusto Pinochet—are the easiest with which to begin, given that each openly admitted its desire to subordinate organized labor to government wishes. In seizing power in 1976, the Argentine military suspended the right to strike, made work slowdowns or industrial sabotage punishable by lengthy jail terms, and arrested and murdered several hundred labor leaders (Gallitelli and Thompson, 1982: 145–157). Through a chronological analysis of union leader arrests, one may determine that the number of arrests declined from the initial high of 268 in 1976, to 69 in 1977, 7 in 1978, 10 in 1979, and none thereafter (see Fernández, 1985: 113–134). The trend of declining coercion is obvious.

After 1964, the Brazilian generals operated in a situation where legal strikes were virtually impossible. Beginning in the late 1960s, wages were determined by the government through a formula linked to previous inflation and productivity (Erickson, 1977: 158–159; 163–164). The use of torture and deaths occurring under interrogation became routine (Dassin, 1986: 53). When he came to power in 1974, Geisel introduced an element of political toleration. In contrast to earlier military presidents, he greeted the illegal strikes of 1977–1978 with hesitation rather than open repression. His 1979 successor, Figueiredo, however, allowed various military hard-liners a free hand in dealing with labor protests. Figueiredo's 1979 intervention directed at the important metal workers' union, which had sparked the earlier strikes and the arrest of its leaders, represented a temporary return to the use of force meant to intimidate others (Baloyra, 1986: 30, 43; Selcher, 1986: 80).

In Chile, from the time it seized power in 1973, the Pinochet government severely repressed labor and other groups associated with the Left. Collective bargaining was suspended, job tenure provisions diluted, and existing wage agreements, including those for the indexation of earnings against inflation, placed in abeyance (Barrera and Valenzuela, 1986: 236). Only with the Labor Plan of 1979 were some union rights reintroduced. Collective bargaining could occur, but only at the company level, a maximum of sixty days was set for any strike, and the use of strike breakers was legalized (Ruiz-Tagle, 1987: 12–14).

Each of these three regimes encountered increased opposition in the face of economic difficulties. In Argentina, the 1980 financial crisis led to the severe devaluations of 1981, increased factionalism among the military, and a rapid shift of governments. The more frequent strikes continued to be repressed but with less savagery than before. The failure of the Malvinas/Falklands adventure of 1982, however, made the military's now-open divisions unbridgeable except through the decision to relinquish power to civilians at the end of 1983 (Epstein, 1987: 24). In contrast with Argentina, the Brazilian transition to democracy was much more gradual and much less the product of internal political collapse. The 1974 political opening led to the gradual displacement from power of the military hard-liners. In the face of worsening inflation of the 1970s, the huge government electoral defeat for key state governorships in 1982, the post-1982 debt crisis, and the intensity of the 1984 popular campaign for direct presidential elections, the fragmented officer corps decided to permit the 1985 transfer of power to acceptable conservative civilians (Skidmore, 1983; De Góes and Camargo, 1984; Selcher, 1986).

The Chilean case has been different due to the unity derived from Pinochet's personalistic rule and the absence of a single civilian alternative. Although the 1982 economic crisis was as severe as elsewhere, the government was able to make temporary minor concessions to the mass protests of 1983, only to resort to more force as the opposition divided and lost momentum a year later. In terms of organized labor, the copper strike and the general strike of 1983 were met with a return to harsh repression; the 1984 general strike led to the reimposition of the state of siege and a partial resurgence of death squad activity (Ruiz-Tagle, 1987: 25, 27; Brown, 1985: 57–59). As had been true in the mid-1970s, the new economic crisis brought a return to massive unemployment, this time officially in the area of some 20 percent of the work force. Joblessness of this magnitude was far greater than anything experienced in either Argentina or Brazil (ECLA, 1986: 16). Unlike those countries, the Chilean military has been able to maintain itself in power.

The treatment of organized labor under popular authoritarian and conservative democratic regimes has been less visibly brutal and has focused on efforts to induce the unions to participate in governmental structures, in which worker demands could be diluted and radicals co-opted. Such institutionalization has gone farthest in Mexico where ties developed over the last forty years between the single-party authoritarian regime and a conservative national union bureaucracy able to secure membership cooperation by threats to withhold welfare services, to expel individuals who in the context of "closed shop" rules would lose their jobs, or to use occasional violence against dissidents (Trejo, 1979: 130–131; Carr, 1983: 97–99).[3] Even here, the old guard union leaders saw their once monolithic control erode in the 1970s with the emergence of independent unions initially encouraged by the populist Luis Echeverría administration as part of its democratic opening (Trejo, 1979: 135–143; Roxborough, 1984: 32–33). With the twin economic crises of 1976 and 1982 and the austerity policies introduced by the José López Portillo and Miguel de la Madrid governments, labor was forced to accept falling real wages (Reyna, 1979: 394). Whereas the independent unions have continued their protests, if much less visibly than before, less sympathetic governments since 1976 have allowed traditional union leaders to re-capture some of the political initiative with periodic rhetorical denunciations of official policy (Carr, 1983: 101, 106–107, 113–115).

Similar efforts to control labor in Peru by the 1968–1975 Juan Velasco Alvarado reformist military government failed because of the resistance of an already highly politicized work force, the highly limited economic resources available to win worker support, and the hesitance of military leaders to use sufficient coercion to replace the ideologically pluralist existing trade unions with a single government-run body (Stepan, 1978: 293, 303–304). The much more probusiness and antilabor Francisco Morales Bermúdez military presidency alienated the trade unions through its efforts to use emergency powers to limit strike activity including the general strikes of 1976 and 1977, its dilution of the job security law, and its weakening of the industrial communities, which had provided for future possible worker ownership of major companies (Sulmont, 1980: 205; Scurrah and Esteves, 1980: 14). The increasingly discredited military ultimately decided to hold elections to allow a democratic transition. Attempts by the conservative Fernando Belaúnde Terry administration elected in 1980 to talk the workers into accepting nominal wage hikes less than inflation were rejected by the trade unions. The new wave of general strikes, declared illegal, would only be undercut by the sharp rise in unemployment noticeable after 1982 in the key industrial sector (Yepes and Bernardo, 1985: 33–35; Parodi, 1986: 330–332). Belaúnde's presidency would also be marked by an increasing climate of general human rights violations linked to the Sendero Luminoso guerrilla insurgency (Brown, 1985: 215–218).

In Colombia, the López Michelsen government moved away from the attempts of earlier governments to control wage disputes through compulsory binding arbitration and deals with the more orthodox unions toward efforts at involving all of the major labor confederations, including the newly recognized Communists, in tripartite negotiations with the state and private business (Moncayo and Rojas, 1978: 238, 244, 274). The failure of the unions to accept the lower wages that had been in evidence since 1971 and a resulting government intransigence led to the temporary coalescence of the highly fractionalized labor movement in support of the 1977 general strike, or *paro cívico*. Having failed to persuade the traditional unions to defect or to intimidate the strikers, the government used repression to crush the strike (Gómez et al., 1986: 126). The resort to force reflected the growing influence of the Colombian military that would culminate in a virtual ultimatum to López in December 1977 and the resulting introduction of the highly restrictive Security Statute by the next administration (Gabriel Turbay's) in September 1978 (Leal, 1984: 261, 267; Valencia, 1984: 135–136). Turbay only deigned to negotiate with the unions when he was faced with the threat of a new general strike in 1981 (Gómez et al., 1986: 65); although earlier governments had made extensive use of the state of siege,[4] his position seemed unduly harsh in its attacks on dissidents (Gallón, 1986: 129–150; Brown, 1985: 227–228).

The populist-tinged Belisario Betancur government, elected in 1982, raised the possibility of national reconciliation and social reform but ultimately was unable to deliver on many of its promises, given the tenacity of its opponents in the military and elsewhere and the growing seriousness of the economic recession. During the early 1980s, the unions were to suffer a massive dropout of members due to unemployment, which became severe from 1983 onward (Gómez et al., 1986: 109, 145).

In contrast with the occasional use of coercion in both popular authoritarian and conservative democratic regimes, the populist variant of democracy has generally avoided such excesses. The Alfonsín government in Argentina initially sought union electoral reform that would have given the non-Peronist minority some representation at the leadership level. When that strategy was blocked in the congress, the government turned to the more conventional policy of tripartite negotiations with labor and business, but enjoyed little success. From the point of view of state control or official use of coercion, Alfonsín exercised little direct restraint on the unions other than his retention of the power to set wage limits, inherited from his military predecessors. Despite the serious condition of the economy in 1984, the new populist government openly supported the recuperation of wages that had suffered severely under authoritarian rule (Epstein, 1987: 17, 19).

Recent populist Venezuelan governments utilized a highly co-optive structure, where labor leaders agreed to accept a high level of state control over the use of the strike in return for favorable economic treatment and job security. Most worker complaints have been settled through the official mediation process, short of a work stoppage; binding arbitration is the rule for the crucial petroleum industry. Where strikes have occurred, most have been officially declared illegal. This theoretically permits workers to be dismissed and sanctions the official use of force. Nevertheless, such draconian actions seem to have been imposed rarely (Davis and Coleman, 1987: 11–12, 20). The typical short duration of most illegal strikes as well as the close union connections with the two political parties that have alternated in power may explain such government moderation. With the economic crisis in effect since the late 1970s, real wages have fallen sharply and job loss has risen to high levels. Union efforts to work through the parties to obtain price controls have had minimal effect on the deteriorating standard of living (McCoy, 1986: 25; Lucena, 1986: 184–185).

The foregoing discussions of coercion under varying political regimes in each of the seven countries under study have been meant to provide information that allows construction of a series of seven-point scales to be used to test the political hypothesis linking the degree of government control over labor to the level of strike activity (see Table 8.7). Although the judgments used in such scales embody a considerable subjective element, my opinion is that the scoring should provide a reasonable

Table 8.7 Official Control,[a] 1976-1984

	1976	1977	1978	1979	1980	1981	1982	1983	1984
Argentina	7	7	6	6	5	5	4	3	2
Brazil	5	5	4	4	5	4	3	3	3
Chile	6	6	6	5	4	4	4	5	5
Colombia	4	5	5	4	4	4	4	3	5
Mexico	4	5	5	4	4	4	5	5	5
Peru	5	4	3	3	3	3	3	4	4
Venezuela	2	2	2	2	2	2	2	2	2

a Official Control refers to the usage of various forms of government or government-linked repression as it affects union members, with scores falling between a maximum of 7 and a minimum of 1.
Sources: Control scores represent this author's evaluation as based on the sources cited in this chapter.

Table 8.8   Official Control and Strike Behavior, 1976-1984

	Number of Strikes[a]			Number of Strikers[b]		
	Low	Medium	High	Low	Medium	High
Control						
Low	7	5	8	9	3	4
Medium	9	4	2	5	4	5
High	11	0	2	6	1	0

[a] Gamma = −.63.
[b] Gamma = −.17.
Source: Tables 8.2 and 8.3

measure of changes within individual countries over time, as well as comparisons among each of the different nations.

Again, the political hypothesis to be tested suggests that strike activity should be *negatively* correlated with the degree of control. That is, the more control—as indicated by a higher score—the fewer the number of strikes and strikers. I have followed the same procedure in Table 8.8, recategorizing the data as used with Table 8.4 and 8.5 in order to permit the use of the gamma statistic to measure the statistical association between "control" and the number of strikes and strikers. The divisions of the control variable, however, occur between 2 to 3 for the low category, 4 for medium, and 5 to 7 for high, so as to produce a reasonable number of cases in each table cell.

Even with the obvious crudeness of the measure, the strong (−.63) gamma suggests that *knowledge of what is here referred to as "official control"*—itself based on the regime type and the efforts by those running the state to restrict trade union behavior—*seems a reasonable predictor of the number of strikes* in the seven case countries. The measure is a much more weakly correlated (−.17) with *the number of strikers* participating in those strikes. Here the political variable can be strengthened by bringing in the additional effect of unemployment. By controlling for or only using the years of medium and high unemployment, there is an increase in the gamma measure to a moderately strong −.39.

Conclusion

Two explanations have been offered for the pattern of trade union strike behavior in seven Latin American countries between 1976 and 1984. Whereas the *economic hypothesis* links strikes to falling real wages and rising unemployment (the latter a result of austerity), the *political hy-*

pothesis focuses on the effect of variations in regime type and official control of the unions by states needing to cut expenditures. The examination of the data provided suggests that the ideal predictor of the frequency of strikes and the level of militancy measured by the number of strikers is some measure of such political control strengthened by the addition of the effects of the more sensitive aspect of the economic variable, unemployment (for discussions of the economic versus the political, see Torre, 1974: 18–19; Zapata, 1977: 16–17).

If a case can be made to include the political in the analysis of union behavior, a major problem encountered has been the relative absence of available comparative measures of an acceptable reliability. Official control, the measure I have used here, is still a crude indicator of this important political variable.

Notes

1. For a detailed study of the link between regime type and austerity policy in Argentina, see Epstein, forthcoming.

2. The Freedom House annual surveys published in *Freedom at Issue*, especially those dealing with civil rights, are the only alternative that was available here. Given their presumed conservative bias, I discounted them (Méndez, 1987).

3. Mexican labor leaders did gain credibility from the rank and file as a result of the continuous rise in wages in the 1946–1975 period (Roxborough, 1984: 27).

4. The use of the state of siege was justified by various Colombian governments by citing the continuous existence of a limited guerrilla insurrection.

References

Baloyra, Enrique. "From Moment to Moment: the Political Transition in Brazil, 1977–1981," in Wayne Selcher (ed.), *Political Liberalization in Brazil*, Boulder, Colorado: Westview Press, 9–54, 1986.

Barrera, Manuel, and J. Samuel Valenzuela. "The Development of Labor Movement Opposition to the Military Regime," in J. Samuel and Arturo Valenzuela (eds.), *Military Rule in Chile*, Baltimore: Johns Hopkins University Press, 1986.

Brown, Cynthia (ed.). *With Friends Like These: The Americas Watch Report on Human Rights and U.S. Policy in Latin America*, New York: Pantheon, 1985.

Carr, Barry. "The Mexican Economic Debacle and the Labor Movement," in Donald Wyman (ed.), *Mexico's Economic Crisis*, La Jolla, California: Monograph Series #12, Center for U.S.-Mexican Studies, University of California, San Diego, 91–116, 1983.

Joan Dassin (ed.). *Torture in Brazil*, New York: Vintage, 1986.

Davis, Charles, and Kenneth Coleman. "Political Control of Organized Labor in a Semi-consociational Democracy: the Case of Venezuela," in Edward

Epstein (ed.), *Trade Unions and the State in Latin America*, Winchester, Massachusetts: Allen and Unwin, 1987.

de la Madrid, Miguel. *Quinto Informe de Gobierno*, México, D.F.: Government of Mexico, 1987.

Delgado, Alvaro. *Política y Movimiento Obrero, 1970–1983*, Bogotá: Editorial CEIS, 1984.

De Góes, Walder, and Aspásia Camargo. *O Drama da Sucessão*, Rio de Janeiro: Nova Fronteira, 1984.

Dornbusch, Rudiger. *Dollars, Debts, and Deficits*, Cambridge, Massachusetts: MIT Press, 1986.

ECLA. *Economic Survey of Latin America, 1980*, Santiago, Chile: United Nations, 1982.

——— . *Economic Survey of Latin America and the Caribbean, 1984*, Santiago, Chile: United Nations, 1986.

——— . *Balance Preliminar de la Economía Latinoamericana, 1986*, Santiago, Chile: United Nations, 1987.

Epstein, Edward. "Labor Populism and Hegemonic Crisis in Argentina," in Edward Epstein (ed.), *Trade Unions and the State in Latin America*, Winchester, Massachusetts: Allen & Unwin, 1987.

——— . "What Difference Does Regime Type Make? Economic Austerity Programs in Argentina," in Howard Handelman and Werner Baer (eds.), *Paying the Costs of Austerity in Latin America*, Boulder, Colorado: Westview Press, forthcoming.

Erickson, Kenneth. *The Brazilian Corporative State and Working Class Politics*, Berkeley, California: University of California Press, 1977.

Fernández, Arturo. *Las Prácticas Sociales del Sindicalismo (1976–1982)*, Buenos Aires: CEAL, 1985.

Gallitelli, Bernardo, and Andrés Thompson. "La Situación Laboral en la Argentina del Proceso, 1976–1981," pp. 141–190 in Bernardo Gallitelli and Andrés Thompson, *Sindicalismo y Régimenes Militares en Argentina y Chile*, Amsterdam: CEDLA, 1982.

Gallón, Gustavo. *Quince Años de Estado de Sitio en Colombia*, Bogotá: FEDE-SARROLLO and CERC, 1986.

Gómez, Hernando, Rocío Londoño, and Guillermo Perry. *Sindicalismo y política económica*, Bogotá: FEDESARROLLO AND CERC, 1986.

ILO. *Yearbook of Labor Statistics*, Geneva: United Nations, 1986.

IMF. *Government Finance Statistics Yearbook*, Washington, D.C.: International Monetary Fund, 1986.

Jelin, Elizabeth. "Conflictos Laborales en la Argentina, 1973–1976," *Estudios Sociales*, (9), Buenos Aires: CEDES, 1977.

Keck, Margaret. "Labor and Politics in the Brazilian Transition," paper presented at the meetings of the Latin American Studies Association (LASA), Albuquerque, New Mexico, 1985.

Kim, Kwan, and David Ruccio (eds.). *Debt and Development in Latin America*, Notre Dame, Indiana: University of Notre Dame Press, 1985.

188   Edward C. Epstein

Lucena, Héctor. "Para Conjurar la Crisis Económica," pp. 181–188 in CLACSO, *El Sindicalismo Latinoamericano en los Ochenta*, Santiago, Chile: CLACSO, 1986.

Leal, Francisco. *Estado y Política en Colombia*, Bogotá: Siglo XXI and CERC, 1984.

McCoy, Jennifer. "The Politics of Adjustment: Labor and the Venezuelan Debt Crisis," paper presented at the meetings of the Latin American Studies Association (LASA), Boston, Massachusetts, 1986.

Méndez, Juan. Telephone communication with director of Washington, D.C., office of Americas Watch, the human rights group, November 1987.

Moncayo, Victor, and Fernando Rojas. *Luchas Obreras y Política Laboral en Colombia*, Bogotá: la Carreta, 1978.

Munck, Ronaldo, Ricardo Falcon, and Bernardo Gallitelli. *Argentina from Anarchism to Peronism: Workers, Unions and Politics, 1855–1985*, London: Zed Books, 1987.

O'Donnell, Guillermo. "Corporatism and the Question of the State," pp. 47–88 in James Malloy (ed.), *Authoritarianism and Corporatism in Latin America*, Pittsburgh: University of Pittsburgh Press, 1977.

Parodi, Jorge. "La Desmobilización del Sindicalismo Industrial Peruano en el Segundo Belaundismo," pp. 325–336 in CLACSO, *El Sindicalismo Latinoamericano en las Ochenta*, Santiago, Chile: CLACSO, 1986.

Reyna, José Luis. "El Movimiento Obrero en una Situación de Crisis: México, 1976–1978," *Foro Internacional* (75), January–March: pp. 390–401, 1979.

Roxborough, Ian. *Unions and Politics in Mexico*, Cambridge: Cambridge University Press, 1984.

Ruiz-Tagle, Jaime. "Trade Unions and the State under the Chilean Military Regime," in Edward Epstein (ed.), *Trade Unions and the State in Latin America*, Winchester, Massachusetts: Allen & Unwin, 1987.

Scurrah, Martin, and Guadalupe Esteves. "The Peruvian Organized Working Class After the Military Revolution," paper presented at the meetings of the Latin American Studies Association, Bloomington, Indiana, 1980.

Selcher, Wayne. "Contradictions, Dilemmas and Actors in Brazil's *Abertura*, 1979–1985," pp. 55–96 in Wayne Selcher (ed.), *Political Liberalization in Brazil*, Boulder, Colorado: Westview Press, 1986.

Skidmore, Thomas. "From *Descompressão* to *Abertura*: The Decline of Brazilian Authoritarianism, 1973–1982," paper presented at the Yale Conference on "Democratizing Brazil?" New Haven, Connecticut, 1983.

Stepan, Alfred. *The State and Society: Peru in Comparative Perspective*. Princeton, New Jersey: Princeton University Press, 1978.

Sulmont, Denis. *El Movimiento Obrero Peruano (1890–1980)*, Lima: La Tarea, 1980.

Taavares de Almeida, Maria Hermínia. "O Sindicalismo Brasileiro entre a Conservacão e a Mudançao", paper presented at the VI meeting of the Associação Nacional de Pos Graduação e Pesquisa em Ciéncias Sociais, 1982.

Thorp, Rosemary, and Lawrence Whitehead (eds.). *Latin American Debt and the Adjustment Crisis*, London: Macmillan, 1987.

Torre, Juan Carlos. "El Proceso Político Interno de los Sindicatos en Argentina," Documento de Trabajo (89), Instituto Torcuato de Tella, Buenos Aires, Argentina, 1974.

Trejo, Raúl. "El Movimiento Obrero," pp. 121–151 in Pablo Gonaález Casanova and Enrique Florescano (eds.), *México, Hoy*, México, D.F.: Siglo XXI, 1979.

Urrutia, Miguel. *The Development of the Colombian Labor Movement*, New Haven, Connecticut: Yale University Press, 1969.

Valencia, Enrique. "El Movimiento Obrero Colombiano," pp. 9–151 in Pablo González Casanova (ed.), *Historia del Movimiento Obrero in América Latina*, volume 3, México, D.F.: Siglo XXI, 1984.

Wionczek, Miguel (ed.), with Luciano Tomassini. *Politics and Economics of External Debt Crisis: The Latin American Experience*, Boulder, Colorado: Westview Press, 1985.

Wynia, Gary. *Argentina in the Postwar Era*, Albuquerque, New Mexico: University of New Mexico Press, 1978.

Yepes, Isabel, and Jorge Bernardo. *La Sindicalización en el Perú*, Lima: Pontifica Universidad Católica, 1985.

Zapata, Francisco. "Strikes and Political Systems in Latin America," paper presented at the meetings of the Latin American Studies Association (LASA), Houston, Texas, 1977.

9

The Response to Austerity: Political and Economic Strategies of Mexico's Rural Poor

Merilee S. Grindle

Periodically throughout history, peasants have acted collectively and violently to alter the economic and political conditions that affect their daily lives.[1] Similarly, peasants have had frequent recourse to an array of protest activities short of open rebellion—sabotage, passivity, and dissimulation (see Scott, 1985). In addition to rebellion and more subtle forms of resistance, rural inhabitants have also attempted to alter their relationships to larger economic and political institutions through such conventional activities as organizing to represent rural interests, joining political parties, and voting. Far from being passive victims of the expansion of capitalism or the emergence of urban and industrial dominance, peasants have helped shape these processes by organizing, protesting, and rebelling.[2] In doing so, they have often carved out niches of persistence and adaptation in societies dominated by more powerful classes and interests.

In Mexico, the history of peasant protest and rebellion is extensive. In the twentieth century, this history includes the dramatic Zapatista uprising that played a prominent part in the Revolution of 1910 (see especially Womack, 1968). In the 1920s, the Cristero Rebellion pitted peasant-based armies against a secularizing and centralizing state apparatus (Meyer, 1976; Quirk, 1973), and in the 1930s, local groups organized massively to demand land and to support the agrarian reform initiated under the leadership of President Lázaro Cárdenas (Craig, 1983; Ronfeldt, 1973; Warman, 1980). Peasants were also stimulated to organize in the early 1970s to demand greater access to land and state resources (see Sanderson, 1981). In the late 1970s, peasant protests called attention to the depredation of land and ecology caused by the national oil company's rapid expansion and its trampling of local and communal rights (Alcántara Ferrer, 1986). In the 1980s, peasants joined popular protest movements against inflation and declining standards of living and mobilized to protest against prices set by the government for inputs and crops (Fox, 1987; Carr, 1986; Prieto, 1985–1986). In these cases, mobilization emerged during periods of crisis in the rural economy— either regionally or nationally—when peasants were pressed by larger economic forces and particularly when access to land was at issue.

Given this history of claims against the state and the institutions of capitalist society, it could be predicted that under conditions of extreme economic crisis in the 1980s, rural Mexico would again be characterized by mobilization and protest. The systemwide economic crisis of the 1980s has been called the worst in modern history and its effects are noted to be particularly egregious for the urban and rural poor (see World Bank, 1986; Altimir, 1984; Bortz, 1986).[3] Despite expectations of widespread rural mobilization, the predominant pattern in the countryside after the onset of the severe economic crisis of 1982 was not community or regional organization and protest (although some such activities did occur), but rather a series of adaptations within rural households to ensure economic survival. Moreover, in responding to the crisis, peasant households did not invent new ways of dealing with hardship. Rather, they redoubled long-standing efforts to manage and diversify complex economics of households that were increasingly pinched by the effects of inflation and austerity.

Economic responses to crisis occur within the peasant household, not in the public arena, and are often overlooked in the search for more dramatic evidence of collective political protest. Household-based strategies for economic survival attest to the increasingly multifaceted ways the rural poor are linked to regional, national, and international economies as producers, consumers, and wage earners. Efforts to cope with the crisis have involved household-level strategies to mobilize economic linkages at regional, national, and international levels. Where political mobilization has occurred, it has also reflected the increasingly complex nature of economic interaction of peasant households beyond the village. Collective protest has emerged less over traditional issues of access to land and more over issues that affect the rural poor as producers, consumers, wage earners, and citizens. Thus, the basis for collective action among the rural poor in the past—access to land—has become attenuated by the changing nature of the peasant household economy. This chapter indicates that more complex economic relations and greater penetration of state-sponsored activities have increased the ways of adapting to hardship within peasant communities, have increased the dependence of rural areas on national and international economies, and have reduced collective demand making around the issues that have traditionally defined peasant protest activities.

Crisis, Austerity, and the Poor

On August 5, 1982, Mexico closed its foreign exchange market. Later in the same month, the country formally acknowledged that it was unable to service its foreign debt of more than U.S. $62 billion (see Trebat, 1985). Expansionary government spending in the 1970s—encouraged to tremendous proportions during the oil boom years of 1977–1981—falling oil prices, and rising international interest rates were significant factors in precipitating this situation (see Wyman, 1983: 12; Trebat, 1985).[4] But the debt crisis only served to unmask a crisis of major proportions affecting the economy. In the years after 1982, analysts became convinced that the problem was not a momentary "blip" in the country's impressive postwar economic growth, but a crisis deeply embedded in the structure of economic development that could only be addressed over the long term (see Cornelius, 1986).

A number of indicators attest to the severity of the crisis—a situation made worse by a devastating earthquake in 1985 and a precipitous further decline in international oil prices in 1986. Growth in the economy, which had averaged 8–9 percent a year between 1987 and 1981, declined by 0.5 percent in 1982 and 5.3 percent in 1983. The GDP recovered to a positive 3.7 percent growth rate in 1984, slowed to 2.7 percent in 1985, and was estimated to have declined by 4 percent in 1986 (see Table 9.1). Total investment declined by 36 percent between 1981 and 1984 (World Bank, 1986: 5). Export earnings fell steadily and capital flight—reported to have reached U.S $55 billion between 1979 and 1982—continued apace (World Bank, 1986: 64). Mexico's external debt rose to over $102.6 billion in 1986, with interest payments due of $8.6 billion for that year, some 37.5 percent of total export earnings (SCHP, 1986). Oil exports dropped from 16.5 billion dollars in 1982 to $6.3 billion in 1986 (SCHP, 1986). Moreover, inflation refused to diminish in accordance with government policy objectives, reaching over 100 percent by 1986. The peso continued to drop against the dollar from 30.5 in 1981 to 1,129.6 in 1986 (IMF, 1987b: 348).

The impact of macroeconomic conditions on Mexico's population was extensive. Although the middle class grew significantly during the 1970s and the oil boom years, the majority of the county's population remained poor. And although the middle class witnessed a severe deterioration in its standard of living, the poor—on the margins of subsistence to begin with—found mere survival increasingly difficult to ensure (see

Table 9.1 Growth of GDP, Public Sector Deficit, Employment, and
Labor Force, 1982-1987

	1982	1983	1984	1985	1986[a]	1987[b]
Real GDP growth	-0.5	-5.3	3.7	2.7	-4.0	3.5
Overall public sector deficit % of GDP	17.1	8.9	7.7	8.4	15.8	12.3
Employment growth rate	2.0	-3.9	2.6	2.5	-1.5	3.9
Labor force growth rate	3.5	3.6	3.6	3.6	3.6	3.6

[a] Estimates.
[b] Projections.
Source: SCHP (Secretaria de Hacienda y Credito Publico), Mexico's
Development Financing Strategy (Mexico City, 1986).

World Bank, 1986; Altimir, 1984). Real wages fell precipitously in the
years after 1982, dropping 9.6 percent in 1982, 18 percent the following
year, a further 7.4 percent in 1984, and 1.3 percent in 1985 (IDB, 1986:
314). In agriculture, the minimum wage declined 31.3 percent in real
terms between 1981 and 1983 (World Bank, 1986: 16–17). Official
unemployment rates rose to 12.3 percent in 1986, with underemployment
estimated to affect 45 percent of those working (LAM, 1987: 38). According
to a World Bank study,

> [T]he labor force increased from 22.7 million in 1981 to 24.7 million in
> 1984, yet gainful employment remained at 20.1 million. . . . Not a single
> job was created during these years (on a net basis), while the labor force
> kept on increasing by 2.8 percent each year. Consequently, open unem-
> ployment went up from 2.7 million in 1981 to 4.6 million in 1984. Open
> unemployment was particularly acute among young people (World Bank,
> 1986: 11).

The expansion of the informal sector undoubtedly absorbed a considerable
amount of otherwise idle labor, as suggested by the fact that wage
earners, who composed 83 percent of those employed in 1982, accounted
for only 76 percent in 1985. Simultaneously, those who claimed to be
self-employed or unpaid family labor increased from 17 to 24 percent
of those considered employed (World Bank, 1986: 14). Government
projections for 1990 indicate that 7.8 million out of a total of 28 million

economically active people would find jobs in the informal sector (Nacional Financiera, 1986: 27). Fragmentary evidence on the nutritional impact of the crisis indicated that the composition of the diet of the average person has been altered and that the urban poor have suffered declines in their level of food intake (World Bank, 1986: 22–23).

Government policies aimed at stabilizing the economy have been tough. Under the first of a series of agreements with the International Monetary Fund, the Mexican government agreed in November 1982 to a program of fiscal austerity considered necessary by the international bankers to deal with the mounting rate of inflation, to secure foreign exchange activities, and to pay the interest on the debt. In consequence, the budget deficit of 14.6 percent of GDP in 1982 was forced down to 7.6 percent in 1983, 6.7 percent in 1984, and 7.4 percent in 1985 (IDB, 1986: 314). Total expenditures of the federal government were cut back by 10.5 percent in 1983 and by an additional 5.3 percent in 1984 (see Table 9.2). Budgetary sectors most affected by these stringency measures were communications and transportation, agriculture and natural resources, education and culture, and administration. Expenditures for public works fell by 50 percent in 1983 alone. The government also committed itself to cutting back subsidies on a number of basic consumer goods. The price for most of the products consumed regularly by low-income people rose precipitously in relation to the minimum wage (see Table 9.3). Undeniably, the crisis has taken a significant toll in the living standards of the vast majority of Mexicans and has required the poor to struggle even harder to ensure basic household subsistence. In rural areas the crisis forced many to increase their efforts to diversify sources of income and to become significantly more dependent on remittances from labor migration.

Crisis and Austerity in Rural Mexico

Life has never been easy for Mexico's rural poor. Even before the economic crisis of the 1980s, many scholars had come to the conclusion that conditions in rural areas were growing ever more difficult because of population pressure on the land, a poor and declining natural resource base, and discriminatory government policies that favored the development of large scale modern commercial farming (see Grindle, 1986; 1988). Recent evidence suggests that population pressure on the land is severe, with an average of about 1.9 hectares of cultivated land available to each person considered to be economically active in agriculture in the 1970s (SALA, 1983: 47, 75). According to the agricultural census of 1970, 22.1 percent of all farmers in Mexico had farms of 1

Table 9.2 Budget Expenditures of the Federal Government (billions of 1970 pesos)

	1977	1978	1979	1980	1981	1982	1983	1984	1985
Total expenditure	103.9	113.0	130.3	160.9	206.5	259.0	231.7	219.5	229.5
% change		8.7	15.3	23.5	28.3	25.4	-10.5	-5.3	4.5

Source: Derived from Nacional Financiera, La economía mexicana en cifras (Mexico City, 1986).

Table 9.3   Subsidies for Basic Consumption Goods

Product Cost	Annual & average growth rate	
	Nominal	Real
Tortilla	62.5	−6.6
Bread	119.0	25.8
Milk	75.0	0.6
Eggs	76.5	1.4
Sugar	67.0	−4.0
Cooking oil	58.7	−8.8
Beans	128.1	31.1
Rice	93.3	11.1
Minimum Wage	57.5	−9.5

Source: SCHP (Secretaria de Hacienda y Credito Publico), **Mexico's Development Financing Strategy** (Mexico City, 1986).

hectare or less and 42.4 percent had farms of between 1 and 5 hectares (Yates, 1980: 150).[5] Moreover, the land itself is often poor. Population increase, a harsh climate, and centuries of pressure on land mean that much of Mexico suffers from extensive erosion. In many areas, there is sufficient rainfall during four or five years of every ten; in the other years, drought is a major threat. The risks inherent in farming such marginal lands are great.

Thus, although the country's development has encouraged zones of highly productive commercial agriculture, much of the rural sector is marked by high population density, poor soils, erratic and insufficient rainfall, and a long history of periodic crop failure. Land distribution is highly inequitable, and the rural population of 23 million people continues to grow in size, as does the incidence of landlessness, poverty, and malnutrition. Government policies to control the price of basic food items and to channel credit, appropriate technology, technical assistance, and infrastructure to zones of highly profitable agriculture have also played a major role in creating an underproductive sector. Primarily dedicated to corn and beans, small farms in Mexico are unable to generate more than subsistence or sub-subsistence income (CEPAL, 1983: 151–159). Costs of production on marginal lands are high and increasingly require purchased inputs of seeds, fertilizer, insecticides, and at times hired labor. For the landless—who constitute almost 50 percent of the rural population—opportunities for wage labor are also extremely limited, both on the farm and off (see Grindle, 1988).

Thus, conditions were bad in rural areas even before the economic crisis of 1982 began to be felt. Then, with the crisis came high rates of inflation, sharply declining wages, and cutbacks in state programs, cutbacks that affected the poor in rural areas much as they did the poor in urban zones. In spite of these general conditions, agriculture performed more favorably than the overall economy did between 1983 and 1986. The sector increased its contribution to GDP from 8.8 percent in 1982 to 9.7 percent in 1986 (see Table 9.4). This more positive performance reflected in part the effect of good weather, in part the more favorable exchange rate for agriculture exports, and in part official price increases for food. For peasants who had access to land and especially those who produced an agricultural surplus, the impact of the crisis was somewhat muted, although input supply subsidies were also reduced, offsetting an improved price for many producers. Rural producers of basic crops also had access to subsistence food supplies, giving them an advantage over the urban poor (see Cook, n.d.). Because of the stronger performance of the sector, jobs may have been more available in rural areas than in many urban ones.

Nevertheless, to the extent that rural inhabitants were consumers (and almost all of them are) or wage earners (an increasing proportion of them are) or recipients and beneficiaries of government programs and projects (few rural communities are without access to some government programs) they were as adversely affected by the crisis as their urban counterparts, and in some cases they were even more disadvantaged. Consumer prices have always been higher in rural areas than in urban zones. High prices for basic consumer goods were a particular hardship for peasants who worked for wages because the official rural minimum wage was maintained at 6 to 18 percent below that of the important urban zones of Mexico City, Guadalajara, and Monterrey (Nacional Financiera, 1986: 52). Moreover, rural inhabitants continued to hire themselves out for considerably less than the full minimum wage. In addition, most of those who receive the "social wage" of benefits that include subsidized housing, food, transportation, and social welfare services reside in urban areas (Carr, 1986: 3). Rural diets, already less rich in protein than those in urban areas, relied increasingly on corn and beans and substitutes with little nutritional content. In terms of social welfare benefits provided by the government, rural inhabitants have always had less access to health care and educational facilities than people in urban areas, a situation that persisted with budget cutbacks for social services. Public works, an important employer of rural people, were significantly reduced under austerity measures. Sim-

Table 9.4 Real GDP Growth and Composition, 1971-1986

	1971-1975	1976-1977	1978-1981	1982	1983	1984	1985[a]	1986[a]
Growth								
Gross Domestic Product	6.5	3.8	8.4	-0.5	-5.3	3.7	2.7	-4.0
Agriculture, livestock, & fishing	3.0	4.3	4.2	-0.6	2.9	2.5	2.2	-1.3
Mining	6.0	6.8	16.6	9.2	-2.7	1.8	1.0	-5.7
Manufacturing	6.7	4.2	8.6	-2.9	-7.3	4.8	5.8	-5.8
Construction	6.9	-4.7	12.4	-5.0	-18.0	3.4	2.5	-12.6
Commerce	6.5	2.5	9.0	-1.9	-10.0	3.0	1.8	-5.2
Transport & communications	12.2	5.8	13.2	-3.7	-4.8	6.4	2.7	2.9
Financial services, insurance, and real estate	5.7	3.8	4.8	2.9	2.1	2.9	2.5	-2.4
Community & personal services	6.7	4.7	7.4	4.4	0.3	3.2	-0.5	1.1
Composition								
Gross Domestic Product	100.0	100.0	100.0	100.0	100.0	100.0	100.0	100.0
Agriculture, livestock, & fishing	11.2	10.1	9.2	8.8	9.6	9.5	9.4	9.7
Mining	1.4	1.5	2.9	3.8	3.9	3.8	3.8	3.7
Manufacturing	25.9	24.4	24.7	24.1	23.6	23.8	24.6	24.3
Construction	5.1	5.2	5.3	5.4	4.7	4.7	4.7	4.3
Electricity	1.2	1.4	1.5	1.6	1.7	1.8	1.8	2.0
Commerce	24.6	24.9	25.0	25.5	24.2	24.0	23.8	23.6
Transport & communications	5.5	6.3	7.3	7.4	7.5	7.7	7.7	7.8
Financial services, insurance, and real estate	11.0	10.7	10.0	9.8	10.6	10.5	10.5	10.7
Community & personal services	14.0	14.5	14.1	13.5	14.2	14.2	13.7	13.9

a Preliminary estimate.
Source: SCHP (Secretaria de Hacienda y Credito Publico), Mexico's Development Financing Strategy (Mexico City, 1986).

ilarly, the construction industry virtually collapsed as a source of migratory and seasonal jobs in 1982 and 1983. For most of the rural poor, an already difficult situation became more difficult after 1982 (see Cook, n.d.).

Throughout Mexico, the poor have been tenacious in developing means to respond to the increasing insecurity of rural life. Much recent research output has indicated the prevalence of economic strategies for maintaining a precarious standard of living or for accumulating capital to expand the resource base of the household (Dinerman, 1982). So pervasive is the search for sources of income that one analyst has noted that "creating employment, inventing ways of working harder, is part of peasant leisure" (Warman, 1980: 238). Another researcher noted that as conditions of life worsen in rural communities peasant household activities become increasingly oriented toward "survivability" (Cook, n.d.).

Some peasants, of course, have been able to take advantage of locally favorable conditions for agriculture to grow crops that provide greater returns than corn and beans (see de la Peña, 1981; Schryer, 1980). In many rural communities, there has emerged a group of wealthier small landowners that has become linked to urban and international markets for fruits, vegetables, feed grains, livestock, and other products. For most, however, increasing insecurity has meant a search for multiple sources of income. Wage labor in rural areas or nearby urban zones frequently contributes to household income. Commercial pursuits and the production of handicrafts also provide additional income (see Cook, n.d.). Most frequently, however, labor migration on a massive scale has been the rural response to a declining natural resource base, increasing population pressure, discriminatory government policies, and worsening maldistribution of wealth. For hundreds of thousands of families, the search for work outside the local community has become a critical component of complex strategies for ensuring survival, for coping with unexpected economic demands, and for investing in a more secure future.

The prevalence of labor migration means that remittance income is increasingly the key to the persistence and survival of rural households (see Grindle, 1988). For example, in one village in north-central Mexico, over half of household income was derived from temporary labor migration in the 1970s (Mines, 1981: 47). Similar dependence on migration income was discovered by Cornelius (1976) in his study of nine communities in rural Jalisco, where at least 50 percent of the economically active population has engaged in labor migration. Studies of communities in the states of Michoacán, Nuevo Leon, Oaxaca, and Mexico also reported that high rates of temporary labor migration were common (see Gregory, 1986: 109, 113). In one village in Oaxaca, over 90 percent of households were reported to depend in some part on income from migration, and in Zacatecas, a similar situation was faced by nearly 80 percent of village families (Stuart and Kearney, 1981: 35; Mines, 1981: 24). Migration and the income it generates have been a major way in which rural areas have become more incorporated into regional, national, and international economic interactions. It has also been a principal means for adjusting to the economic crisis of the 1980s.

Data gathered in four rural *municípios* in 1985 indicated the extent to which diversifying the household economy through migration and other means has been relied upon to manage or minimize the impact of the crisis. The field research, undertaken as part of a book-length study of the phenomenon of labor migration in rural Mexico, sought to generate an economic and political profile of each of the *municípios* in terms of the daily life of the municipal center and two, three, or four villages ascribed to it (see Grindle, 1988). The purpose of the research was to generate a brief descriptive overview of each in order to highlight its development in the past, the dilemmas its inhabitants face in the present, and the alternatives that exist for it in the future. The *municípios* are briefly described below in this chapter, focusing on how their inhabitants have responded to the crisis. What is significant about all of the cases is the extent to which the crisis accelerated trends already occurring in these rural areas, particularly the increasing dependence on labor migration.

Tepoztlán, Morelos

More than half of Tepoztlán's total population lived in the bustling municipal center in 1980. Tourism had generated considerable growth in the *município* in the 1970s and the labor force had increased by drawing on the villages surrounding the center. Over eighty commercial establishments offered an impressive array of goods and services in 1985. In addition, a weekly market filled the central plaza with more than a hundred stalls selling a wide variety of foods and consumer goods. The transport, services, and construction industries grew rapidly in the 1970s, reflecting the growth of the tourist industry and manufacturing in the period after 1960. In response to new opportunities, many rural households began to draw income from jobs in these sectors of the local economy. They were also able to find employment in public works in the 1970s and early 1980s, when potable water was brought to the entire town and roads were paved. But the crisis brought such activities to a near halt and severely constrained the availability of investment capital that might have been used to develop the construction materials and furniture industries for which raw materials were available locally. Increasingly, Tepoztecans set their eyes on jobs in Cuernavaca,

Mexico City, and the United States. They complained bitterly about the futility of looking for jobs in the *município* and of the need to look far and wide for sources of income.

In Tepoztlán's rural villages, economic conditions were even more difficult. Poor soils and the virtual absence of irrigation meant that most farm households in surrounding communities produced little surplus. Of the total land available in Tepoztlán, only 16 percent is suitable for agriculture. In the villages, many *ejidatarios* sharecropped their own land and the very poorest supplemented family income through the sale of wood.[6] Young men commuted to an industrial park in Cuernavaca, supplying income to make it possible for their families to remain in the villages, and young women were sent to Cuernavaca and Mexico City as domestic servants. As economic conditions worsened in the 1980s, temporary migration to the United States increased considerably as local opportunities became more scarce. In one village, 32 workers went to the United States and Canada in 1984; in 1985, 130 left for these destinations. A change in the use of remittance income also paralleled the impact of the crisis. Prior to 1982, remittances were often used to purchase construction materials for housing. Many also used this money to pay for their children's education or to invest in small businesses. Increasingly in the 1980s, however, remittances were needed to ensure mere subsistence and fewer investments in the long-term sustainability of the household were made.

Jaral del Progreso, Guanajuato

It is hard to escape the overall impression that Jaral is a prosperous and modern rural region, even in the midst of a severe economic crisis. Its richness is most evident in the late summer and early fall when the extensive fields surrounding the municipal center are green with the approaching harvest. Production on the flat valley land is irrigated, mechanized, and technically advanced. The *município* is set deep within the Bajío, the richest and most technologically advanced agricultural area of central Mexico (see Roberts, 1985). It is in this area that the green revolution and irrigation facilities introduced in the 1950s and 1960s combined to create a dynamic agricultural sector firmly embedded in national and international markets. Sorghum, white corn, sunflower, wheat, vegetables, and fruit are grown with modern techniques even on *ejido* lands. Irrigation is extensive and two agricultural cycles mark each year. Where vegetables are grown, three crops are produced. Sorghum is sold in the nearby towns of Queretaro, Irapuato, and Salamanca to companies such as Purina, and vegetables are shipped north to the United States. Wheat is sent to Mexico City, Toluca, and

Puebla. Moreover, in addition to its rich agricultural base, Jaral is located near the industrial centers of Celaya, Salamanca, and León, which provide jobs for residents of the *município*.

Jaral is a *município* that has been favored rather than discriminated against by government policies for agricultural and industrial development and one that is in the lead in the utilization of modern agricultural techniques. Nevertheless, the area is marked by extensive labor migration to the United States, a characteristic found frequently in poorer rural regions. In Jaral, few families have not sent someone to "the other side." And in spite of the evident richness of the area and the access that *ejidos* have to irrigation and modern technology, the level of poverty of a large portion of its population is similar to that found in much more depressed zones. The reason why these conditions have developed obviously cannot be a poor local resource base. Instead, the source of the extensive evidence of poverty in Jaral is found in the inequitable distribution of economic and political power in the region, structures that grew directly out of the modernization of the agricultural economy. The crisis beginning in 1982 did not alter these structures; it only made them more apparent.

The *município* is clearly divided between those who have adequate land and irrigation and those who have only small plots of land and no irrigation. In addition, a growing sector of the population is landless. A small and wealthy class of farmers emerged from the introduction of highly commercialized agriculture in the region in the 1950s and 1960s. This economically advantaged class owns its own land and rents or sharecrops a considerable portion of the *ejido* land. Although statistics that describe actual conditions of access to land are not available, it is widely acknowledged in Jaral that considerable concentration of control occurred in the 1960s, 1970s, and 1980s. Large landowners may control three to four hundred hectares, often by accumulating land in the hands of different family members, while poor farmers are fortunate to have access to three or four hectares. Irrigation and access to national and international markets for local crops became the principal factors differentiating the advantaged from the disadvantaged (Roberts, 1982: 309).

Because of the maldistribution of assets at the local level, a sizable portion of household income of the poor is generated by the young people who migrate and who send remittances to their families. Migratory flows correspond directly to the need for labor in agriculture. In the peak sowing and harvest times (May–June and November–December), demand for labor provides some job opportunities in Jaral. In the months before and after these periods, however, peasants in the area generally have work only one or two days a week. The solution to this problem of seasonal underemployment has been temporary migration. Some go to Celaya and some go to Mexico City, but most go north to the United States. In the 1980s, the world of Jaral's poor was constrained by *los ricos* who controlled the land and who blocked efforts to diversify the local economy. As the poor saw it, their only reasonable option was to migrate. Jaral del Progreso is a rich *municipio*. Nevertheless, its very richness created obstacles to its development: concentration of land-holding, seasonal unemployment, displacement of labor by machines, and dependence on migration. The economic crisis of the 1980s did not create these dilemmas of regional development. It did, however, draw attention to the relationship between economic stratification and dependence on migration.

Unión de San Antonio, Jalisco

Just as the poverty of Jaral was difficult to understand, the source of the evident prosperity of Unión de San Antonio is not easy to identify. The fields and hills surrounding Unión are sparsely covered with semidesert-type flora. There is much less evidence of agricultural production; where cultivated fields are to be found, they are farmed far less than those of Jaral. Cattle graze in groups of five or ten on sparse pastures throughout the landscape. Few people can be seen working in the fields, nor can they be found congregating in the central plaza of Unión, an attractive square of green leafy trees and white benches surrounded by Spanish colonial style buildings. In spite of the lack of visible economic pursuits, even in outlying villages and ranchos, television antennas sprout from the roofs of brightly painted stucco houses.

The source of this apparent prosperity is not to be found in agriculture. The average size of an *ejido* plot is seven hectares, too small to ensure subsistence on such arid land, and not very promising for cattle ranching in an area in which one hectare of grazing land is required at a minimum for each head of cattle. This clearly suggests that *ejidatarios* suffer from a shortage of land, especially given its poor quality and the extensive erosion that affects agricultural potential. In fact, however, in recent years farmers have left about 15 percent of their land uncultivated, often renting it out to cattle ranchers, most of whom are small private producers. Most of the livestock is in dairy cows and local industry, focused on the production of milk, cheese, and other dairy products, reflecting the economic importance of this livestock sector. Milk production is relatively modernized and the influence of large processing plants owned by Nestlé and Danesa is considerable.

The dairy industry provides some explanation for the apparent prosperity of Unión de San Antonio, but this is not the entire picture. There are household industries such as sewing and knitting and small commercial outlets for food, clothing, shoes, and household and agricultural goods. A number of taxis and buses service the community. In one village, women knit and crochet baby clothes for sale to intermediaries in Lagos de Moreno, León, and Guadalajara. Each of these activities contributes a small amount to the income of rural households. But the real solution to the economic puzzle of Unión is migration, perhaps the most important industry of the *município*. Migration to the United States became significant in the late nineteenth century and has become firmly embedded in the local economy. The stimuli to this migratory pattern are clear to local inhabitants: a poor natural resource base, an under-developed agricultural sector, and a dairy industry that employs few people, either on the farms or in the food-processing sector. By the mid-1980s few local inhabitants considered that their economic problems could be resolved through access to land. In some ways, then, Unión is a rural town that has given up on agriculture, and for most households, migration continues to be a recurrent necessity, especially during a period of crisis.

Villamar, Michoacán

In Villamar, migrants leave for the United States in February; until November, the municipal center is virtually a ghost town. The migrants return faithfully each year in order to spend the holidays with their families. In the past, they used their earnings to buy an animal, to improve their houses, and to consume a considerable amount in local cantinas. Villamar's seasons are marked by the rhythm of the migratory cycle, not by the needs of local agriculture, as one would expect in a rural area. In fact, the *município* has never enjoyed a vigorous local agricultural economy. About a third of the available land in Villamar is dedicated to cropping, another third is used for dairy cattle, and the remainder is in forests. *Ejidatarios* and small farmers grow corn, wheat, beans, saffron, and garbanzo on small plots. Only recently have vegetables and sorghum been introduced, and few farmers have adopted the production of these crops. The size of *ejido* plots varies between two and five hectares, although smallholders may have access to as much as twenty to fifty hectares. Even on the larger plots, however, few modern techniques are employed. The terrain is not suitable for extensive mechanization and individual plots are fractionalized. The majority of those with small plots produce only for self-sufficiency.

Agriculture does not provide much opportunity for generating income in Villamar. Moreover, the widespread experience of going to "the other side" has created a situation of virtual dependence on the migratory cycle for the income needs of a large portion of the population. For much of the year, in fact, Villamar is populated by women, children, and the elderly. Even commercial activity is stagnant because local entrepreneurs see little point in investing in an area in which economic activity is minimal and erratic. Universally, low salaries in local agriculture and lack of alternatives are blamed for the migration. In Villamar, the problems of agriculture have generated the strong migratory tradition; migration in turn creates conditions in which there is little incentive to invest in agricultural or nonagricultural pursuits. In this *município*, the response to the crisis of the 1980s has been more of the same—migration to the United States and subsistence based on remittances.

The cases of Tepoztlán, Jaral del Progreso, Unión de San Antonio, and Villamar attest to the incorporation of rural households in economic transactions at the regional, national, and international levels. For producers, consumers, and wage earners, the boundaries of the *município* and local community have little meaning. Indeed, rural households are increasingly difficult to categorize in terms of their economic activity because many generate income and subsistence from the land, from small commercial and manufacturing pursuits, and from wage labor. The crisis of the 1980s has intensified the integration of rural households into broader economic relationships. In the case of notably increased labor migration, integration has amounted to increased dependence on transfers of resources from elsewhere. Many rural areas managed to weather the worst of the crisis through greater efforts to generate remittances.

Most studies of rural areas and their development take as axiomatic that rural households have access to land and that they generate a major portion of their income from the land. Increasingly, this is a distorted view of what occurs in vast numbers of rural communities. In Mexico, landlessness and declining employment opportunities in agriculture are particularly marked. Nonfarm employment, much of it through temporary labor migration, makes it possible for rural inhabitants to maintain themselves in rural areas. These factors have also brought about changes in how the rural poor relate to the political system. In recent years, when peasants have responded collectively to egregious economic conditions, they have done so by organizing around issues that connect them directly to national and regional economies, issues such as their status as consumers and wage earners, or around issues that define their relationship to the state.

Collective Rural Protest and Mexican Politics

The extensive interaction with regional, national, and international economies was striking at Tepoztlán, Jaral del Progreso, Unión del San

Antonio, and Villamar. Equally interesting was the lack of political activity beyond endemic factionalism over the allocation of positions in local institutions. The most common responses to questions about political activities indicated cynicism and apathy about the potential to resolve problems through organization and collective protest. When asked what could be done to respond to local economic problems, the rural poor characteristically responded that "the government *should* do something." This statement was consistently followed by reasons why the government would not act, based on their own experiences of unfulfilled expectations in the past. For many in these *municípios*, collective protest did not offer a promising solution to their economic problems.

Such attitudes, which are widely held among a broad cross-section of the Mexican population, reflect an objective appreciation among the rural poor of their marginal position within the political system. Despite occasional and localized gains, the political system since the 1940s has sought consciously to demobilize and disaggregate independent political initiatives at the same time that it has sought to incorporate organized groups into the official party in order to control their activities (see, for example, Stevens, 1974; Hellman, 1983; Collier, 1982; Warman, 1980). Such activities are an important reason why peasants, who have benefited least of all economic sectors from Mexico's historically impressive economic development, have remained the most enduring support group for the regime (see, for example, Reyna, 1974). Throughout rural areas, local bosses trade allegiance to the political system in return for the economic and political benefits that ensure their continued ability to control local clienteles.

Thus, the Mexican government almost always has a captive and verbal support group in rural areas; however, such support rarely runs deep, is often pro forma, and is accompanied by considerable political cynicism (see, for example, Cook, n.d.: 19–22). In fact, peasants have long been manipulated, co-opted, or threatened by the political institutions of the state—the Institutional Revolutionary Party (PRI), the National Confederation of Peasants (CNC), or its local and regional affiliates (Ronfeldt, 1973; de la Peña, 1981; DeWalt, 1979; Anderson and Cockcroft, 1972). Similarly, they have frequently been swindled or abused by the state institutions responsible for rural development initiatives (see Grindle, 1977; 147–163). In practically every community, there are vividly recalled examples of official credit agencies overcharging for services, of state-supplied fertilizer arriving too late for the harvest or seriously altered in content, of officials of the state marketing agency underweighing grain delivered to them by peasants, or of the PRI determining who the beneficiaries of the state services should be.

Indeed, experiences in the 1970s increased rural awareness of the activities of the state at the same time that these experiences confirmed skepticism about the ability of the state to resolve severe problems of rural underdevelopment. Early in the decade the government began to assign significant resources to increase the productivity of rain-fed agriculture in order to ensure national food self-sufficiency. The programs introduced were legion; from the mid-1970s through the early 1980s, the government spent annually about 15 percent of the central budget for agricultural, forestry, and fishing development. But the results of this history of heavy investment were disappointing. Agricultural production on rain-fed plots remained practically stagnant throughout the 1970s and the need to import massive amounts of basic staples remained a major problem for the government. Perhaps more important, levels of rural unemployment, underemployment, and landlessness all increased despite markedly increased government investment.

The impetus to accord high priority to the rural sector died with the onset of the severe economic crisis of 1982, due in large part to stringent austerity measures and to preoccupation among government planners and decisionmakers with macroeconomic adjustments.[7] Austerity measures meant that the state had neither the economic nor the administrative capacity to continue its strongly interventionist role in rural areas. Mindful of the potential for rural protest, however, the government initiated efforts to decentralize control over government activities in the mid-1980s. In so doing, it reversed a trend toward centralization of decisionmaking power and control that has characterized Mexico in the twentieth century.[8]

Until the 1980s, the proportion of public spending accounted for by state and municipal governments was declining. In the 1970s, for example, state governments accounted for 12.1 percent of all public spending; by 1980, this proportion was 8.8 percent. Conditions for municipal governments were especially penurious and growing worse; in 1970, municipalities accounted for only 1.6 percent of public spending (SPP, 1982; 455). A long history of small budgets and poor career mobility opportunities also left state and local governments starved for qualified and committed human resources.[9] Then, in the 1980s, State Development Planning Committees, bringing together officials from local, state, and national levels serving in the same state, were given the responsibility to plan and program development initiatives in the state, in the expectation of promoting greater regional equity at the same time that administrative and fiscal decentralization was to be achieved (see SPP, 1982: 175). Trends in the centralization of budgetary expenditures were reversed. By 1985, 11 percent of the federal budget was being transferred to the states. An employment service was part of the new responsibilities of the state governments, and in 1986, some 66,000 individuals received jobs or were placed in training programs through this service (de la Madrid, 1986: 92). A municipal reform also transferred significant authority and resources to the nearly 2,400 *municípios* in the country. These changes increased considerably the capacity of local and state governments to respond to instances of tension and organization in rural areas. In a similar vein, CONASUPO, the state marketing agency, began to rely more on selling basic staples (Fox, 1987).

And despite the lack of interest in politics evidenced by the rural poor in Tepoztlán, Jaral, Unión, and Villamar, the 1980s were not devoid of collective rural protest. Where it emerged, the rural poor generally mobilized in response to increasing government penetration of rural areas and to economic concerns that they shared with other low-income groups in Mexico. Rural protest in the 1980s was primarily concerned with issues of agricultural prices, access to markets, wage rates, the delivery of basic services, and the impact of inflation on goods and services utilized by poor people. These concerns reflected the fact that rural communities had become more differentiated in their economic interactions and more vulnerable to conditions affecting national and international economies. They had also become more subject to a variety of government policies and programs that affected daily life in rural villages.

Juchitán, Oaxaca, is an interesting case of the changes occurring in collective protest activities. In a notable instance of collective response to changing economic conditions, official corruption, and local factionalism, workers, peasants, and students in the *município* organized under the banner of a broad-based coalition in the 1970s.[10] In 1981, they succeeded in winning a municipal election and presided over a leftist town hall for two years. Partisans of the Coalition of Workers, Peasants, and Students of the Isthmus (COCEI) demanded improvements in municipal services, payment of the minimum wage, and fair treatment from government agencies that were responsible for providing goods and services to the population. They were assisted in their protest by the Mexican Communist party, and once in power, COCEI succeeded in making a number of changes that reflected the goals of its membership.

The capacity of COCEI to sustain itself as a viable forum for collective protest was related to the existence of issues that affect poor people broadly. The organization initiated efforts to mobilize peasants in the early 1970s around issues of land tenancy. By the latter years in the decade, these concerns had been significantly replaced by broader issues of credit, processing, wages, and relationships to markets for agricultural and nonagricultural goods. In large part, changing concerns reflected changes in the rural economy, such as increased cash cropping and intensified interaction and domination by state agencies controlling credit, processing, and marketing. In consequence, COCEI found a basis for linking rural concerns to those of poor people living in the municipal center.

> Since Juchitán is a rural city, virtually every extended family unit has some members who own and work land, others who work in industrial, commercial, or bureaucratic jobs, and still others who buy and sell in the city's central market or in their neighborhoods. The COCEI can thus appeal to the general interest of the poor and lower-middle-class people without at any point favoring peasant families over worker or market families or vice versa (Rubin, 1987: 159).

A number of conditions unique to Juchitán account for its success in mobilizing poor people in protest against economic and political exploitation. Nevertheless, the factors responsible for stimulating collective action are reiterated elsewhere in Mexico. In the late 1970s, in fact, innovative political organizations encouraged the rural poor to identify common interests as producers, consumers, wage earners, and citizens and to achieve and maintain independence from the organizational control of the state. In the years after 1982, these organizations became a focal point for protesting against the impact of economic depression and austerity (see Carr, 1986: 15). The National "Plan de Ayala" Coordinating Committee (CNPA) served as an umbrella organization for regional and local groups of *ejidatarios*, agricultural workers, and women concerned about access to economic resources and goods and services provided by the state (Carr, 1986; Prieto, 1985–1986). Many such groups were initially formed to press for access to land, but with time, activists "linked this demand with others, including a halt to corruption and authoritarianism in rural governmental agencies; democratic governance and the provision of adequate services at the level of the municipio; improved credit and market facilities; control on real estate speculators; and an end to repression" (Prieto, 1986: 83; see also Aguado Lopez, Torres Franco, and Scherer, 1983). In October 1983 and June 1984, the CNPA and counterpart organizations representing the urban poor participated in two civic strikes intended to elicit official response to the impact austerity was having on the living conditions of the poor (Carr, 1986). In many communities peasants organized to acquire access to subsidized food products distributed by the government through CONASUPO (see Fox, 1987).

The extent and importance of rural mobilization in the 1980s should not be overstated. A large majority of the rural population remained cynical and politically quiescent as they pursued household-based strategies for economic survival. In addition, rural organizations continued to confront serious impediments to effective demand making. The government, in decentralizing control over decisionmaking and development and social welfare resources, heightened its capacity for timely action to demobilize local tensions and protests. And although innovative, organizations such as the CNPA have yet to demonstrate their capacity to deliver results to their component groups. Nevertheless, the very existence of the CNPA signifies the extent to which peasants have come to identify their interests in terms of issues beyond access to land. Political activities among the rural poor increasingly reflect the dependence on state largesse and the market economy for their survival. This trend is likely to become stronger in the future, whether the economic crisis is resolved or not.

Conclusion

When economic conditions worsen suddenly, social scientists, journalists, and other observers of conditions in developing countries become alert for signs of discontent and protest, especially among the groups affected most significantly by the crisis. Under conditions of heightened interest and social tensions, events such as a strike or a protest march take on revolutionary potential in the eyes of many beholders. Under conditions of extreme economic dislocation in Mexico, however, the search for political protest activities can obscure the extent to which the poor in rural areas have had recourse to household-based strategies for economic survival. In part, the retreat into the household reflects the possibilities for "getting by" that are offered by diversification and relationships to national and international markets. Peasant households in Mexico are no longer primarily dependent on the land. Instead, their livelihood is determined by their success in combining sources of income from agriculture, commercial, industrial, and migratory pursuits. To the extent that they have sought political redress for declining economic conditions, their pursuits have come to reflect their more complex economic activities, as well as the increased relevance of the state in their daily routine.

If the experience of Mexico's peasants is valid for those in other parts of the Third World, then understanding rural areas will increasingly require analysis of the linkages between rural households and nonlocal economic institutions, the possible trade-offs between political activism and investment in household economic strategies, and the expanding presence of the state in rural areas. Conventional assumptions about the nature of peasant populations and the content of rural protest movements may well be altered in consequence.

Notes

Guillermo Prieto Trevino of Harvard's John F. Kennedy School of Government provided expert research assistance for this chapter and his valuable contributions are gratefully acknowledged. Jonathan Fox of MIT was helpful in providing material and commenting on an earlier draft of this paper.

1. The term "peasant" is used broadly in this chapter to refer to the rural poor, including smallholders, tenants, sharecroppers, *ejidatarios* (see note 6), and landless workers. My usage of peasant corresponds to the use of the Spanish term "campesino" and is adopted because of the difficulty of differentiating clearly among sectors of the rural population when an increasing proportion of households engages in multiple income-generating activities (see Grindle, 1986: Ch. 6).

2. Scholars are divided over the extent to which such rural rebellion is a defensive reaction to changes that threaten accepted subsistence levels in a community—such as the expansion of commercial agriculture or the claims of a centralizing state—or represents a more calculated effort of individual decisionmakers to shape alternative futures for peasant classes (see Scott, 1976; Popkin, 1979).

3. In 1980, Mexico had a total population of 66.8 million people, 63 percent of whom were classified as urban (that is, living in localities of 2,500 or more). Between 1970 and 1980, the annual population growth rate was 3.3 percent. For urban areas, it was 4.6 percent and for rural areas, it was 1.2 percent (Nacional Financiera, 1986: 12). In 1980, 5.7 million people were considered economically active in the primary sector (Nacional Financiera, 1986: 28).

4. Thomas Trebat indicated the extent of public spending and lack of appropriate macroeconomic policies to control the oil windfall of the late 1970s. "The public deficit overwhelmed domestic savings, spilling over into inflation, which accelerated rapidly after 1980, and rapid increases of the current account deficit and external indebtedness. The boom in Mexico was further fueled by a loose monetary policy and by exchange rate policy, especially the rapid appreciation of the peso in real terms from 1977 through 1981. Domestic interest rate policy and exchange rate policy encouraged borrowing by the private sector abroad and, especially after 1980, significant capital flight" (Trebat, 1985: 37).

5. One study found that 61 percent of the production units in the central region of the country could be classified as infrasubsistence, that is, incapable of providing for the subsistence needs of the farm household; an additional 15.3 percent of the units was classified as subsistence (CEPAL, 1983: 119).

6. An *ejidatario* is a legally recognized beneficiary of the right to farm lands belonging to an *ejido*, a corporate landholding community. Some *ejidos* are farmed collectively, but the vast majority allocate plots to individual *ejidatariaos*. *Ejido* land cannot be sold or mortgaged.

7. The shift in emphasis was less evident in rhetorical pronouncements than it was in terms of activities actually pursued. Early in the administration of Miguel de la Madrid, the National Development Plan for 1983–1988 was produced.

In it, the government reaffirmed commitment to the importance of rural areas in feeding the population, and it pledged to pursue the medium-term goals of social welfare, integrated agrarian reform, agricultural production, and the improvement of employment and income levels in rural areas. Shortly thereafter, the National Food Program (PRONAL) announced with significant fanfare that its strategy, programs, and projects would resolve long-standing conditions of underdevelopment in rural areas. Two years later, the National Integrated Rural Development Plan (PRONADRI) made its appearance and echoed the government's commitment to the priority of rural development, especially in rainfed areas. In fact, neither strategy was put into effect.

8. Prior to the 1980s, state and local governments were systematically starved of resources and denied a significant role in policy and/or program initiative. Historically, this created a system in which "each successive level of government is weaker, more dependent, and more impoverished than the level above" (Fagen and Touhy, 1972: 20).

9. Nevertheless, state and local governments were not completely excluded from the policy process. In fact, state and local authorities were regularly assigned important responsibilities for maintaining the political and social peace at local levels, intervening in resource allocation decisions, providing information on local power relationships, and distributing jobs and contracts with an eye to political support building.

10. Rubin (1987) presented an excellent analysis of events in Juchitán in the 1970s and 1980s, indicating their relationship to leftist politics in the country. The description here is drawn from this source.

References

Aguado Lopez, Eduardo, José Luís Torres Franco, and Gabriela Scherer. "La Lucha por la tierra en Mexico (1976–1982)." *Revista Mexicana de Ciencias Políticas y Sociales* 28:113–114 (July-December), pp. 43–64, 1983.

Alcántera Ferrer, Sergio. "Selected Effects of Petroleum Development on Social and Economic Change in Tabasco," in Ina Rosenthal-Urey, ed., *Regional Impacts of U.S.-Mexican Relations*. La Jolla: University of California, San Diego, Center for U.S.-Mexican Studies, Monograph 16, pp. 103–118, 1986.

Altimir, Oscar. "Poverty, Income Distribution and Child Welfare in Latin America: A Comparison of Pre- and Post-recession Data," in Richard Jolly and Giovanni Andrea Corina, eds., *The Impact of World Recession on Children*. Oxford: Pergamon Press, pp. 91–112, 1984.

Anderson, Bo, and James Cockcroft. "Control and Cooptation in Mexican Politics," in James Cockcroft, André Gunder Frank, and Dale L. Johnson, eds., *Dependence and Underdevelopment: Latin America's Political Economy*. Garden City, New York: Anchor Books, pp. 219–244, 1972.

Bortz, Jeffrey. "Wages and Economic Crisis in Mexico," in Barry Carr and Ricardo Anzaldria Montoya, eds., *The Mexican Left, the Popular Movements, and the Politics of Austerity*. La Jolla: University of California, San Diego, Center for U.S.-Mexican Studies, Monograph 18, pp. 33–46, 1986.

Carr, Barry. "The Mexican Left, the Popular Movements, and the Politics of Austerity, 1982–1985," in Barry Carr and Ricardo Anzaldria Montoya, eds., *The Mexican Left, the Popular Movements, and the Politics of Austerity.* La Jolla: University of California, San Diego, Center for U.S.-Mexican Studies, Monograph 18, pp. 1–18, 1986.

CEPAL (Comision Economica para America Latina). *Economia campesina y agricultura empresarial.* Mexico: Siglo Veintiuno, 1983.

Collier, Ruth Berins. "Popular Sector Incorporation and Political Supremacy: Regime Evolution in Brazil and Mexico," in Sylvia Ann Hewlett and Richard S. Weinert, eds., *Brazil and Mexico: Patterns in State Development.* Philadelphia: ISHI, 1982.

Cook, Scott. "Inflation and Rural Livelihood in the Oxaca Valley: An Exploratory Analysis." Unpublished Ms., Department of Anthropology, University of Connecticut, n.d.

Cornelius, Wayne A. "Outmigration From Rural Mexican Communities," *The Dynamics of Migration: International Migration.* Washington, D.C.: Smithsonian Institution, Interdisciplinary Communications Program, Occasional Monograph Series No. 5, Vol. 2, pp. 1–40, 1976.

———. *The Political Economy of Mexico Under de la Madrid: The Crisis Deepens, 1985–1986.* La Jolla: University of California, San Diego, Center for U.S.-Mexican Studies, Research Report No. 43, 1986.

Craig, Ann L. *The First Agraristas: An Oral History of a Mexican Agrarian Reform Movement.* Berkeley: University of California Press, 1983.

de la Madrid, Miguel. *Fourth State of the Nation Report.* Mexico, D.F., 1983.

———. *Primer Informe de Gobierno, Sector Agropecuario Y Forestal.* Mexico, D.F., 1986.

De la Peña, Guillermo. *A Legacy of Promises: Agriculture, Politics, and Ritual in the Morelos Highlands of Mexico.* Austin: University of Texas Press, 1981.

Dewalt, Billie R. *Modernization in a Mexican Ejido.* Cambridge: Cambridge University Press, 1979.

Dinerman, Ina R. *Migrants and Stay-at-Homes; A Comparative Study of Rural Migration from Michoacán, Mexico.* La Jolla: University of California, San Diego, Center for U.S.-Mexican Studies, Monograph No. 5, 1982.

Fagen, Richard, and William S. Touhy. *Politics and Privilege in a Mexican City.* Stanford, California: Stanford University Press, 1972.

Fox, Jonathan. "Popular Participation and Access to Food: Mexico's Community Supply Councils, 1979–1985," in Scott Whiteford and Ann Ferguson, eds., *Food Security and Hunger in Central America and Mexico.* Boulder, Colorado: Westview Press, 1987.

Gregory, Peter. *The Myth of Market Failure: Employment and the Labor Market in Mexico.* Baltimore, Maryland: Johns Hopkins University Press, 1986.

Grindle, Merilee S. *Bureaucrats, Peasants, and Politicians in Mexico: A Case Study in Public Policy.* Berkeley: University of California Press, 1977.

———. "The Implementor: Political Constraints on Rural Development in Mexico," in Merilee S. Grindle, ed., *Politics and Policy Implementation in the Third World.* Princeton, N.J.: Princeton University Press, pp. 197–223, 1980.

_____. *State and Countryside: Development Policy and Agrarian Politics in Latin America.* Baltimore, Maryland: Johns Hopkins University Press, 1986.

_____. *Searching for Rural Development: Labor Migration and Employment in Mexico.* Ithaca, N.Y.: Cornell University Press, 1988.

Hellman, Judith Adler. "The Role of Ideology in Peasant Politics: Peasant Mobilization and Demobilization in the Laguna Region" *Journal of Inter-American Studies and World Affairs* 25:1, pp. 3–30, 1983.

IDB (International Development Bank). *Economic and Social Progress in Latin America.* Washington, D.C.: International Development Bank, 1986.

IMF (International Monetary Fund). *International Financial Statistics Yearbook.* Washington, D.C.: International Monetary Fund, 1987a.

_____. *International Financial Statistics.* Washington, D.C.: International Monetary Fund (May), 1987b.

LAM (Latin American Monitor). *Mexico 1987: Annual Report on Government, Economy, and Business.* London: Latin American Monitor, Ltd., 1987.

Meyer, Jean A. *The Cristero Rebellion: The Mexican People Between Church and State, 1926–1929.* Cambridge: Cambridge University Press, 1976.

Mines, Richard. *Developing a Community Tradition of Migration: A Field Study in Rural Zacatecas, Mexico, and California Settlement Areas.* La Jolla: University of California, San Diego, Center for U.S.-Mexican Studies, Monograph No. 3, 1981.

Nacional Financiera. *La economia mexicana en cifras.* Mexico, D.F., 1986.

Popkin, Samuel. *The Rational Peasant: The Political Economy of Rural Society in Vietnam.* Berkeley: University of California Press, 1979.

Prieto, Ana. "Mexico's National Coordinadoras in a Context of Economic Crisis," in Barry Carr and Ricardo Anzaldria Montoya, eds., *The Mexican Left, the Popular Movements, and the Politics of Austerity.* La Jolla: University of California, San Diego, Center for U.S.-Mexican Studies, Monograph 18, pp. 75–94, 1985–1986.

Quirk, Robert E., *The Mexican Revolution and the Catholic Church.* Bloomington: Indiana University Press, 1973.

Reyna, José Luís. *Control Político, estabilidad y dasarrollo en México.* Mexico: El Colegio de México, Cuadernos del CES 3, 1974.

Roberts, Kenneth. "Agrarian Structure and Labor Mobility in Rural Mexico." *Population and Development Review* 8:2, pp. 299–322, 1982.

_____. "Household Labor Mobility in a Modern Agrarian Economy: Mexico," in Guy Standing, ed., *Labour Circulation and the Labour Process.* London: Croom Helm, pp. 358–381, 1985.

_____. "Technology Transfer in the Mexican Bajio: Seeds, Sorghum, and Socioeconomic Change," in Barry Carr and Ricardo Anzaldria Montoya, eds., *The Mexican Left, the Popular Movements, and the Politics of Austerity.* La Jolla: University of California, San Diego, Center for U.S.-Mexican Studies, Monograph 18, pp. 37–70, 1986.

Ronfeldt, David. *Atencingo: The Politics of Agrarian Struggle in a Mexican Ejido.* Stanford, California: Stanford University Press, 1973.

Rubin, Jeffrey. "State Policies, Leftist Oppositions, and Municipal Elections: The Case of COCEI in Juchitan," in Arturo Alvarado, ed., *Electoral Patterns and*

Perspectives in Mexico. La Jolla: University of California, San Diego, Center for U.S.-Mexican Studies, Monograph 22, pp. 127–160, 1987.

SALA (Statistical Abstract for Latin America). Published annually by the Latin American Center, University of California at Los Angeles, 1983.

Sanderson, Steven E. *Agrarian Populism and the Mexican State.* Berkeley: University of California Press, 1981.

SCHP (Secretaria de Hacienda y Credito Publico). *Mexico's Development Financing Strategy.* Mexico, 1986.

Schryer, Frans J. *The Rancheros of Pisaflores: A History of a Peasant Bourgeoisie in Twentieth-Century Mexico.* Toronto: University of Toronto Press, 1980.

Scott, James. *The Moral Economy of the Peasant: Rebellion and Subsistence in Southeast Asia.* New Haven: Yale University Press, 1976.

———. *Weapons of the Weak: Everyday Forms of Peasant Resistance.* New Haven: Yale University Press, 1985.

Spalding, Rose. "Structural Barriers to Food Programming: An Analysis of the Mexican Food System," *World Development* 13:2 (December), pp. 1249–1262, 1985.

SPP (Secretaria de Programacion y Presupuesto). *Anuario Estadistico de los Estados Unidos Mexicanos 1981.* Mexico, 1982.

Stevens, Evelyn P. *Protest and Response in Mexico.* Cambridge, Mass.: MIT Press, 1974.

Stuart, James, and Michael Kearney. *Causes and Effects of Agricultural Labor Migration from the Mixteca of Oaxaca to California.* La Jolla: University of California, San Diego, Center for U.S.-Mexican Studies, Working Paper No. 28, 1981.

Trebat, Thomas J. "Mexico's Foreign Financing," in Peggy B. Musgrave, ed., *Mexico and the United States: Studies in Economic Interaction.* Boulder, Colorado.: Westview Press, pp. 33–70, 1985.

Warman, Arturo. *"We Come to Object": The Peasants of Morelos and the National State.* Translated by Stephen K. Ault. Baltimore: Johns Hopkins University Press, 1980.

Womack, John, Jr. *Zapata and the Mexican Revolution.* New York: Vintage Books, 1968.

World Bank. *Poverty in Latin America: The Impact of Depression.* Washington, D.C.: The World Bank, 1986.

Wyman, Donald L. *Mexico's Economic Crisis.* La Jolla: University of California, San Diego, Center for U.S.-Mexican Studies, Monograph 12, 1983.

Yates, P. Lamartine. *Mexico's Agricultural Dilemma.* Tucson: University of Arizona Press, 1980.

10

Austerity and Dissent: Social Bases of Popular Struggle in Latin America

John Walton and Charles Ragin

Since August 1982, debt and austerity have become the watchwords of underdevelopment in Latin America and, indeed, in poor countries from Africa to Eastern Europe. The debt crisis is a global problem both in its origins and its effects. Striking miners in Romania and food rioters in Zambia's copperbelt towns respond in locally conditioned ways to the common experience of austerity measures implemented by states facing a towering international debt.

Latin America holds certain distinctions among the world's debtor regions. It shares roughly one-half of the world's external debt owed to private banks, multilateral agencies, and governments. (Current estimates peg Latin America's external debt at U.S. $1 trillion.) Although bankrupt foreign exchange reserves appeared in Egypt, Jamaica, and Peru as early as 1976, it was the threatened default of Mexico in summer 1982 that forced international recognition of the debt crisis—often as a characteristically Latin problem. In the past five years, moreover, Latin America has pioneered political responses to the crisis: popular protests in many countries, precedent-setting limits on debt service in Peru, a moratorium on payments in Brazil, negotiated concessions in Mexico and Argentina, and regional cooperation on increasingly forceful demands for debt relief, beginning with the Cartegena Consensus of 1984. A close analysis of debt politics in Latin America suggests emerging world patterns of the response that mobilized groups have fashioned to redress their condition.

A great deal has been written about the origins of the debt crisis (see, e.g., Block, 1977; Honeywell, 1983; Moffit, 1983; Stallings, 1987; Wood, 1986) and the effects of various policies for economic stabilization (see, e.g., Cline and Weintraub, 1981; Diaz-Alejandro, 1981; Frenkel and O'Donnell, 1979; Haggard, 1986; Killick, 1984; Pastor, 1987; Sutton,

Figure 10.1

Austerity Protest Events Around the World, 1976–1987

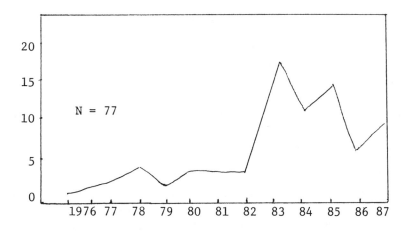

1984; Williamson, 1983). This literature is enormously valuable, documenting, for example, the roots of the problem in an accumulation crisis of the advanced countries (e.g., Brett, 1983) and the socially regressive consequences of austerity programs (e.g., Foxley, 1981). Despite these varied contributions, social scientists and policymakers alike have analyzed the problem from an economistic vantage point. Debt is understood as the result of an inexorable logic of accumulation unsullied by political motives, and the revealingly named "stabilization" programs are evaluated for their macroeconomic effects rather than their interplay with social action. In this way standard analyses of the debt crisis replicate an incomplete understanding of history as the playing out of a series of choices made exclusively "at the top" and suffered through by allegedly powerless groups below. Whatever the general limitations of this perspective, it is particularly inappropriate for analyzing today's crisis, in which massive popular protests have accompanied, and indeed have shaped, efforts to cope with the burden of indebtedness.

From 1976 to the present, austerity protests have occurred in 26 debtor countries around the world (13 in Latin America and the Caribbean), often repeatedly, for a total of 77 separate incidents of strikes, riots, and demonstrations (see Figure 10.1). The protests have been called "IMF Riots" because they typically are responses to austerity measures recommended by the International Monetary Fund as presumably "stabilizing" conditions that justify new or rescheduled loans. These measures, however, affect people in demonstrably unstabilizing ways: Reduced public spending eliminates jobs, currency devaluations elevate domestic prices, and subsidy cuts do away with cheap food and petroleum for the poor. Whatever the economic rationale for such measures—and selectively they sometimes make good economic sense—they are frequently perceived as penalties imposed on the poor as a solution to problems created by the political and economic elites' profligate borrowing. Hence the moral energy that prompts demonstrators against austerity programs to shout "Out with the IMF!" and "Let the ones who stole the money pay the debt!"

Among the small number of studies devoted to the politics of austerity, only a fragmentary picture of oppositional movements has appeared. Several fascinating case studies of resistance in North Africa refrained from generalizing beyond the specific national political context in which economic hardship activates social divisions (Brown, 1986; Seddon, n.d.; Seddon, 1984). Austerity protest in Mexico has been muted by organized labor's preference for maneuvering within the theater of official institutions, by a defensive Left, and by industrialists' exploitation of the crisis as an occasion to increase productivity (Carr and Anzaldua, 1986). Yet popular protest has occurred in many other countries, rising in tandem with the debt burden and the rate with which austerity measures are adopted.

Journalists and scholars alike have proposed explanations for the wave of protest, albeit on the basis of impressionistic evidence. This informed speculation can be refashioned as a set of hypotheses and then evaluated in light of a systematic inventory of Latin American austerity protests. The purpose of this chapter is to specify the causes of austerity protests, and thereby achieve a first step toward understanding the social crisis in Latin America and its implications for the future.

Explaining Austerity Protest

The most obvious and plausible hypothesis holds that protest varies directly with *hardship* as indicated by depredations directly linked to debt and austerity (such as the debt burden, cost of living, unemployment, wage freezes, devaluations, subsidy cuts). Critical treatments of the international monetary crisis often cite social unrest as a characteristic contradiction of the policies intended to restore stability (e.g., Moffitt, 1983). Journalistic accounts from the *Wall Street Journal* (22 June 1984) to the *Monthly Review* (February 1985) identified "social upheaval" and "political turmoil and riots" as a direct consequence of the debt crisis.

In more qualified treatments, the *urban austerity* hypothesis holds that generalized hardship is less the source of protest than are specific measures prescribed by IMF adjustment programs and aimed at urban groups. The *Christian Science Monitor* (16 April 1985) reported a "link between aid terms and riots in Africa" in which IMF pressure for the elimination of food subsidies, reduced public deficits, and agricultural self-sufficiency led to predictable results in African cities: "If bread price increases are too sudden . . . they act as a trigger to explode social discontent." Discussing IMF shock treatments, economist John Loxley (1984:30) argued "usually the urban working class is worst affected, by lay-offs induced by restraint and by deteriorating real incomes in the face of inflationary pressures resulting from devaluation, subsidy cuts, and the imposition or raising of fees and prices for public sector services. In extreme cases this has given rise to what are now called 'IMF Riots' which are, essentially, an urban phenomenon."

The third, the *legitimacy* hypothesis, discounts the effects of hardship per se in favor of an analysis of the state's ability to control unrest and engender legitimacy. James Petras and Howard Brill (1986:440–41) argued:

> An extremely important factor shaping the impact of IMF policies is the relationship between state and private institutions. Some states in Latin America are characterized by relatively limited linkages between institutions while others will have dense linkages. State institutions can be deeply integrated with other institutions and pervade all aspects of social life. States with dense linkages tend to be able to control and channel dissent and conflict with selective use of direct coercion or rapid changes in the redistribution of the surplus, while states with weak linkages are either easily destabilized or are forced to resort to more extreme measures of direct coercion or to the cementing of social compromises by relatively large expenditures of surplus . . . the response of the populace cannot be gauged by the harshness of the austerity programmes, but by the degree of state legitimacy and the density of linkages with civil society.

Fourth, the *power of capital and labor* hypothesis in some ways takes the opposite position from the legitimacy argument. According to Petrass and Brill's reasoning, weak linkages between the state and civil society, however those are measured, would result in less state capacity to control conflict and more austerity protest. Robert Kaufman (1986:194), by contrast, argued that the combination of concentrated capitalistic economic power and a populist tradition in labor and politics (both seeming to involve strong state-civil linkages) would produce "antistabilization co-alitions." Generalizing from the cases of Argentina, Brazil, and Mexico, two conditions are required:

> one . . . sharp concentration of capitalist economic power, characterized in recent decades by increasingly close cooperation between state enterprises,

international banks, and large transnational and domestic industrial companies. The second feature . . . is a politicolegal space and organizational infrastructure that politicians and union leaders can employ to defend the distributive interests of their constituents. This combination . . . creates the potential for unusually combustible, politicized, and persistent conflicts over stabilization.

Kaufman revised another hypothesis that claimed that authoritarian states were more disposed toward and capable of implementing stabilization programs in the first place (e.g., O'Donnell, 1978; Frenkel and O'Donnell, 1979; Skidmore, 1977; Sheahan, 1980). Although germane to this discussion, the authoritarianism hypothesis provides no unique explanation for protest except, perhaps by implication, to minimize its importance in authoritarian regimes.

Excluding the authoritarianism hypothesis, the remaining four hypotheses summarize the limited number of explanations that have been offered for popular movements organized around the regressive consequences of the debt crisis and austerity regimes. How well do they explain the incidence of protest?

Methods

The first task in evaluating these hypotheses is to develop a systematic inventory of protest events and the attributes of the national settings in which they appear. Austerity protests are large collective actions that oppose state economic reform policies aimed at reducing foreign debt and qualifying debtor nations for new or rescheduled loans. Since 1976, many of these protests have been the subject of detailed journalistic accounts appearing in the international press, financial journals, and weekly magazines and newsletters. Illustrative cases include the April 1983 demonstrations and looting in São Paulo (*Veja*, 13 April 1983), the April 1984 price riots in Santo Domingo (*Latin American Weekly Report*, 11 May 1984), and the regular strikes and demonstrations from 1976 through the mid-1980s in Peru (for example, "Peruvians Battle Police in Five Cities in Protests over Austerity Measures," *New York Times*, 23 June, 1977).

To obtain an exhaustive inventory of these events we used several cross-validating methods. First, we searched the *New York Times Index* for reports on austerity protests for all countries of Latin America and the Caribbean (excluding very small countries with less than two million people) from 1976 through 1987. Second, the *Latin American Weekly Report* was consulted for the same period to supplement and elaborate the first listing. Third, we attempted to track down purported events mentioned in a variety of sources (such as the *Economist, Business Week*) and to recover past incidents in the course of following current events in the U.S. press from 1984 onward. Then, on the basis of relatively complete accounts for each country, we coded the reports for each event and combined them in country summaries of the frequency of protest, size, duration, locations (number of cities involved), "form" (riot, strike, demonstration), and other features.

For the purposes of this analysis, protest was measured in two ways. First, we simply divided countries into two classes: those that have experienced one or more protests and those that have had none. Second, we measured variation in the severity of protest for countries in the first category. Given many possible indicators and the subjective nature of the journalistic accounts—the primary source of our data—protest severity is difficult to measure. Multiple indicators and low reliability suggested the use of a factor analytic approach to combine correlated measures and increase reliability.

We used four indicators of severity: (1) an ordinal measure (four categories) that distinguishes countries according to the reported number of deaths and arrests, (2) an interval measure of the number of distinct episodes of protest in the 1976–1987 period, (3) a dichotomous measure of the presence of rioting, and (4) an interval measure of the spread of protest—number of cities involved. The resulting factor analysis showed that these indicators correlate positively with one another and form a strong one-factor solution. The four variables were standardized (that is, converted to Z scores) and then summed to form a single index of severity. Protest and nonprotest countries and the scores of the protest countries on the severity index are shown on Table 10.1.

Next we assembled data on a variety of cross-national variables both for descriptive purposes and for evaluating suggested explanations of austerity protest. Many of these are familiar concepts with widely accepted indicators (for example, development based on GNP per capita, urbanization using percent living in urban areas, size of the tertiary sector defined by percent employed in service occupations, strength of organized labor based on percent of the labor force unionized, and so forth). Several of our independent variables, however, required special attention.

First was the matter of "IMF Pressure" or the extent to which individual countries have been the object of external encouragement for austerity reforms. Here, again, we used factor analysis to justify the combination of four correlated indicators of possible IMF conditionality: number of debt renegotiations, number of debt restructurings, use of the Extended Fund Facility, and loans as a percent of quota contributions—an indicator of "tranches." (See the Appendix, Table 10A.1, for data sources.) These indicators have strong loadings on a single factor and were combined

Table 10.1   Austerity Protest in Latin America and the Caribbean,
1976-1987

Countries	Severity
Protest	
Dominican Republic	1.84
El Salvador	-4.00
Guatemala	-1.28
Haiti	-.65
Jamaica	.37
Mexico	-4.00
Panama	-3.69
Argentina	.10
Bolivia	2.49
Brazil	1.79
Chile	2.28
Ecuador	.60
Peru	6.61
Nonprotest Countries	
Costa Rica	
Cuba	
Honduras	
Nicaragua	
Uruguay	
Venezuela	

Note: Negative standard scores such as Mexico's -4.00 indicate low
severity.

to form a single index of IMF pressure after converting them to common
units (Z scores).

Second was the matter of debt burden. The best indicator is debt
service as a percentage of exports, but this figure can vary substantially
from year to year for a given country. Thus, we averaged each country's
values over the 1976–1982 period when the debt crisis emerged. This
averaging procedure corrects for year-to-year fluctuations over the most
relevant period of observation.

Finally, scholarly and journalistic interest in the urban origins and
bases of protests required that we address the issue of "overurbanization."
A central concern in the literature on urbanization in the Third World
is the degree to which countries have experienced excessive urbanization
(see Bradshaw, 1987), which is often seen as a sign of distorted development. *Excessive* is usually defined relative to level of development.
Countries with low levels of GNP per capita, according to this reasoning,
should have comparably low levels of urbanization. This line of thought
cautions against assessing the effect of urbanization in isolation from
the effect of development. That is, the effect of urbanization ideally
should be addressed in multivariate analyses that include controls for
level of development. Of special interest here is a pattern of results

Table 10.2   Correlations of Debt and IMF Pressure

	Average Debt Correlation	N	IMF Pressure Correlation	N
Multinational penetration 1973	-.342	18	.152	18
Export commodity concentration 1980	-.108	18	.238	18
Import partner concentration 1980	-.256	18	.015	19
Export partner concentration 1980	-.301	18	-.042	19
Raw material export 1980	-.132	18	-.521[a]	19
Consumer price index 1983	.483[a]	18	.112	18
Average inflation 1973-1984	.426[b]	18	.149	18
GNP per capita 1981	.288	18	-.086	18
Urbanization 1980	.504[a]	18	.046	18
Tertiary employment 1980	.364	18	.266	18
Manufacturing employment 1980	.340	18	.074	18
Unionization 1975	.409	17	.136	18
Protest events/population 1948-1977	-.295[c]	18	-.646[c]	19
State sanctions/population 1948-1977	-.602[c]	18	-.510[a]	19
Civil rights index 1973-1979	.233	18	-.199	19
Political rights index 1973-1979	.262	18	-.143	19
Government revenue/GNP 1980	.229	18	.281[b]	18
Direct taxation/revenue 1980	.347	18	.401[b]	18

[a] $p < .05$
[b] $p < .10$
[c] $p < .01$

showing a positive effect for urbanization and a negative effect for the indicator of development (for example, GNP per capita). This pattern indicates that high scores on the outcome variable (for example, severity of austerity protests) are displayed by countries that combine a high level of urbanization and a low level of development—countries that are overurbanized.

Results

We begin with a descriptive picture of the distribution of debt and IMF pressure in Latin America, correlating these two measures with a number of independent variables (see Table 10.2). Average debt is strongly correlated with measures of hardship (consumer price index and inflation), urbanization, and, to a lesser extent, with unionization. This provides an implicit account of the distribution of debt. Among several political variables, debt is negatively associated with a measure of repressive "state sanctions" (Taylor and Jodice, 1983), suggesting an inverse relationship between authoritarianism and debt burden—less authoritarianism, by this measure, correlated with more debt, contrary to some hypotheses about the bureaucratic-authoritarian state.

IMF pressure shows strong negative correlations with the frequency of past protest events (that is, general domestic unrest) and with state

Table 10.3   Correlations of Presence/Absence of IMF Protest[a] and
Severity of IMF Protest[b] with Various Indicators of
Economic, Social, and Political Conditions

	Presence/Absence of Protest Correlation	Severity of Protest Correlation
I. Indicators of IMF conditional/debt		
Number of renegotiations	.169	.633[c]
Number of restructurings	.065	.688[d]
Use of extended fund	.251	.092
Loans/IMF quota	.464[e]	.021
IMF pressure index	.301	.448
Average debt service/exports	.247	.306
II. Indicators of dependency		
Multinational penetration 1973	-.185	-.082
Export commodity concentration 1980	-.142	-.285
Export partner concentration 1980	-.007	-.411
Import partner concentration 1980	.030	-.398
Raw material export 1980	-.347	.247
III. Indicators of hardship		
Consumer price index 1983	.278	.278
Average inflation 1973-1984	.215	.309
IV. Social structural indicators		
GNP per capita 1981	-.242	-.041
Urbanization 1980	-.144	.257
Tertiary employment 1980	-.150	.117
Manufacturing employment 1980	-.208	-.070
Unionization 1975	-.281	.589[c]
V. Political indicators		
Protest events/population 1948-1977	-.061	-.106
State sanctions/population 1948-1977	-.237	.016
Civil rights index 1973-1979	.088	.053
Political rights index 1973-1979	.096	.257
Government revenue/GNP 1980	-.101	.283
Direct taxation/revenue 1980	-.184	.002

[a] All countries, N = 18-19.
[b] Protest countries, N = 13.
[c] $p < .05$
[d] $p < .01$
[e] $p < .10$

sanctions. IMF pressure also bears a strong inverse relation to one measure of dependency, the level of raw material export. Conversely, a significant positive correlation obtains between pressure and a measure of state strength, direct taxation. Overall, this suggests that strong independent states with a history of less protest mobilization and of less repression enjoy the most IMF attention and, with that, external pressure for austerity reforms.

Table 10.3 displays correlates of the two measures of austerity protest, presence versus absence and, for countries with protests, severity. Here, independent variables are grouped into five conceptual categories. The first set measures external involvement in the national debt situation and the extent of IMF pressure to implement austerity measures. These conditionality variables are positively correlated with both measures of protest. Proportionately higher IMF loans (based on each country's quota contribution) shows a strong positive correlation with the presence of protest, and three other measures (use of extended fund, pressure index, debt service) have moderate associations in the same direction. For protest countries alone, the severity index is very strongly correlated with the number of restructurings and renegotiations, whereas pressure and debt service modestly complement the pattern. The clear result is that the greater the external pressure for austerity reforms, the more likely and more severe the protest. This supports, in part, the urban austerity hypothesis.

Measures of economic dependency show consistently modest and negative, but not significant, correlations with both measures of protest. The individual negative correlations between raw material export and presence of protest and those between export partner and import partner concentration and severity are moderately strong (significant at the .20 level). The data suggest that the less the dependency, the more likely and more severe the protest.

Hardship indicators are associated with both protest measures in a weak positive pattern. The correlations, however, are not strong enough to recommend acceptance of the hardship hypothesis. The structural indicators relating to development and urbanization have no clear relationship to protest with the notable exception of a very strong positive correlation between unionization and severity. Urbanization is unexpectedly weak as a predictor, based on previous results, but this is due to a confounding of separate measures, as we show below.

Finally, the political indicators show no strong or consistent association with protest. The result is instructive. A history of social unrest ("protest events") does not predict austerity protest, suggesting that the latter is a distinctive phenomenon rather than a continuation of traditional recusancy. Several measures that, taken together, fairly capture the ideas of legitimacy and authoritarianism (for example, state sanctions, civil rights, political rights) bear no consistent relationship to protest and provide no support for those hypotheses.

The problem of confounded independent variables can be addressed by unpacking the associations with protest severity via multiple regression. As noted, some relationships (such as those between urbanization and protests) are assessed best in multivariate designs. The very small N of thirteen protest countries makes multiple regression risky, however, even with only two independent variables. To compensate we use a

Table 10.4   Regression Analysis of Variation in Protest Severity

Equation#		Constant	GNP per Capita 1981	% Urban 1980	Unioniza- tion 1975	Corrected R-Squared
1.						
	B	-6.44	-5.63	.27	.26	
	Beta		-1.42	1.53	.89	.34
	P	.05	.02	.02	.01	.05
2.						
	B	-.62	-2.35			
	Beta		-.57			.49
	P	.68	.05			.02

strategy of substituting correlated measures in separate regression equations.

Table 10.4 displays the results of an analysis assessing the explanatory power of urbanization while controlling for GNP per capita. As noted, this procedure evaluates the contribution of urbanization beyond its close association with GNP per capita. The equation shows a strong overurbanization pattern because the effect of urbanization is strongly and significantly positive, while the effect of GNP per capita is strongly and significantly negative. (The multiple regression unpacks a suppressor relation.) The results show that countries that are highly urbanized relative to their levels of GNP per capita experienced the most severe austerity protests.

Urbanization is strongly correlated with unionization, which, in turn, is one of the strongest correlates of protest severity (see Table 10.3). Thus, the effect of urbanization reported in Table 10.4 may simply be a surrogate for unionization. We address this confounding in equation 2 of Table 10.4 by substituting unionization for urbanization. (The small N and high degree of collinearity make a three variable multiple regression hazardous.) A comparison of equation 2 with equation 1 shows that the pattern of results is identical, and the corrected R-squared value is greater in equation 2. These results indicate that countries that are highly unionized relative to their levels of development experienced the most severe austerity protests.

It is impossible to disentangle these variables with our small sample. They may be impossible to separate in reality as well. Our findings should be viewed as support for a causal complex centered on relatively high levels of urbanization and unionization. Other forces are involved in this causal complex. The IMF pressure or conditionality measures, for example, are confounded with these variables. (The multiple correlation of number of restructurings with urbanization and GNP per capita is .687.)

Discussion

Summarizing these results, we have found, first, that hardship, urbanization, less dependency, and a less repressive state are associated with greater average debt. Stated differently, the debt burden is greatest for countries that enjoy more economic independence and political tolerance but suffer excess urbanization and declining real income. Mexico and the new Southern Cone democracies fit this picture. Ironically, perhaps, external pressure to implement regressive austerity programs is directed, not systematically at the countries with the same high average debt profile, but at countries that reflect only a subset of those characteristics. IMF pressure is correlated with less dependency and less repression, as before, and with the additional indicators of less previous unrest and a strong state (at least on the direct taxation measure). Here countries like Jamaica, Ecuador, the Dominican Republic, and Peru more closely fit the image. One possible explanation for this discrepancy between debt burden and austerity pressure is that the smaller, democratic, and less explosive countries are made the object lessons for disciplining debtors by international banks and agencies because they are less able to resist external pressures and less implicated in the welfare of the developed countries (via trade, for example). Jamaica's unfortunate experience with externally imposed reforms conforms to this interpretation (Bernal, 1984; Girvan et al., 1980).

The correlates of austerity protest present a clear pattern in which hardship is a contributing factor, but pressure for stabilizing reforms in combination with excess urbanization and its inextricable features such as unionization has the more decisive impact on both the presence and severity of unrest. Economic dependency is negatively related to protest, and political factors such as authoritarianism are unrelated.

The various explanations of protest have mixed success. The urban austerity hypothesis is best supported, involving as it does partial support for the hardship hypothesis. The legitimacy hypothesis receives little direct support, although its vaguely formulated notion of dense linkages between the state and civil society may correspond to other social structural factors such as unionization. Authoritarianism does not work as an explanation and is even refuted in its expectations about debt burden. Finally, the power of labor and capital hypothesis is at least half right because unionization is strongly related to austerity protest. Nevertheless, as we have seen, the real relationship between unionization and protest derives from the former's confounding with urbanization and other measures of the extent to which countries have a high proportion of people affected by austerity. Overall, therefore, the urban austerity hypothesis is the best available explanation. In any case, previous explanations of protest fail to incorporate those factors we have found to be the strongest predictors. A new explanation is needed.

The debt crisis generates a three-sided political struggle. The state in Third World countries confronts new developmental dilemmas—capital export in debt service and diminishing public resources, for example— at the very time when innovative policies are most needed. On one side, international actors (banks, advanced-country governments, the IMF) exert differential policies and pressures on debtor countries in the interests of managing (or recovering) a stable international monetary system, which means, at a practical level, making austerity examples of some countries and negotiating political compromises with others. On the other side, states now have to contend with domestic political considerations, particularly the mobilized opposition to austerity coming from the urban poor, working-class, and even middle-class victims (for example, public employees) of retrenchment.

Our results clarify these links between the state in Latin America and the political forces that converge on the state from above and below (cf. Cardoso and Faletto, 1977). We have shown the determinants of differential austerity pressure on states (such as less mobilization and repression), determinants that derive from the international realm. And we have shown the conditions under which popular forces mobilize to challenge the socially regressive effects of austerity (for example, pressure, urbanization). The appropriate hypothesis for describing this process must incorporate the interplay of global politics and urban mobilization as they are mediated by the state—what we shall call for simplicity a global-urban interplay hypothesis. In contrast to previous reflection on the debt crisis, this notion provides a more exacting explanation for the systematic variation in the conditions and consequences of austerity.

Conclusion

From its inception in the mid-1970s and its general recognition in 1982, the debt crisis has become the centerpiece of Latin American under-development, the problem around which all other problems take their relational places. The crisis has eluded solution despite an evolving series of policies that promised a return to stability but delivered only a punitive regimen for the poor, accompanied by actual increases in the debt burden (from about U.S. $700 million in 1984 to $1 trillion by late

1987). At first, the crisis was denied or was attributed to mismanagement in some of the smaller countries that practiced strong state intervention in the economy. Mexico's near default forced a redefinition. The crisis was now seen as a general condition growing out of some combination of oil shocks, falling commodity prices, ill-fated state corporations, ill-conceived uses of borrowed funds, and a reluctance to let the free market work its generative effects. Whatever the presumed causes of the crisis, it was agreed that the debt could be paid and growth restored through market-oriented stabilization programs. The first four years of the crisis were marked by a series of debt restructurings coupled with austerity reforms, and with protest, all of which failed to reverse the growing debt burden. In late November 1987 at a meeting of Latin American presidents in Acapulco, a perceptive observer reported, "There is a consensus on two things. One is that the debt has to be paid, and the other is that the debt cannot be paid" (*New York Times*, 30 November 1987).

That paradoxical truth summarized the national responses to the crisis. It began to dawn on participants in the Cartegena Consensus of 1984 and has progressed with Peru's limitation of debt service payments to a percentage of exports, Ecuador's emergency moratorium, and Brazil's more persevering resistance to IMF agreements, followed by suspension of interest payments on foreign commercial debts in February 1987. By April of the same year the largest U.S.-international banks (Bank of America, J.P. Morgan, Manufacturers Hanover, Citicorp, and Chase Manhattan) began reclassifying their Latin, and specifically Brazilian, debts as nonaccruing—a move designed to accept losses and begin unloading discounted paper through a variety of mechanisms (such as debt-equity and debt-commodity swaps, secondary loan markets, exit bonds). By year's end even the U.S Treasury had abandoned its Baker Plan of 1985 and proposed an unprecedented arrangement for discounting Mexico's debt with special Treasury bonds acting as the medium between the Mexican government and the banks. As banker Felix Rohatyn observed, "For the first time the Treasury is participating directly in a debt-swapping transaction so that the U.S. Government is becoming a partner in debt restructuring at below par" (*New York Times*, 31 December 1987).

The catalog of reasons for this policy shift, from austerity and repayment to de facto default and internationally managed discounting, begins with sheer necessity. Debt service mounts faster than foreign exchange, and onerous austerity packages have not worked even where they have been energetically implemented (for example, Mexico). The continuing crisis not only results in dramatic declines in the standard of living of the poor countries but also returns to limit the economic and political objectives of the developed countries—the former exponents of austerity.

Self-interest comes to recognize another direction of reform. The growing U.S. trade deficit, for example, is exacerbated by austerity-dictated import restrictions in Latin America, particularly in Argentina, Brazil, and Mexico, where large domestic markets encourage concessions on debt servicing. The United States has an interest in other countries' economic growth —to curb Mexican emigration and Peru's Sendero Luminosa insurrection, or to bolster Jamaica's pliable Edward Seaga administration, the struggling Southern Cone democracies, and sundry other exceptions to hard-line policies on the debt.

Austerity protests, dramatic as they have been, are but one term in the debt politics equation. Yet we believe that dissent is strategic both in its own right and as an analytic means for deciphering broader changes. In the first instance, IMF riots have contributed to the downfall of governments (Peru in 1980 and 1984, Brazil in 1983, Panama in 1985, Haiti in 1986) and pressured other regimes to resist austerity policies in the interests of political peace. In a revealing turnabout, popular governments in Argentina, Brazil, and Peru have consolidated their domestic support through vocal resistance to creditors and their austerity demands. In cross-nationally varied ways, political stability is a consideration that overrides debt payment, and austerity protest is perhaps the most effective way in which political stability has been brought to the forefront.

We should guard against romanticizing the protest. Its principal objective of ameliorating new forms of poverty has not been achieved, and it is susceptible to cooptation by governments willing to strike their own bargains with dependent development. Yet rarely have the urban poor spoken in such a menacing voice to the national and international elites who control their fortunes. At least the opportunity is open for a renegotiation of the costs and benefits of development. Much will depend on whether the mood of injustice that prompts riot can be converted to sustained political initiatives by and for the urban poor.

References

Bernal, Richard L. "The IMF and Class Struggle in Jamaica, 1977–1980." *Latin American Perspectives* 11 (Summer): pp. 53–82, 1984.

Brown, Richard. "International Responses to Sudan's Economic Crisis: 1978 to the April 1985 Coup d'Etat." *Development and Change* 17: pp. 487–511, 1986.

Block, Fred L. *The Origins of International Economic Disorder: A Study of United States International Monetary Policy from World War II to the Present.* Berkeley: University of California Press, 1977.

Bradshaw, York. "Urbanization and Underdevelopment: A Global Study of Modernization, Urban Bias, and Economic Dependency." *American Sociological Review* 52 (April): pp. 224–239, 1987.

Brett, E. A. *International Money and Capitalist Crisis: The Anatomy of Global Disintegration.* London: Heinemann, 1983.

Cardoso, Fernando H., and Enzo Faletto. *Dependency and Development in Latin America.* (Original Spanish edition, 1969). Berkeley: University of California Press, 1977.

Carr, Barry, and Ricardo Anzaldua. *The Mexican Left, the Popular Movements, and the Politics of Austerity.* San Diego, California: Center for U.S.-Mexican Studies, University of California, Monograph Series 18, 1986.

Cline, William. "Economic Stabalization in the Developing Countries: Theory and Stylized Facts," pp. 175–208 in John Williamson (ed.). *IMF Conditionality.* Washington, D.C.: Institute of International Economics, 1983.

Cline, William R., and Sidney Weintraub. *Economic Stabilization in Developing Countries.* Washington, D.C.: The Brookings Institution, 1981.

Diaz-Alejandro, Carlos F. "Southern Cone Stabilization Plans," pp. 119–147 in William R. Cline and Sidney Weintraub (eds.). *Economic Stabilization in Developing Countries.* Washington, D.C.: The Brookings Institution, 1981.

Foxley, Alejandro."Stabilization Policies and Their Effects on Employment and Income Distribution: A Latin American Perspective." pp. 191–225 in William R. Cline and Sidney Weintraub (eds.). *Economic Stabilization in Developing Countries.* Washington, D.C.: The Brookings Institution, 1981.

Frenkel, Roberto, and Guillermo O'Donnell. "The Stabilization Programs of the International Monetary Fund and Their Internal Impacts," pp. 171–216 in Richard R. Fagen (ed.). *Capitalism and the State in U.S.–Latin American Relations.* Stanford: Stanford University Press, 1979.

Girvan, Norman, Richard Bernal, and Wesley Hughes. "The IMF and the Third World: The Case of Jamaica, 1974–80." *Development Dialogue* 2: pp. 113–155, 1980.

Haggard, Stephan, "The Politics of Adjustment: Lessons From the IMF's Extended Fund Facility," pp. 157–186 in Miles Kahler (ed.). *The Politics of International Debt.* Ithaca: Cornell University Press, 1986.

Honeywell, Martin. *The Poverty Brokers: The IMF and Latin America.* London: Latin America Bureau, 1983.

Kaufman, Robert R. "Democratic and Authoritarian Responses to the Debt Issue: Argentina, Brazil, Mexico," pp. 187–217 in Miles Kahler (ed.). *The Politics of International Debt.* Ithaca: Cornell University Press, 1986.

Killick, Tony. *The Quest for Economic Stabilization: The IMF and the Third World.* London: Heinemann, 1984.

Loxley, John. "Saving the World Economy." *Monthly Review* (September): pp. 22–34, 1984.

Moffitt, Michael. *The World's Money: International Banking from Bretton Woods to the Brink of Insolvency.* New York: Simon and Schuster, 1983.

O'Donnell, Guillermo. "Reflections on the Patterns of Change in the Bureaucratic-Authoritarian State." *Latin American Research Review* 13: pp. 3–38, 1978.

Pastor, Manuel. "The Effects of IMF Programs in the Third World: Debate and Evidence from Latin America." *World Development* 15 (2): pp. 249–262, 1987.

Petras, James, and Howard Brill. "The IMF, Austerity and the State in Latin America." *Third World Quarterly* 8 (April): pp. 425–448, 1986.

Seddon, David. "Riot and Rebellion: Political Responses to Economic Crisis in North Africa (Tunisia, Morocco, and Sudan)," unpublished manuscript, n.d.
_____ . "In Tunisia and Morocco," *Merip Reports* (October): pp. 7–16, 1984.
Sheahan, John. "Market-oriented Economic Policies and Political Repression in Latin America." *Economic Development and Cultural Change* 28 (January): pp. 267–291, 1980.
Skidmore, Thomas E. "The Politics of Economic Stabilization in Post War Latin America," in James M. Malloy (ed.). *Authoritarianism and Corporatism in Latin America.* Pittsburgh, Pa.: University of Pittsburgh Press, 1977.
Stallings, Barbara. *Banker to the Third World: U.S. Portfolio Investment in Latin America, 1900–1986.* Berkeley, California: University of California Press, 1987.
Sutton, Mary. "Structuralism: The Latin American Record and the New Critique," in Tony Killick (ed.). *The IMF and Stabilization: The Developing Countries Experience.* London: Heinemann, 1984.
Taylor, Charles Lewis, and David A. Jodice. *The World Handbook of Political and Social Indicators.* New Haven: Yale University Press, 1983.
Williamson, John. *IMF Conditionality.* Washington, D.C.: Institute of International Economics, 1983.
Wood, Robert E. *From Marshall Plan to Debt Crisis: Foreign Aid and Development Choices in the World Economy.* Berkeley: University of California Press, 1986.

Table 10.A1   Data Sources for Tables 10.2 and 10.3

Measure	Source
Number of renegotiations, 1975–1984	World Bank, World Debt Tables
Number of restructuring, 1978–1985	IMF, Occasional Paper No. 40
Use of extended fund, 1975–1986	IMF, Annual Report; IMF Survey
Loans/IMF quota, 1985	IMF, Annual Report
Debt service/exports, 1976–1982	World Bank, World Debt Tables
Multinational penetration, 1973	Ballmer-Cao and Scheidegger, 1979
Export commodity conc., 1980	U.N., Yearbook of Trade Statistics
Export partner conc., 1980	U.N., Yearbook of Trade Statistics
Import partner conc., 1980	U.N., Yearbook of Trade Statistics
Raw material export, 1980	World Bank, World Development Report
Consumer price index, 1983	IMF, International Financial Statistics
Average inflation, 1973–1984	World Bank, World Development Report
GNP per capita, 1981	World Bank, World Tables
Urbanization, 1980	" "
Tertiary employment, 1980	" "
Manufacturing employment, 1980	" "
Unionization ca. 1975	Taylor and Jodice, 1983
Protest events, 1948–1977	" "
State sanctions, 1948–1977	" "
Civil rights index, 1973–1979	" "
Political rights index, 1973–1979	" "
Government revenue/GNP, 1980	World Bank, World Tables
Direct taxation/revenue, 1980	" "

About the Editor and Contributors

William L. Canak is an assistant professor in the Department of Sociology at Tulane University. He holds a joint appointment in the Roger Thayer Stone Center for Latin American Studies, Tulane University. He received his Ph.D. from the University of Wisconsin, Madison. He has written on national development, state structure and policy in Latin America and Asia, urbanization, agrarian development, and collective bargaining laws. His current Fulbright-supported research focuses on strategic planning and policy implementation in Argentine health care institutions. His publications include articles in *Latin American Research Review, Annual Review of Sociology, Political Power and Social Theory, Social Problems, Journal of Contemporary Asia,* and others. A manuscript titled *Desarrollo Nacional: Colombia* is forthcoming (1989) and a coauthored (with Berkeley Miller) book titled *New Labor, New Laws: The Passage of Public Sector Collective Bargaining Laws in the United States, 1966-1979* will be published by Westview Press in 1989.

Edward C. Epstein is an associate professor of political science at the University of Utah where he specializes in comparative public policy in Latin America. A book he edited, *Trade Unions, the State, and Autonomy in Latin America,* will appear in 1989. He has published in various journals, including *Comparative Politics, Comparative Political Studies, Latin American Research Review, World Development,* and *Economic Development and Cultural Change.*

Franklin W. Goza received his Ph.D. in sociology from the University of Wisconsin, Madison in 1987 and is currently a Rockefeller post-doctoral fellow at the Center for Analysis and Planning (CEDEPLAR) in Belo Horizonte, Brazil. His recent publications examine refugee and immigrant adaptation among Asian migrants to the United States. At present, he is working on a study of circular labor migration in central Brazil.

Merilee S. Grindle, a political scientist at the Harvard Institute for International Development, received her Ph.D. from MIT. She is a specialist on issues of policy making and implementation in developing countries, focusing much of her attention on agricultural and rural development policies. She has studied such issues extensively in Mexico and has written widely on this topic. She is the author of *Bureaucrats, Politicians and Peasants in Mexico: A Case Study in Public Policy* (1977), *State and Countryside: Development Policy and Agrarian Politics in Latin America* (1986), and *Searching for Rural Developments: Labor Migration and Employment in Mexico* (1988). She edited *Politics and Policy Implementation in the Third World* (1980), and is the author of numerous journal articles about development issues in Latin America and elsewhere. At the Kennedy School of Government, Professor Grindle teaches about the politics of development policy in developing countries.

Ralph Hakkert is a demographer. He received his Ph.D. from Cornell University in 1984 and while working at the Brazilian Center for Analysis and Planning (CEBRAP), São Paulo, conducted his dissertation research on infant and child mortality trends in Brazil. He later worked at the Center for Population Studies (NEPO) at the University of Campinas. Since 1986 he has been on the graduate faculty in demography at the Federal University of Minas Gerais, Belo Horizonte, Brazil. His research interests include mortality, regional population projections and the demography of small areas.

Michael Johns is a graduate student in geography at Johns Hopkins University. He has worked in Mexico and Nicaragua and is currently investigating aspects of Argentine urbanization between 1880 and 1920.

Adriana Marshall is professor and senior researcher at the Facultad Latinoamericana de Ciencas Sociales (Latin American Faculty of Social Sciences) in Buenos Aires. She received her Ph.D. from the Netherlands School of Economics (Erasmus Universiteit, Rotterdam). Her major publications include *The Import of Labour* (1973), *El Mercado de Trabajo en el Capitalismo Periférico* (1981) and *Políticas Sociales: el Modelo Neoliberal* (forthcoming). She is currently senior researcher at the International Institute of Labour Studies (ILO, Geneva), where she is working on labor market issues in Latin America.

Alejandro Portes is John Dewey Professor of Sociology at Johns Hopkins University. His most recent publications include "Making it Underground: Comparative Material on the Informal Sector in Western Market Economies," *American Journal of Sociology*, July 1987 (with Saskia Sassen-Koob); "Making Sense of Diversity: Recent Research on Hispanic Minorities in the United States," *Annual Review of Sociology*, 1987 (with Cynthia Truelove); and *The Informal Economy: Studies in Advanced and Less Developed Countries*, 1988 (with Manuel Castells and Lauren Benton). He is currently a member of the Joint Committee on Latin American Studies of the Social Science Research Council and chairs the Task Force in U.S.-U.S.S.R. Scholarly Relations of the Latin American Studies Association.

Charles Ragin is professor and chair of the Department of Sociology at Northwestern University. He has written extensively on international development, peasant revolts, ethnic nationalism, and the relation of theory and method in comparative research. His recent book, *The Comparative Method: Moving Beyond Qualitative and Quantitative Strategies* (1987), is widely regarded as the most original work in the field to appear in the last twenty years.

Alejandro Rofman received his Ph.D. in economics from the Universidad de Córdoba, Argentina. He is a senior investigator at the Centro de Estudios Urbanos y Regionales in Buenos Aires, Argentina, and a regular investigator for the Consejo Nacional de Investigaciones Científicas y Técicas, Ministerio de Educacíon, Argentina. His recent books include *Monetarismo y Crisis en el Nordeste* (1983), *Política Económica y Desarrollo Regional en la Argentina* (1983), and *Políticas Estatales y Desarrollo Regional: El Caso del NEA* (1987).

Paul Singer is currently professor of economics at the Universidade de São Paulo, Brazil, and researcher at CEBRAPE (Centro Brasileiro de Análise e Planejamento). He received his Ph.D. in Economics at the Universidade de São Paulo and did postgraduate work at Princeton University. He has written several books on economic development, population dynamics, labor force and employment, income distribution, and inflation. His latest books are: *Formação da Classe Operária* (1985), *Repartição da Renda: Ricos e Pobres Sob o Regime Militar* (1986), *O Capitlaismo: Sua Formação, Sua Dinâmica e Sua Lógica* (1987), and *O Dia da Lagarta: Democratização e Conflicto Distributivo no País do Cruzado* (1987).

William C. Smith received his Ph.D. from Stanford University and currently is an assistant professor in the Department of Politics and Public Affairs at the University of Miami. He has been a visiting researcher at the Instituto Torcuato Di Tella in Argentina (1973–1975) and taught Latin American politics in Brazil at the Federal University of Minas Gerais (1980–1984). His book *Authoritarianism and the Crisis of the Argentine Political Economy* is forthcoming.

John Walton is professor of sociology and director of the Social Theory and Comparative History Program at the University of California, Davis. His major works treat the politics of economic development and urbanization and include *Labor Class in the International System* (with Alejandro Portes) (1981) and *Reluctant Rebels: Comparataive Studies of Revolution and Underdevelopment* (1984), which won honorable mention for the 1984 C. Wright Mills Award.

Index